D1637104

9MM
GUIDE TO
AMERICA'S MOST POPULAR CALIBER

BY ROBERT A. SADOWSKI

Copyright ©2018 Caribou Media

All rights reserved. No portion of this publication may be reproduced or transmitted in any form or by any means, electronic or mechanical, including photocopy, recording, or any information storage and retrieval system, without permission in writing from the publisher, except by a reviewer who may quote brief passages in a critical article or review to be printed in a magazine or newspaper, or electronically transmitted on radio, television, or the Internet.

Published by

Gun Digest® Books, an imprint of Caribou Media
Gun Digest Media, P.O. Box 12219, Zephyr Cove, NV 89448
www.gundigest.com

To order books or other products call 920-471-4522 or visit us online at
www.gundigeststore.com

CAUTION: Technical data presented here, particularly technical data on handloading and on firearms adjustment and alteration, inevitably reflect individual experience with equipment and components under specific circumstances the reader cannot duplicate exactly. Such data presentations therefore should be used for guidance only and with caution. Caribou Media accepts no responsibility for results obtained using these data.

All photos by Swamp Yankee Media / Small Orchard productions
unless otherwise noted.

ISBN-13: 978-1-946267-19-1
ISBN-10: 1-946267-19-8

Cover design by Dave Hauser
Designed by Jeromy Boutwell
Edited by Corey Graff

Printed in the USA

10 9 8 7 6 5 4 3 2 1

INTRODUCTION

As I look back on my ballistic data, the 9mm and I have had significant range time. Yes, I have a spreadsheet with muzzle velocity, muzzle energy, largest group, smallest group, temperature, wind, notes, and more — my engineering professor would be so proud. I've been writing and shooting — more shooting than writing — and competing with the 9mm more than any other cartridge save for the .22 Long Rifle for a long time. My data logs show scores of pistols, revolvers, derringers, and rifles that have been in my brief possession throughout the years, all chambered for the nine.

I've also had plenty of trigger time with .45 ACP pistols and an assortment of .380 ACP and .40 S&W handguns, but it has mostly been the 9mm when it comes to semi-automatics. I've also reloaded more 9mm cartridges than the .45 ACP and .40 S&W combined. At one time, my net worth was tied up in reloaded 9mm ammo, reloading equipment, and supplies.

The cartridge was introduced in 1902 and soon caught on with military and law enforcement around the globe. It took longer to catch on in the United States. We do love our .45s. It took a while for the round to be embraced by American shooters, but it was firmly entrenched when Uncle Sam opted for a 9mm service pistol in the 1980s. I, too, went through the 9mm cycle of adopting the round, moving on to newer more powerful calibers, and eventually coming back to the nine. I've gone full circle just like law enforcement.

There is hardly a firearm manufacturer that does not produce a 9mm pistol. That includes handguns that run the spectrum from full-size to compact, subcompact and micro models.

Will the 9mm survive another 100 years? Heck, yes. It is a cartridge that has found the sweet spot of moderate recoil, accuracy, power, and availability in pistols ranging from subcompacts to full-size. What's not to like? Make mine a nine!

– Robert A. Sadowski
Hampstead, North Carolina, 2017

TABLE OF CONTENTS

SECTION I: 9MM ORIGINS

1 | The Rise of the World's Most Popular Handgun Cartridge 5

2 | A Pistol in Search of a Cartridge 9

3 | Battle Tested Since World War I 11

4 | Law Enforcement Gears Up With the 9mm 17

5 | Uncle Sam Rethinks the .45 ACP 21

6 | The 9mm in Pop Culture 28

SECTION II: BALLISTICS & CARTRIDGES

7 | 9mm Specifications and Performance 36

8 | Why the 9mm Beats the .40 S&W and .45 ACP 42

9 | Current Trends in 9mm Ammunition 46

SECTION III: GUNS

10 | Iconic Nines: Game-Changing 9mms 65

11 | Wonder Nines 97

12 | The Striker-Fire Cometh 109

13 | 9mm Subcompacts and Micro Pistols for Deep Concealment 127

14 | Cocked and Locked Nines — Single-Action 9mms 146

15 | Super-Sized Handguns — Braced Pistols 157

16 | Transitional-Trigger Nines — DA/SA Models 168

17 | Rotary Barrel Nines 183

18 | Revolver-Inspired DAO 9mms 188

19 | Nines that Got Game — Competition 9mms 192

20 | Optics-Ready 9mm Handguns 199

21 | Wheelgun Nines — 9mm Revolvers 205

22 | 9mm ARs: Pistol-Caliber Firepower 215

SECTION IV: ACCESSORIES

23 | Reflex Sights, Lights & Lasers 228

24 | Carrying Heavy Metal — Holsters for Full-Size 9mms 241

25 | Suppressing the 9mm: Silencers Go Mainstream 252

SECTION V: RELOADING

26 | Reloading 9mm Ammo — Cranking Out Nines 259

27 | 9mm Components — Powder, Bullets, Cases 261

28 | Progressive Presses for High-Quantity Reloading 268

CHAPTER 1

THE RISE OF THE WORLD'S MOST POPULAR HANDGUN CARTRIDGE

We all know it simply as the 9-millimeter, or 9mm, but it goes by a variety of names: 9mm Luger is the official SAAMI and C.I.P. name, 9mm Parabellum by *Deutsche Waffen- und Munitionsfabriken,* the original manufacturer of the round, 9x19mm, 9mmP, and I'm sure there are more depending on which patch of dirt or city street you happen to be standing upon in this world.

The story of the 9mm is a German one. The German military at the turn of the 19th century needed a sidearm. During both the first and second World Wars, the U.S. and nearly every other country involved in the conflict witnessed the prowess of the 9mm cartridge firsthand. It was at this time that the 9mm became embraced by other nations. However, it took the cartridge longer to establish a foothold in the U.S. and reach the popularity it has today.

The 9mm cartridge is adaptable to many bullet types and weights. (Left to Right): Civil Defense 50-gr. HP, Speer 115-gr. FMJ, Aguila 124-gr. FMJ, Hornady 135-gr. FTX, and Hornady 147-gr. XTP.

In 2015, the FBI selected the 9mm Speer Gold Dot G2 147-grain as the new duty round, replacing the .40 S&W. Photo: Speer

During the late 1970s through the 1980s — the "Wonder Nine" era — we Americans began to embrace the small German centerfire cartridge. After all, we are Americas and we like our centerfire cartridges in .38 Special, .357 Magnum, .44 Special, .44 Magnum and .45 ACP — big-bore calibers that can stop bear and man. The shift to the 9mm by the U.S. military and domestic law enforcement made the cartridge what it is today. There are more 9mm pistols produced by U.S. and foreign manufacturers than any other centerfire caliber, and so the 9mm found its balance and became the most popular centerfire pistol cartridge in the U.S. and the world.

To really know the 9mm, you need to understand the profound impact a German-designed pistol had on arms and cartridge development, and grasp the cartridge's

The Smith & Wesson Model 39 was the first U.S.-manufactured semi-automatic pistol and ushered in the acceptance of the 9mm round with American shooters. The Model 39 (top) is an early aluminum alloy frame 9mm with a long extractor. Note the shorter extractor on the Model 39-2 (bottom). Photo: Smith & Wesson

The CZ 75 is a very popular double-action or "DA" 9mm pistol overseas. It offers a high-capacity magazine, double-action/single-action trigger, and full metal receiver. Photo: CZ USA

tendency to reinvent itself, especially at moments in the recent past when it was nearly written off as inadequate. In 2018, the cartridge will have been around for 116 years. That makes it older than the .45 ACP, which debuted in 1904. The 9mm is closer in age to the .38 Special, which was introduced in 1889. There are reasons the 9mm cartridge is as popular as ever: it has plenty of power, offers decent accuracy, has minimal recoil, is inexpensive, and can be adapted to a variety of platforms from full-size to subcompact pistols, revolvers, and carbines.

The ability to sustain fire without reloading is a plus in a gunfight, and more military forces and law enforcement departments started to do the math: .38 Special with less power and maximum 6-round capacity in a revolver versus a 9mm semi-automatic with more power and 9-round capacity.

The 9mm started life with a 124-grain FMJ bullet loaded to about 1,200 fps. That was a hot load then, even as it is now. Part of the reason it was loaded so hot was to reliably operate the Luger pistol's toggle action. More modern and powerful variations include a 9mm+P and 9mm+P+, versions that came

Revolvers have also been chambered in 9mm and this Ruger LCR9 is a current example of adapting a revolver to a semi-auto pistol cartridge.

out in the 1990s. But don't think the 9mm has been immune to other calibers trying to take its place. The .40 S&W unseated the 9mm in the mid- to late-20th century, but the 9mm has staying power. Just when some would discount it, new propellants and bullet design propelled the round ahead and away from the maddening crowd of other calibers. In the 9mm cartridge's favor are milder recoil and higher magazine capacity than larger calibers.

Here in the U.S., the 9mm did not catch on as fast as it did in Europe and Asia, as domestic firearm manufacturers simply were not building guns in the caliber. Well after World War II in 1954, the U.S. Army kicked around the idea of changing to the 9mm but abandoned the search. Despite this initial resistance, Smith & Wesson introduced the Model 39 to their commercial lineup and courted the law enforcement (LE) market. The ice cracked. In 1967, the Illinois State Police adopted the Model 39 and the 9mm cartridge. It wasn't long before other U.S. manufacturers were chambering handguns in 9mm. In the 1980s, agencies started to take notice of the nine and traded their 6-shot revolvers for pistols like the Beretta 92, SIG P226, Glock 17, and others. The floodgates opened, the era of Wonder Nines arrived. It seemed like law enforcement geared up with 9mm pistols from coast to coast. Beretta, Glock, and SIG are part of that genus of Wonder Nines — high-capacity 9mm handguns with double-action/single-action (DA/SA) triggers. These were higher capacity than the single-stack magazine pistols for sure. Today, nearly every domestic and foreign handgun manufacturer produces a high-capacity 9mm.

Over half of all LE agencies — 60 percent at last check, including the FBI —use the 9mm round. In fact, the FBI switched back to the 9mm cartridge in 2015, which is ironic since the bureau in 1986 gave the caliber a black eye in law enforcement circles after the 1986 Miami shootout.

When I talk to firearms trainers, officers, competition shooters, and concealed carry holders, they more than likely use a 9mm.

The Smith & Wesson M&P M2.0 is but one of many concealable, state-of-the-art 9mms on the market today. Photo: Smith & Wesson

CHAPTER 2

A PISTOL IN SEARCH OF A CARTRIDGE

The destinies of the P.08 Luger pistol and 9mm Parabellum cartridge were on a collision course. In the beginning, the 9mm cartridge was not in search of a pistol, but a pistol, the P.08, was in search of a new cartridge. First came the Luger, then the 9mm.

German Beginning

Georg Luger essentially reworked the design of the Hugo Borchardt C-93 pistol to create the P.08 Luger. The C-93 was designed in 1893 and it, along with other self-loading pistols of the time, was a revelation to shooters, police, and military organizations. The revolver was the sidearm of choice, but self-loading pistols were the future. The C-93 was an awkward-looking thing with a 6.5-inch barrel, a nearly vertical grip that held an 8-round magazine, and a toggle lock system that stuck out the back of the pistol about 3 inches past the grip. Its toggle lock system wasn't new by any means. A toggle system was used in the Maxim heavy machine gun in 1886. Borchardt compacted the design and placed the toggle on top rather than below, as in Hiram Maxim's design. The toggle used a two-piece arm that bent like the knee on your leg when the gun fired. The toggle unlocked the breech, ejected the empty cartridge case, and shoved a fresh cartridge into the chamber. Many military organizations tested this high-tech pistol, and all said in no uncertain terms it was a great gun, but ultimately turned it down. The C-93 was too awkward and delicate for a combat pistol.

Georg Luger was a German designer who reworked the Borchardt pistol to create the Luger pistol. Luger made the pistol smaller and more compact. He also made it more reliable (relatively speaking) and chambered it in the 7.65x21mm, also known

An excellent example of a World War II Luger as issued to German Army troops.
Photo: Rock Island Auction Company

as 7.65 Parabellum and .30 Luger to us cartridgephiles. The year was 1898. Self-loading pistols, what we call semi-automatic today, were weapons of the future. The Luger used a toggle system, which was as odd to revolvers shooters of that time, just as polymer-frame pistols were odd to us shooters some 30 years ago.

Before we go further I should clear up some names, since the cartridge and the pistol are entwined and can be confused. The pistols designed by Georg Luger are called, among other names, the Luger, P.08, Pistole 08, Pistole 04, Pistole 1900, Lange Pistole 08, and Parabellum. The name Parabellum for the pistol was mostly used in Europe, like how we use "Forty-Five" in the U.S. The cartridge is most commonly referred to as the 9x19mm Parabellum, 9mm NATO, 9mm Luger, 9x19mm, 9mmP, and 9x19.The Swiss Army snapped up the new Luger in 7.65mm caliber and bought a crate full. Being the small, neutral country they were, the Swiss contract was not the payday DWM had in mind, but it was a start. The German military was the contract Georg Luger and his employer DWM most wanted. That deal would not only mean crates, but containers and railroad cars filled with pistols and ammunition. The German military wanted a bigger, more powerful cartridge, so DWM and Luger took the 7.65mm Parabellum cartridge case, shortened it, blew out the bottleneck to accept a larger diameter bullet and more powder, and a new cartridge was born. They named it the 9x19mm Parabellum, which we call today the 9mm.

The German Navy was sold on the new pistol and cartridge and adopted both in 1904. The German Army adopted the pistol and cartridge in 1908, hence the Pistole 08 and P.08 designations. It was pay dirt. DWM secured a lucrative military contract and, unknown to them at the time, introduced a pistol cartridge that would become popular

LATIN LESSON: *Si vis pacem, para bellum*

The name Parabellum is derived from the Latin phrase: *Si vis pacem, para bellum*, which translated to English means "If you seek peace, prepare for war." Deutsche Waffen- und Munitionsfabriken (DWM), the original manufacturer of the P.08 pistol, used the Latin phrase as its company motto.

around the globe. Other countries like Bolivia, Russia, Netherlands, Portugal, Norway, China, Spain, Turkey, and others all adopted the pistol and caliber.

By 1900, the Luger pistol chambered in 9mm was available in the U.S. The reception to the newfangled contraption was tepid at best. Civilian shooters purchased some, while cowboys and lawmen of the day posed with their high-tech Lugers along with Colt Single Action Army revolvers and Winchester lever-action rifles. The initial U.S. military response to seeing the Luger in field trials was promising, calling the pistol/caliber combination "…far superior to any other handgun … well balanced, shoots very well and fast." What they disliked about the Luger was the magazine. Many who tried loading Luger magazines felt as though they had busted their thumbs, thanks to the stiff magazine spring. The U.S. Ordnance Department said that the pistol was too hard for a mounted soldier to load with cold fingers. This was the era when Calvary meant horses. But by this time the U.S. military wanted .45 caliber handguns and, in 1907, the U.S. Ordnance Department tested Lugers chambered in .45 ACP. But that never happened — Uncle Sam passed on the Luger and adopted the 1911, but that's another story.

CHAPTER 3

BATTLE TESTED SINCE WORLD WAR I

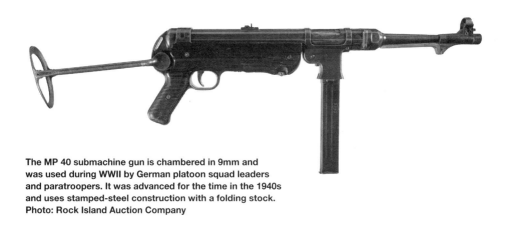

The MP 40 submachine gun is chambered in 9mm and was used during WWII by German platoon squad leaders and paratroopers. It was advanced for the time in the 1940s and uses stamped-steel construction with a folding stock. Photo: Rock Island Auction Company

The 9mm cartridge gained traction in 1904 when the German Navy ordered Lugers, which they officially called the Pistole 04. Such naval organizations were typically quicker to adopt new technology — think submarines — and the Luger pistol chambered in 9mm was cutting-edge weaponry at the time. The Pistole 04 is characterized by the German Navy's specification of a 5.9-inch barrel and two-position rear sight with 100- and 200-meter adjustments. Armies typically take longer to adopt new weaponry, and in 1908 the German Army adopted the pistol and issued it to troops as the Pistole 08 or P.08. The Army requested a 3.9-inch barrel model. Other countries started to place orders for the new self-loading 9mm Luger.

Mauser and Steyr, competitors of DMW, knew that the acceptance of the Luger was due to the 9mm cartridge. They retooled the C96 and M1912 in 9mm. Others would follow suit. European firearm manufacturers soon offered even more pistols in what had become the popular chambering of the time.

The 9mm cartridge had its baptism by fire in the trenches of World War I, where it was employed via the Luger and other pistols. The Imperial German Army was in desperate need of sidearms. Production of the standard issue P.08 was slow, so the Germans contracted with Mauser to produce the C96 pistol in 9mm. This variant was named the "Red 9" due to a large number "9" burned and painted red into the grip panels. This indicated it was chambered

This Mauser Model 1896 Cone Hammer Broomhandle was high-tech firepower circa 1900. The wooden stock also served as a holster. Photo: Rock Island Auction Company

in 9mm and not 7.63mm, which was also used during the war.

The Walther Model 6 was introduced by Walther around the same time, but it was more of a Ruby pistol on steroids. It used a simple blowback action and fired the then-new 9mm cartridge, but saw limited use and the design was scrapped shortly after it was introduced.

Revolvers were still the sidearm of choice for armies during the early 20th century, and when World War I started in 1914 the most popular sidearm was the Lebel M1892 revolver. It is a 6-shot, 8mm double-action/single-action revolver with about the same power as the .32 ACP. Officers in France, Belgium, Spain, Switzerland, and Czechoslovakia were armed with it.

The .32 ACP caliber was also very common at the time and many small, compact pistols were chambered in the caliber. Many of these semi-automatic handguns were generically called the Ruby pistol and were manufactured in France and Spain.

Of note is that a pistol was very much a status symbol in armies around the world during this era. A sidearm denoted rank and a commissioned officer. The typical enlisted man was not issued one. Non-commissioned officers in various armies across Europe purchased their own sidearms. In fact, many different pistols were used during the Great War. A common self-loading handgun was the aforementioned Ruby, which again was chambered in 7.65x17mm (.32 ACP). These small-caliber pistols were rugged and designed after the Colt M1903. Indeed, quality control was spotty with the Ruby. The advantage it had over other revolvers of the time was extra capacity. It held nine cartridges. The primary disadvantage of the Ruby was the stopping power of the cartridge. It was weak.

British forces were armed with 6-shot, break-top Webley Mk V revolvers chambered in .455 Webley. The revolver had been used with good success in the Boer War from 1899 to 1902. The caliber offered far more power than the French revolver and the numerous examples of Ruby self-loading pistols. The break-top design allowed it to be unloaded quickly and reloaded. As the Great War continued, the Webley MK IV evolved into the Mk V and Mk VI. All were chambered in .455 Webley.

When the U.S. entered World War I in 1917, the Colt M1911 in .45 ACP had been adopted, and while the demand for the M1911 was high, the supply on hand was low. There was plenty of .45 ACP ammo in U.S. Army inventory but not many pistols to fire it. Colt needed to gear up production on the M1911, but the Army decided to increase production of the M1917 revolver, which was produced by both Colt and Smith & Wesson. Even in the U.S., revolvers were the bread and butter of most handgun manufacturers during this time. The M1917 revolvers were chambered in .45 ACP and used moon clips to allow the semi-automatic pistol cartridges to be fired in the cylinders.

While the British and American revolvers offered more power, the revolver platforms were slower to shoot and reload than the German P.08. Fast shooting and reloading, light recoil, accuracy, and an 8+1-round capacity gave the P.08 advantages over British and French revolvers and pistols.

During trench fighting in World War I, armies became more aware of the 9mm pistol as a fighting tool. There was no ignoring the compactness and maneuverability of the new handguns within the confines of a trench.

A new, far more efficient weapon was being developed during World War I, and the 9mm cartridge was tapped to fuel it. The Bergmann MP 18 was the first successful submachine gun and was deployed late during the Great War. While the Maxim and Browning M1917 machine guns worked well for troops dug in and defending, the submachine gun was lighter and did not need a crew of men to operate it. Chambered in 9mm, it was the tool needed for newer 20th-century warfare tactics. As warfare changed from open battlefields to urban areas, the sub-

machine gun became the tool of choice. The 9mm moved up in status — not only was it a cartridge for handguns but for lightweight, fully automatic carbines.

Employed late in the war, the Bergmann MP 18 proved its usefulness in the 1918 Spring Offensive. Though the Germans gained territory, their war machine was depleted. The MP 18, however, proved the submachine gun concept in trench fighting. Its basic design had a great influence on later submachine gun innovations. This small, compact weapon, capable of firing 500 rounds per minute and fed from a 32-round magazine, proved superior in modern urban warfare to the longer, heavier standard-issue infantry rifle. The MP 18 valued speed and mobility. The modern M4 and AK-47/74 are direct descendants of the submachine gun.

By the second World War, the 9mm was in use with many military forces across the globe: England, France, Spain, Belgium, Bulgaria, Finland, Poland, Sweden, Netherlands — fair to say nearly all of Europe, plus Canada and countries in South America like Brazil, Malaysia, China and more. Those not using the 9mm were the United States, some South American countries, Mexico, and a few others who opted for the .45 ACP in the M1911 or M1911A1 platform. The U.S.S.R. adopted the TT-30 pistol chambered in 7.62x25mm Tokarev. Meanwhile, the Empire of Japan issued the Nambu Model 14 in 8x22mm Nambu, and fascist Italy the Beretta M1934 in 9x17mm Court, what we call .380 ACP. Nazi Germany stuck with the nine. The Luger P.08 pistol, however, was dated.

The P.08 took time to build, for most of its parts were hand fitted. At peak production, DWM could produce 700 pistols a day. In 1944 it cost the Reich about $19 per pistol. Even though P.08 production was spread across many manufacturers, the demand for a 9mm semi-auto far exceeded the ability to produce the P.08.

The revolver as a combat handgun had conceded to more modern semi-automatic designs that were less expensive to manufacture and offered more firepower, meaning a higher magazine capacity and faster shooting, with reliable operating systems to boot. Semi-automatic pistols were in, revolvers were out. By 1930, Germany knew they needed a replacement for the P.08. Submachine guns followed suit. While the MP 18 saw use in the 1930s with German police and paramilitary, the future was in new, more modern designs. The modern submachine gun and pistol were about to be born.

In 1939, the *Blitzkrieg* was set in motion by Germany and countries around the globe were poised for another world war. Many armies took with them handguns chambered in 9mm. Germany adopted the Walther P.38 as an inexpensive alternative to the P.08 Luger. In 1944, the cost to the Reich for a P.38 was just over $14. The P.38 was a reliable pistol that was just as cutting edge as the Luger had been 40 years prior.

The P.38 was designed for mass production using stamped steel, alloys, and composite grips. The German military wanted a reliable, rugged pistol suitable for combat. Though the P.38 was designed for ease in manufacturing, the design introduced technical innovations that were cutting edge for 1938. Many current handgun designs use features that were first employed on the P.38.

Use of submachine guns peaked during WWII. Britain issued the Sten, Germany the MP40, Italy the Beretta Model 38, and Finland the Suomi M31. These were all chambered in 9mm. U.S. troops were issued the Thompson submachine gun and the less-costly M3, which was nicknamed the "Grease Gun," as it looked like a mechanic's ... grease gun. These weapons were chambered in .45 ACP.

Probably the most iconic of 9mm German weapons during the war was the MP 40 submachine gun. While the MP 18 proved the concept of compact, full-auto weapon, the MP 40, also called the *Schmeisser*, was the epitome of the modern combat weapon of the time.

Made of stamped steel and spot welded, the MP 40 is a simple open-bolt, blowback system. The stock folded under the receiver to make the weapon compact. The MP 40 had one mode of fire — full auto — but the slow rate of fire allowed experienced operators to squeeze off controlled bursts and single shots. The detachable, double-column, single-fed magazine holds 32 rounds of 9mm firepower and doubles as a grip for the support hand when firing. The MP 40 has an effective firing range of 100 to 200 meters, but it is most effective in close-range urban combat. During the Battle of Stalingrad, both Russian and German units effectively used submachine guns in street battles. Combat had changed from long distance encounters to engagements under 100 meters. The submachine gun in 9mm offered low recoil and controllable suppressive fire. The compromise was a pistol cartridge instead of a rifle round. The compact size of the MP 40 meant it was easier to maneuver in cramped environments like doorways, buildings, or in vehicles. The firepower the MP 40 could provide over the typical manually operated bolt-action rifle and even the M1 Garand semi-automatic is stunning. The typical German soldier carried six magazines for a total of 192 rounds. The 9mm shined in combat.

The TEC-9 and its variants were easily manufactured pistols made with a mix of polymer and stamped-steel parts. Photo: Rock Island Auction Company

As mentioned, back in the U.S. the M1A1 Thompson and M3 "Grease Gun" were chambered in the same caliber as the 1911A1 — .45 ACP — but on the Allied side there were other 9mm submachine guns.

Great Britain introduced the Sten Gun into service in 1941. Built with simplicity and ease of production, the minimalist Sten used an open-bolt, blowback operating system. Cheaply made with stamped metal parts and welded together like the German MP, it required little manufacturing time. The Sten could be manufactured in about five hours. It is a spartan weapon compared to the German MP models and has a rate of fire of about 500 to 600 rounds per minute. The 32-round magazine is like that of the MP 28 and protrudes horizontally out the left side of the weapon.

Early Sten Guns were not as reliable as the MPs but were produced in the millions. There are several variations, with the Mk II being the most common.

The other 9mm submachine gun worth noting at this time is the Suomi KP/-31 produced by Finland. The compact Suomi KP/-31 features a wood stock and a longer barrel than the MP and Sten. It also employs a 40- or 70-round drum magazine and fires at a staggering rate of 750 to 900 rounds per minute. Plus it can be fed from stick magazines. This weapon was reliable in some of the coldest environments encountered during the war and it was copied by the Soviets in the PPD-40 and PPSh-41 submachine guns, although the Soviet guns were chambered in 7.62x25mm Tokarev. The Suomi KP/-31 ushered in a submachine gun with a blistering rate of fire.

Europe was a hotbed of pistol development at the time with many 9mms being produced. In Poland, the Radom-manufactured FB Vis — basically a Browning 1911 design knockoff — was chambered in 9mm. Canada took to arms with the High Power and, as ironic and incomprehensible as war is, a small number of German units also carried the High Power after capturing the factory in Belgium. The Swiss had the SIG P210 — perhaps the most accurate of all 9mm pistols then and since. Italy, Britain, Japan, Soviet Union, and others used indigenous-caliber pistols during the war, but afterward there was a major trend for all modern standing armies to convert to the 9mm. The U.S. resisted, until 1985 when the U.S. Army finally adopted the 9mm.

After World War II, pistol designs in 9mm grew out of nearly every country not under Soviet influence. The Soviets had their own version of the 9mm, the 9x18mm Makarov, which uses a shorter case but same bullet diameter. In the mid- to late-20th century, SIG, FN Herstal, Steyr, Beretta, Smith & Wesson, Ruger, and nearly every other small arms manufacturer produced a 9mm pistol. And don't forget Glock. They debuted their first pistol, the G17, in 9mm. Submachine guns evolved, too. The Israeli UZI and Heckler & Koch MP5 are just two of the more iconic submachine guns of recent history. Even the AR-15/M16 was adapted to fire the 9mm.

Machine pistols are literally pistols with select fire. They are highly concealable and can spray lead fast and furious. Two iconic machine pistols are the UZI and MAC-11/9. The MAC-11/9 (originally the MAC-10) was manufactured by Military Armament Corp — hence the MAC — and was used by security and special forces. The MAC-11/9 has a cyclic rate of 1,250 rounds per minute, or in other words, it will fire a 32-round magazine nearly instantly if you don't control the trigger. The UZI pistol is a compact version of the already small UZI submachine gun. Using a closed bolt blowback system and equipped with a 20-round magazine, the UZI can be hidden as easily as a full-size pistol, yet it burps out bullets at a blistering rate.

On the civilian side, manufacturers like Intratec and Cobray Industries produced semi-automatic 9mm pistols that defied the conventional thinking of the day about such handguns. The TEC-9 and variants were easily manufactured pistols made with a mix of polymer and stamped steel parts. That in-and-of-itself was not new, nor was the simple blowback system. What set these pistols apart was firepower. The TEC-9 was produced from 1985 to 1994 and held a 20- or 32-round stick mag in front of the trigger guard. The magazine could be held with the support hand while the firing hand did all the work. I've shot the TEC-9, and let me tell you, the pistol was able to throw lead downrange at a ferocious rate. Unfortunately, the pistol was employed by gangs and was one of the more lethal weapons used in drive-by shootings. For better or for worst, the TEC-9 and similar pistols were banned by name in the now-expired Federal Assault Weapons Ban in 1994. The Cobray M11 saw a similar fate. The M11 is a semi-automatic version of the MAC-10, another stamped steel, blowback pistol but with the magazine housed in the grip. These pistols, among others, were specifically singled out in the ban.

CHAPTER 4

LAW ENFORCEMENT GEARS UP WITH THE 9MM

Currently in the U.S., over half of all law enforcement agencies — some 60 percent, including the FBI — use the 9mm. That wasn't always the case. In law enforcement circles, the shift from revolver cartridges to the 9mm evolved slowly. When the 9mm was deemed inadequate and underpowered, law enforcement quickly changed gears and adopted the more powerful .40 S&W. Now, real-world use has the pendulum swinging back to the 9mm. In fact, the FBI switched back to the 9mm cartridge in 2015, which is ironic since the FBI was the agency that called the 9mm's effectiveness into question in 1986 after the infamous Miami shootout.

The change from revolvers did not happen overnight in law enforcement circles. There were departments ahead of the curve, like the Illinois State Police, who adopted the S&W Model 39 in 1967, but by and large, most departments were equipped with .38 Special revolvers. I distinctly remember the Connecticut State Police adopting the .357 Magnum when I was growing up in the 1970s.

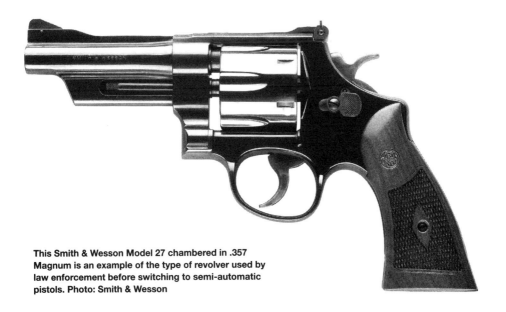

This Smith & Wesson Model 27 chambered in .357 Magnum is an example of the type of revolver used by law enforcement before switching to semi-automatic pistols. Photo: Smith & Wesson

Speer Gold Dot was the first handgun ammunition loaded with bonded-core bullets. The jacket is bonded to the core to virtually eliminate core-jacket separation. Photo: Speer

This move was smart. State Troopers typically encountered altercations with drivers. The .357 Magnum round could penetrate glass or vehicle doors. I also remember Connecticut State Troopers trading their service revolvers for Beretta 92SB pistols in 1981. The switch to semi-automatic pistols was gaining momentum around the country. Connecticut's State Troopers were just one of many agencies around the country that made a major shift in weaponry. Even though the 9mm Beretta is not as powerful as the Smith & Wesson .357 Magnum revolvers, it offered more firepower. Troopers now had a handgun that carried 15 rounds in the magazine compared to six rounds in a revolver. They easily doubled ammunition in spare magazines on their duty belts. Why did law enforcement need to gun up? Cocaine.

In the 1980s cocaine was becoming a billion-dollar industry for drug cartels in South America. President George H.W. Bush declared a war on drugs in 1989, which was carried on by President Bill Clinton in the early 1990s. Drug cartels had lots of cash and could arm their smugglers and enforcers with top-of-the-line weaponry. U.S. law enforcement was forced to play catch-up. On the West Coast, the LAPD adopted 9mm Beretta 92 pistols in the 1980s. On the East Coast, the Miami Police Department adopted 9mm Glocks in 1987. Other agencies took longer. The headline of a *New York Times* article in August 1993 read, "New York City Police to Replace Revolvers with Semiautomatics." According to that article, the NYPD, "resisted the quicker, more powerful weapons," due to New York City's "crowded urban settings." Suffice it to say the semi-automatic pistol did eventually displace the revolver. However, following the 1986 shootout in Miami, the 9mm was labeled as ineffective.

The 1986 Miami shootout involved eight FBI agents and two bank robbers.

During the shootout, two agents were killed, five were wounded. The suspects were also killed in the gunfight and the ensuing investigation found the 9mm pistols that agents used in the fight lacked penetration. The suspects were hit numerous times with 9mm rounds. The FBI needed a fix and fast. That resulted in the Bureau adopting the more powerful 10mm Auto cartridge, but it proved too powerful and difficult for the average agent to control. That debacle resulted in the 10mm being downsized to the .40 S&W, a cartridge that nearly drove the 9mm out of existence with LE agencies.

The most common load for law enforcement, prior to the development of the Federal Hydra-Shok load, was a 115-grain+P+ cartridge using a JHP bullet. Sometimes referred to as the "Illinois State Police load," this cartridge offers a muzzle velocity of 1,300 fps and 432 ft/lbs. Some ammunition manufacturers still produce this load. The Illinois State Police was the first major law enforcement agency to adopt the 9mm cartridge and their S&W Model 39 pistols were loaded with the cartridge. Hydra-Shok bullets feature a center post and notched jacket

FBI Protocol – Minimum Requirements

- *Minimum penetration into ballistic gelatin of 12 to 18 inches*

- *Expansion of bullet to at least 1.5 times original diameter*

- *100% weight retention of expanded bullet*

with a non-bonded lead core. This bullet design offers more reliable and predictable expansion and deeper penetration than the hollowpoint bullets used back then.

What was the turning point that had major law enforcement agencies switching back to the 9mm after they shunned it? As FBI goes, law enforcement follows.

In 2015, the FBI announced it was reverting to the 9mm. Actually, the swinging back to the nine took several years. In fact, the FBI had been reconsidering the 9mm since 2007 because of advancements in ballistic technology. One of the facts the FBI considered in its evaluation of the cartridge is that law enforcement officers in an incident miss targets on average 70 to 80 percent. More ammo on hand can increase the hit rate, plus the 9mm has less recoil, so in theory, officers should shoot it more accurately.

The science of terminal ballistics (or wound ballistics) is what drove law enforcement and the FBI to look at the 9mm a second time. Terminal ballistics studies the behavior and effects of a projectile when it hits and transfers its energy into the target. Studying wounds renewed focus on bullet design and velocity to create an effective wound channel in a target. Where the rubber hit the road, so to speak, or perhaps where the bullet hit the gel, was in examining the projectile's impact on the target. This helped determine the effectiveness of the bullet.

The FBI Ballistics Protocol probably had the most influence on the decision to use the 9mm. The Protocol created a science around wound ballistics. Soon after the shootout in Florida, the FBI developed the protocol for testing ammunition and set a new standard for evaluating defensive ammunition. Tests were conducted at a set distance with a block of 10 percent ordnance-grade ballistic gel, which simulates human

FBI Protocol – Test Events

1. Bare Gelatin at 10 ft.

2. Heavy Clothing at 10 ft.

3. Steel at 10 ft.

4. Wallboard at 10 ft.

5. Plywood at 10 ft.

6. Auto Glass at 10 ft.

7. Heavy Clothing at 20 yds.

8. Auto Glass at 20 yds.

flesh. The protocol called for ammunition to be tested through numerous events involving different material and into gel.

The backstory of the FBI's adoption of the 9mm is that pistol design advancements outpaced ammunition technology. By the late 2000s, bullet designs were better performing. Common 124-grain FMJ rounds were the NATO standard pushing the bullet with a 1,140 fps muzzle velocity and delivering 358 ft/lbs. of muzzle energy. The Speer Gold Dot G2 is literally the gold standard in new 9mm cartridge technology. It is loaded with a 147-grain JHP bullet. The typical hollowpoint features a large cavity that is instantly filled with glass, wood, sheetrock, clothing and a multitude of other target materials when it hits a barrier, preventing it from expanding properly. When the cavity fills it does not expand as well — or as much — depending on the target media. The G2 bullet features a shallow elastomer-filled dish in lieu of a deep cavity. On impact, the flexible elastomer material is forced into fissures designed in the bullet cavity to start the expansion process. This means the G2 bullet provides more consistent expansion in any type of target media.

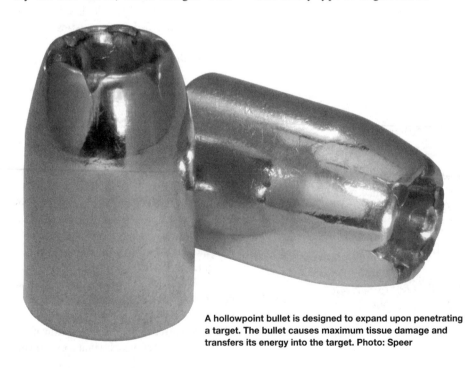

A hollowpoint bullet is designed to expand upon penetrating a target. The bullet causes maximum tissue damage and transfers its energy into the target. Photo: Speer

CHAPTER 5

UNCLE SAM RETHINKS THE .45 ACP

The Beretta M9 chambered in 9mm has been the standard-issue U.S. military sidearm since 1985.
Photo: DoD

The Thompson-LaGarde caliber tests in 1904 involved five unsuspecting cattle at the Nelson Morris Company Union Stockyards. These bovine were the unwitting participants in a test that eventually brought our military to the conclusion that a .45-caliber handgun provided the best shock and stopping effect. The test also used bovine carcasses suspended in the air to measure the sway and movement of the bodies as they were hit with different calibers from varying distances. The wounds the calibers caused in the cattle and carcasses were examined in detail. Science does not always yield data in nice, clean methods. Several different calibers were considered: 7.65×21mm Parabellum also known as .30 Luger, 9×19mm Parabellum, .38 Long Colt, .38 ACP, .45 Long Colt, .476 Eley, and .455 Webley. So why back in 1911 was the M1911 chambered in .45 ACP and not 9mm? The reason: subpar bullet design and cartridge technology of that era. Back then, most pistol bullets were made of lead and the .45 Long Colt proved effective.

While some in the U.S. military prefer the .45 ACP, a 9mm means less recoil and more magazine capacity. Photo: DoD

That is why the .45 ACP was created. A compromise was to fit a cartridge like the .45 Long Colt into a semi-automatic pistol. Uncle Sam was happy until the 1980s.

Most current militaries issue sidearms chambered in 9mm. To the angst of some members in our own U.S. military, the .45 ACP was deep-sixed in favor of the 9mm in 1985. (With the exception of the Marines, who did purchase some new M45CQB 1911s, mostly for Special Forces. For the most part, though, the Marines use a 9mm.)

Users of the 9mm found that it underperformed compared to the .45 ACP. In fact, some sarcastically say that the reason 9mm handguns have twice the magazine capacity is that you need to shoot the enemy at least twice to put them down.

The Beretta 92 was officially adopted by the U.S. Army as the M9 in 1985 and has been used by our troops since then. Generations of soldiers have been trained on the platform. The Model 92 first saw daylight in 1972 and has been produced continuously from 1975 to date in many model versions. Its origins are from early 20th-century Berettas like the Model 1934, with its characteristic open-slide design, which ensures smooth cartridge feeding and ejection plus allows for easy clearing of obstructions. As the design of the Model 92 developed, it borrowed elements from the WWII-era Walther P.38 and Browning Hi Power. Original Model 92s featured a thumb safety on the frame, much like the 1911. That would change.

Where the U.S. military and Beretta crossed paths was the Model 92S in 1978, when the JSSAP (Joint Services Small Arms Program) evaluated the handgun. The 92S variant incorporated a slide-mounted safety at the request of the Italian military. The new safety acted as a

The Beretta M9 (Model 92) represented a major change in U.S. military thinking when it came to sidearms. It literally ushered in the era of the 9mm for the U.S. Army, and later other branches of the service. Photo: Beretta USA

safety and decocking lever. The Model 92S started to get the attention of other military organizations. In fact, the U.S. Air Force tested a variant with the magazine release button relocated from the butt of the pistol to just below the trigger guard on the left side — like nearly all U.S. centerfire pistols. This variant also incorporated a firing pin block and won the USAF trials and was named the Model 92SB.

You might come across a Model 92 SB-F, which indicates a variant for U.S. military testing. A Model 92G denotes yet another variant submitted for French military testing. The Model 92 was gaining traction among some of the largest military organizations in the world, and the model was modified to the specifications given by the test military organizations. That's how the Model 92FS evolved.

The M9 field strips into five major components. Assembled and with an unloaded magazine, it weighs slightly over 33 ounces. Photo: Beretta USA

The U.S. military decided the aging M1911A1 platform needed to be replaced. They tested the Model 92 SB-F with high-pressure test ammunition — not the ammo the 92 was designed to run, nor any 9mm pistol. These were essentially proof loads used to test chamber and barrel. A pistol must be able to withstand a test load, but a steady diet will tear a pistol apart. You've probably heard the expression, "You're not a Navy SEAL until you eat Italian steel." That's one of the negative remarks the Beretta pistol does not deserve. The hammer pin failed with the high-pressure loads and the response was to increase the hammer pin to prevent the slide from flying off a cracked receiver.

While the military was deciding which sidearm to procure, law enforcement agencies were looking to replace their .38 Special and .357 Magnum revolvers. The Connecticut State Police adopted the Model 92 in 1980 and thereafter Florida, Indiana, Maryland, North Carolina, Pennsylvania, South Dakota, Utah and Wyoming all equipped their troopers with Model 92s or variants like the Model 96 chambered in .40 S&W. Some 25 state police agencies ended up acquiring the pistol.

On January 14, 1985, the U.S. Army announced the Beretta 92 SB-F had won the trials. In military parlance, it would come to be called the M9. Uncle Sam bought over 300,000 of them in the first contract worth about $75 million. By 2009, another 450,000 pistols were ordered by the government, along with spare parts, making the $220 million deal the largest U.S. military pistol contract awarded since World War II.

Since the 92 was adopted it has seen tours of duty in 36 countries, from Panama to the Persian Gulf War, and from Bosnia to Somalia, Afghanistan and Operation Iraqi Freedom.

The Beretta 92FS (left) was adopted by the U.S. military in 1985 as the M9. The M9A3 (right) was introduced by Beretta as a replacement for the M9 in 2015.

SPECIFICATIONS

MODEL: Beretta M9

CALIBER: 9mm

ACTION: Semi-Automatic, Open-Slide, Short Recoil-Operated

TRIGGER: DA/SA

BARREL LENGTH: 4.9 in.

OVERALL LENGTH: 8.5 in.

WEIGHT: 34.2 oz. (unloaded)

GRIPS: Checkered Polymer

SIGHTS: Fixed, Notch Rear/Blade Front

FINISH: Black Bruniton

CAPACITY: 15+1, Double-Stack Magazine

The M9 — the militarized version of the Beretta 92FS that it is — was a major departure from the M1911A1, the traditional U.S. military sidearm since 1911. The M1911A1 pistol has a single-stack magazine with a capacity of 7+1 rounds, employs a single-action trigger, and is chambered in .45 ACP. The M9 is chambered in 9mm and has a 15+1 capacity with a double-stack magazine. The M9's trigger system also operates in DA/SA mode.

In 1985, when the contract was awarded, Beretta sold the M9 design to the U.S. Army who now manages the pistol's Technical Data Package (TDP). One of the recent modifications to the M9 is a change to the surface finish to be compatible with dry film lubricant. Beretta still owns and controls the design of the Beretta Model 92.

The M9 was thoroughly torture tested prior to adoption, and survived temperatures from −40°F to 140°F, salt water, drops on concrete, plus being buried in sand, mud, and snow. The average reliability of M9s tested at Beretta U.S.A. is about 17,500 rounds without a stoppage. During testing, some samples shot 168,000 rounds without a malfunction. The average durability of M9 slides is over 35,000 rounds and frames are over 30,000 rounds. Locking blocks last on average about 22,000 rounds.

The M9A1 variant, which is an enhanced M9, has been used by the U.S. Marine Corps since 2006. The M9A1 variant differs mainly from the standard M9 in that the frame features an integrated Picatinny MIL-STD-1913 rail for attaching a tactical light or other accessories. It also uses magazines with a PVD coating that reduces friction. In addition, the magazine body is designed to be sand- and grit-resistant. Ask Marines about the M9A1 and they'll say they really don't have a need for a handgun. That's why they're issued rifles, they'll say.

More 9mms Considered

In 2016, the Marine Corps Forces Special Operations Command (MARSOC) announced that Marine special operators had the option of carrying the Glock 19. The G19 was chosen because operators needed a pistol for concealed carry and low visibility profile.

They liked the 1911A1 platform and special forces continued to use it, but the Marines concluded the 9mm round suited their needs better since, in their experience during operations, the round could penetrate objects of varying densities and in different environmental conditions.

The NATO 9mm standard rounds are loaded to M882 specifications, meaning a 124-grain FMJ bullet is loaded to a muzzle velocity of about 1,260 fps. The NATO round has more power than the U.S. military 9mm cartridge designated US M882 Ball. The M882 uses a 112-grain FMJ bullet loaded to a muzzle velocity of 1,263 fps out of the M9. The NATO round employs a heavier bullet, but it travels at almost the same velocity as the M882 round.

Since these are military cartridges used in warfare, the bullet is a full metal jacket (FMJ), also commonly referred to as "ball" ammo. This is to comply with the Hague Convention of 1899, which prohibits the use of expanding or "dumdum" flat-tipped ammunition that can cause excessive wounds.

Special Forces, however, shoot several special-purpose 9mm rounds, including a 147-grain JHP bullet that is authorized for special mission units such as the 75th Ranger Regiment as well as military-police units.

Beginning with the Request for Proposals in September of 2015, the XM17 Modular Handgun System (MHS) program conducted by the Army was a search for a replacement sidearm for the M9 and M11 pistols. The U.S. Army requirement called for a non-caliber specific weapon with modular features. 'Modular' is the buzzword, and for the MHS program that meant the adoption of different fire control devices, pistol grips, and alternate magazine options. The weapon was required to fit various hand sizes, allow mounting of targeting enablers like tactical lights and/or laser pointers via Picatinny rails, facilitate the use of a suppressor, and have a non-reflective neutral finish to avoid detection.

The Army's new modular handgun, the XM17 (above), and the XM18 (not pictured) are a 5-inch and 4.5-inch-barreled SIG P320, respectively.
Photo: SIG Sauer

By 2016, U.S. Naval Special Warfare (NSW) adopted the Glock 19 as the official sidearm and secondary weapon of the USN SPECWAR operators — Navy SEALs — replacing the SIG P226.

MHS began in 2011 and results were announced in 2017. The Beretta-made M9 was out and the SIG Sauer P320 pistol was in. On January 19, 2017, the U.S. military made the official announcement that a variant of the SIG Sauer P320 had won the XM17 Modular Handgun System competition. The SIG would become the new M17 pistol.

The P320 was released in 2014 and is a polymer striker-fired pistol. It already had some street credibility by the time the MHS program was in full swing. The P320 is a modular pistol with interchangeable grip modules that can be adjusted in frame size and caliber by the operator.

After the announcement, the SIG P320 went through extensive testing across a large sample of users. Testers at Fort Bragg included soldiers of the Special Operations Aviation Regiment, and some of the military occupational specialties involved such as police, pilots, infantry and crew chiefs. Like my engineering professor said, "Test 'em like you use 'em."

SPECIFICATIONS

MODEL: SIG Sauer P320

CALIBER: 9mm

ACTION: Short Recoil-Operated, Locked Breech

TRIGGER: Striker Fire

BARREL LENGTH: 4.7 in.

OVERALL LENGTH: 8.0 in.

WEIGHT: 29.4 oz. (unloaded)

GRIPS: Textured Polymer

SIGHTS: Fixed, Notch Rear/Blade Front

FINISH: Flat Dark Earth (FDE)

CAPACITY: 17+1, Double-Stack Magazine

CHAPTER 6

THE 9MM IN POP CULTURE

Blockbuster movies can make actors, pistols, and cartridges overnight superstars.

" That's a real badge. I'm a real cop. And this is a real gun." – *Lethal Weapon* (1987). Yes, that could have been the moment when the 9mm went from being a European caliber to one embraced by America. Hollywood had a lot of influence. Remember the other scene when Riggs, the character played by Mel Gibson, is at the police shooting range with Murtaugh, played by Danny Glover. Murtaugh takes his time as he aims, cracks his neck and drills the target right between the eyes with his .357 Magnum Smith & Wesson revolver. Riggs says a lot of older guys still like them. Meaning the revolver.

He then proceeds to shoot as fast as fast can be a smiley face into the target with his Beretta 92 9mm. That was how Hollywood convinced America the 9mm was the new caliber, the new kid on the block. It exuded youth and vitality, speed and destruction the likes of which a revolver could not match. Unless, of course, you are Jerry Miculek.

The following year, Bruce Willis as NYPD officer John McClane in *Die Hard* (1988) fought off German terrorists in a high-rise building in Los Angeles after they took his wife and others hostage during a Christmas party.

Willis' pistol in the flick was a Beretta 92. Throughout the film, the tension rises as the magazine in his Beretta steadily empties and bad guys die. Then there is the scene in which he is down to one last cartridge. The viewer is treated to a closeup of a 9mm cartridge in his hand. It was destiny the 9mm would become a star. Of course, it wasn't just blockbuster movies that pushed the 9mm into America's spotlight. Uncle Sam had influence as well.

The Beretta was the new shiny weapon in Uncle Sam's small arms arsenal, which gave it good face in the movies. What was next? Video games. Pong was a distant memory. Atari had been on nearly every kid's wish list since it debuted in 1972. Our television screens became the arcades, and games like "Maze War" (1973) morphed into a certain genre of video game — the shooter. As game graphics improved, shooter games became more realistic and more violent. Perhaps it was "Doom" (1993) or "Wolfenstein 3D" (1992) when the first-person shooter took players away from the ordinary and had them fight evil Nazis (are there any other kind?) or invading demons from hell. Nine-levels of fierce combat played out with a joystick and button controller. Doom, it is said, was played by 15–20 million people. What does the player start out with in Doom, but a high-capacity pistol — the perfect starter weapon. As the game progresses, as if you didn't know, a chainsaw, shotgun, chain gun, rocket launcher and a plasma rifle (whatever that is) are found or won and are used to fight to the next level. Again, the Beretta and pop culture intersect in "Metal Gear" (1987), "Doom 2" (1995), "Resident Evil" (1996) and more. In "Rainbow Six" (1996) it was even equipped with a suppressor.

TV was the other connection, triangulating the 9mm as the pistol to get the job done. *Spenser For Hire* (1985–1988) and the first season of *X-files* (1991) showcased a Beretta 92 up-close and personal and then other pistols began to appear in the movie theater, TV and video games — SIG, Glock, H&K — the truth was out there, and pop culture embraced the nine.

Rappers took the 9mm and made it their own. The lyrics in the 1987 song "9mm Goes Bang" by Boogie Down Productions raps, "Wa da dang/Wa da dang/ Listen to my 9-millimeter go bang." There are more examples even as rap continues to emerge to this day, such as "Gangstas, bitches, and nines." As some products were called out by rap song lyrics, think Gucci and Hennessy, so too was Glock. While those who work in law enforcement and the military were being trained on 9mm pistols, civilians were being immersed in them from every angle. There was momentum and it has not slowed down.

Hollywood's Trick Gun: Star Model B

Armorers for movies and TV shows want you to think it's a Colt 1911 — but it's a Spanish-made 9mm stand-in, for one very important reason. You might not know what a Star Model B is, but I'm sure you've seen one. Here's a clue:

"Ezekiel 25:17. The path of the righteous man is beset on all sides…"

Not yet? How about this:

"I'd like to make one good score and back off…"

If you've ever seen the movies *Pulp Fiction* (1994) or *The Wild Bunch* (1969), then you've seen a Star Model B pistol, but you may have mistaken it for a Colt 1911. And that was exactly the movie set armorer's intent. It is easy to make such an incorrect assumption since there's a bit of Hollywood magic at play here. The Star Model B is the 1911, which is not a 1911.

This Auto-Ordnance M1911A1 is a replica of a 1911A1. Note the grip safety, arched mainspring housing, and small fixed sights.

As early as the 1950s, the Star Model B began appearing in some notable movies. In *Halls of Montezuma*, the 1951 movie starring Richard Widmark in a story about U.S. Marines fighting Japanese soldiers on a Pacific island during WWII, the Star made its first appearance. Here's why: Back in the old days of movie making, it was difficult for a movie set armorer to run blanks in a .45 ACP-chambered 1911 pistol. The gun will fire blanks, but the slide won't cycle like a semi-automatic pistol. The recoil spring and locking lugs of a .45 ACP 1911 offer too much resistance to the low-pressure blank.

Hollywood's armorers improvised a stand-in for the venerable 1911, and that was the Star Model B. The Star, chambered in 9mm, runs on blanks reliably because there's less resistance from the pistol's mechanism, allowing the action to function. More importantly, the Model B looks a lot like a 1911. In fast-moving gunfight scenes, it is hard to tell the difference between the two.

Steve McQueen used one in *The Getaway* (1972), directed by Sam Peckinpah and based on the Jim Thompson novel. McQueen, playing Carter "Doc" McCoy, uses both a Colt 1911 and a Star Model B. In close-ups, McQueen carries a Colt 1911, but in shooting scenes it's a Star. Peckinpah also directed *The Wild Bunch*, and if you pay close attention to the 1911s in that film, you'll see the external extractor on the right side of the pistol — a dead giveaway that it's a Star Model B, not a Colt 1911.

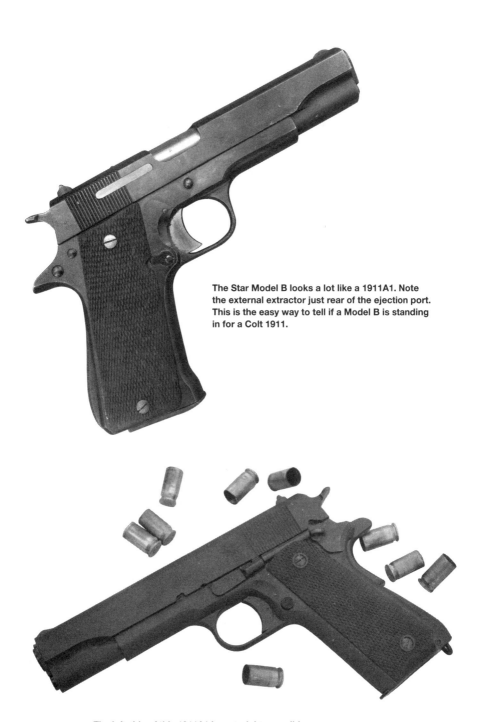

The Star Model B looks a lot like a 1911A1. Note the external extractor just rear of the ejection port. This is the easy way to tell if a Model B is standing in for a Colt 1911.

The left side of this 1911A1 has straight rear slide serrations, the standard slide stop, and thumb safety.

The Star Model B was in a collection of handguns offered to Travis Bickle in *Taxi Driver* (1976). Kevin Costner playing Elliot Ness in *The Untouchables* (1987) used a Model B. Both a blued and a nickel-finish Model B appeared in that film. Even TV shows like *MASH* and *The Walking Dead* have featured a Star Model B as a stunt double.

But perhaps the most memorable use of the Star Model B is in *Pulp Fiction*, when Samuel L. Jackson, playing the character Jules, wields a nickel-plated Star Model B with pearl grips. Jules recites the Ezekiel bible verse before shooting a bad guy with it.

A History Fit for a B Movie

The Star did not start off with all the glitz and glamour but has an interesting background nonetheless. In fact, the story of this odd little 9mm involves a manufacturer in the Basque region of Spain making arms for the Nazis, a seizure by Soviet troops, and

The Star Model B has nearly the exact serrations, slide stop, and thumb safety as the 1911. The trigger also looks like a 1911's, but it pivots instead of sliding.

a trip to America by boat — the road to tinsel town for the Star Model B could itself be a script for a B movie.

Star, short for Star Bonifacio Echeverria, S.A., is a firearms manufacturer in Spain. The Star Model B evolved from the Star Model A, which started off as a Colt 1911 knock-off back in 1922. Even from a distance, you could tell the Model A was not a 1911. The Star Model B, however, received more design inspiration from the Colt 1911, which was obvious when it was introduced in 1931. (Then again, what pistol manufacturer was not influenced or impacted by the 1911 design?) But the Star was as much a Colt 1911 as a Chinatown Rolex has Swiss parts.

The plot thickens a few years after World War II began. Spain was neutral during the war but sold weapons to whoever had the cash. Germany's war machine was in full motion and was producing sidearms for front-line troops, but by 1942 there was a need for pistols to arm police and some military units. Germany bought the Model B by the crate. Those guns were named B.08. Unlike nearly every other weapon issued to German troops and police, the Star Model B did not carry Nazi proof marks. (The serial number code to determine if the Star was German issue will have three digits and a proofing date code with an N, Ñ or O.)

When the war ended, the Soviets scrambled to gather up the machines that made weapons and the handguns themselves, sending them back to the Motherland in preparation for the next war. Numerous Star Model B pistols were captured and confiscated by the Soviets. Back in the Soviet Union, the pistols were disassembled, reblued with a hot dip, and reassembled with no regard to keeping the original parts to the original gun. The telltale Soviet trace can be found on heat-treated, hardened steel parts because the Soviet bluing process changed the color of these parts to a plum color. They

The Star Model B has nearly the exact serrations, slide stop, magazine release, and thumb safety as a 1911A1. The trigger also looks like a 1911's, but it pivots instead of sliding.

Viewed from the business end, the Model B reveals a similar bushing as a typical GI 1911.

From an operator's point of view, the Star has the same sized sights as a GI 1911.

were also dunked in the U.S.S.R.'s version of Cosmoline and stored in wood crates for use in future conflicts.

But that next war never happened. Due to peace, or the semblance of it, and the age of the Model B pistols, arsenal stockpiles in the former Soviet Union made their way to the U.S. on a slow boat from Asia as imported surplus handguns. The Star Model B was produced after World War II for Spain's military and was last made in 1983.

A Star is Born

Chambered in 9mm, the Model B looks a lot like a U.S. military 1911A1 externally. The slide stop, thumb safety, trigger, and magazine release button on the Model B are near dead ringers for the controls on a 1911. The rear grip strap on the frame of a Model B incorporates an arch, making it look like the mainspring housing of a 1911A1.

But the most obvious feature that makes the Star a bogus 1911 is the extractor — a long slender piece of metal set in a cutout on the slide that can be seen on the right side. While some later 1911 builds (such as those from Smith & Wesson and SIG) do feature an external extractor, most, including the original U.S. government-issued 1911, have an internal extractor.

The other obvious difference is the lack of a grip safety. Other than those two features that sharp-eyed 1911 fans can spot easily, the lines, shape and look of the Model B are all 1911A1. With the same sights and similar checkered grip panels, the Model B resembles an ordinary government-issue 1911A1 from the outside. Internally, however, the Model B is quite different.

For instance, the trigger on the Star pivots rather than slides as it does in a

1911. The thumb safety on the Model B can be engaged with the hammer fully forward or fully cocked, whereas a 1911's must be cocked for the thumb safety to be engaged.

Test and Evaluation: Star Model B

My Star Model B has a high serial number and was produced in the 1970s. It is easy to gripe about surplus pistols since most look like they were dragged behind a jeep driving down a gravel road. To say I was jaded going to the range to test a weathered-looking 1911 knockoff is an understatement. But looks can be deceiving.

The importer had long ago cleaned off the Cosmoline that held the ghosts in this pistol. I would rate the finish about 60 percent — a fair condition by NRA standards — and that is being generous. One grip panel is checkered plastic, the other checkered wood, which makes it look like the gun was left in the sun for too long. Racking the slide, it was obvious the Model B was still inebriated with oil. After a squirt of CLP, it started to act like a combat pistol.

I have to say that the Star Model B turned me around. There is a reason why there were so many produced.

The Model B uses a single-stack 8-round steel magazine. The follower and spring were in good condition, and the magazine was easy to load. The magazine dropped free when the magazine release was depressed, similar to a 1911. There was surprisingly very little wiggle between the slide and the receiver. The rear vertical slide serrations offered a good purchase to manipulate the slide. The spur hammer is nicely checkered, making it slip-free. The controls mimic the 1911, so the thumb safety worked the same. The trigger is surprisingly crisp. Either some *hombre* in

Spain or the importer did a great job re-assembling the pistol after the war. The trigger broke at about 4 pounds with little take-up.

Whoever had the gun before me must have had cross-dominant eyes, because the rear sight was pushed way over, and the pistol shot to the left. A brass punch and hammer knocked the rear sight back home — and a real shooter emerged.

I loaded a variety of different 9mm bullet types, anticipating that the ball-style ammo would run while hollowpoint loads would choke the handgun. I also expected stovepipe jams and extraction failures (I had heard that some surplus Star Model Bs were fraught with jams). I found absolutely no glitches with any ammo. It did prefer Aguila ammo with 124-grain FMJ bullets, and at 25 yards put 5 shots into about 3 inches — a nice group. The sights are like a government-issue 1911A1 — small but capable.

I was impressed with the Star Model B. The wannabe 1911 provided a fine performance — which, of course, it has been doing for decades. It's a handgun with rich history and movie and TV credits to its name. You don't need my approval to keep one in the nightstand drawer. "Besides, isn't it more exciting when you don't have permission?" Can you guess what movie that quote came from? Here's a hint, the Star Model B had a starring role.

SPECIFICATIONS

MODEL: Star Model B
CALIBER: 9mm
ACTION: Semi-Automatic, Cameo Locking Lug
TRIGGER: Single Action
BARREL LENGTH: 5 in.
OVERALL LENGTH: 8.5 in.
WEIGHT: 39.6 oz. (unloaded)
GRIPS: Textured polymer
SIGHTS: Fixed, Notch Rear/Blade Front
FINISH: Blued
CAPACITY: 8+1, Single-Stack Magazine

PERFORMANCE: STAR MODEL B				
9mm Ammo	Velocity (fps)	Energy (ft.-lbs.)	Best Accuracy (inches)	Average Accuracy (inches)
Hornady American Gunner 115 XTP	1,138	331	2.0	2.28
Aguila 124 FMJ	1,080	321	2.97	3.2
SIG Sauer 115 FMJ	1,296	429	2.3	2.72

Bullet weight measured in grains, velocity in feet per second, energy in foot-pounds, taken 15 feet from the muzzle by a ProChrono digital chronograph; accuracy in inches averaged from three, 5-shot groups at 25 yards.

CHAPTER 7

9MM SPECIFICATIONS AND PERFORMANCE

The 9mm is the number one handgun cartridge for NATO, the U.S. military, FBI, law enforcement and self-defense handgun owners across the country. To shoot the 9mm is to understand why. The cartridge is well over a century old. When it comes to concealed carry, many new models of compact and subcompact 9mm pistols have been offered, but this handy cartridge is really designed for a full-size handgun with a 4-inch barrel. Even so, significant advancements in cartridge development for self-defense have maximized the performance of pocket pistols.

Though lead-free and frangible bullets may seem new, they evolved as the use of the fledgling 9mm became more widespread during World War II. From a technical point of view, the 9mm is a tapered, rimless cartridge that holds a 9mm (.380 in.) bullet. The case has a length of 19mm (.754 in.) and a rim diameter of 9.96mm (.392 in.). Maximum overall length is 29.69mm (1.169 in.) and it headspaces on the case mouth. The common rifling twist rate for the cartridge is 1:9.84 inches, with six grooves. Original 124-grain FMJ bullets achieved a muzzle velocity of about 1,200 fps with a muzzle energy of 384 ft.-lbs.

Prior to World War I, one of the first 9mm military loads used a bullet with

The ubiquitous 9mm cartridge is available in a wide variety of bullet types and weights.

A Speer Gold Dot 9mm round is fired into bare gelatin.

a conical nose and flat tip. This load was designed to cause more injury than a round-nose bullet. Conflicting stories say this flat-tipped projectile was dropped from German military service after being banned from warfare by The Hague Convention. Other sources say the flat-tip bullet did not feed well in P.08 pistols and the drum magazines some models. Regardless, the bullet's ogive shape was round and slightly tapered, basically, the shape of most 9mm FMJ bullets found today. It was designed to be lethal out to 50 meters. What can be considered the first +P ammo was also developed at this time to be used in carbines. This 9mm load was 15 percent greater than the standard load and not designed for use in handguns.

One of the very first standard 9mm cartridges had a fully jacketed bullet with a weight of about 115 grains. It used a brass case. As the war machine geared up for WWII, all nonferrous metals were conserved, thus lead, brass, and copper were replaced with other materials. About 1940, the first 9mm steel case cartridges were introduced. The German military also tested non-lead bullets made with material like iron, an alloy of sintered steel, which was made of compressed steel particles. Cartridges during WWII were handed out in boxes of 16 rounds, enough to fill two P.08 or P.38 magazines.

The 9mm Federal Premium Law Enforcement HST bullet penetrated the bare gelatin 13 inches and expanded to twice the bullet's original diameter, yet the core and jacket did not separate.

One test in the FBI protocol is to fire a bullet through clothing like denim. Fired from a Glock 43, the 9mm Gold Dot expanded picture-perfectly.

Another test is to fire a round through an angled piece of safety glass to simulate shooting through a windshield.

As much as we think the 9mm is pretty much the same as it was prior to WWI, the fact is that materials and technology have been developed to produce better performing bullets.

As specified by SAAMI (Sporting Arms and Ammunition Manufacturing Institute), the maximum pressure for the 9mm is 35,000 psi; SAAMI maximum pressure for the 9mm +P is 38,500 psi.

In the early 1990s, ammunition manufacturers began loading 9mm+P cartridges. These were attempts to improve the ballistics of the standard round. The +P cartridges had higher pressures and put more wear on firearms. Today, manufacturers include a "+P" and "+P+" ranking on the headstamp of the case to identify them from standard pressure rounds.

One of the areas where modern 9mm ammunition has greatly improved is consistent expansion and penetration of bullets. The Speer Gold Dot is a benchmark in 9mm performance. Gold Dot features a bonded core bullet, meaning the jacket and core do no separate while penetrating the target. The hollowpoint cavity and bullet weight are tuned for the 9mm caliber. Gold Dot works well in compact and full-size pistols, while Gold Dot Short Barrel is further optimized for short subcompact barrels.

Gold Dot ammo passes the FBI handgun cartridge protocol tests, which elevate the bullet's ability to penetrate, expand and retain weight in bare gelatin and through common barriers like denim clothing, glass windshield, pasteboard and more.

The ballistics charts above provide a snapshot of typical 9mm ammo muzzle velocity and muzzle energy by bullet weight and type. The 9mm's sweet spot for bullet weight is 115, 124, and 147 grains. These three weights offer a lot of flexibility in 9mm pistols. There are other bullet weights that are designed for special purposes. Lightweight bullets offer maximum velocity and tend to be used in self-defense loads. Heavier bullets tend to be loaded at subsonic velocities for maximum effect in suppressors. These charts provide a good comparison when looking at the differences between standard, subsonic, +P, and +P+ loads. I included the ammunition manufacturer with the bullet type, but you will note that similar bullet weights between manufacturers have slight differences in muzzle velocity and muzzle energy. Shooting this ammo out of a short barrel subcompact compared to a full-size pistol with 5-inch barrel will also show differences.

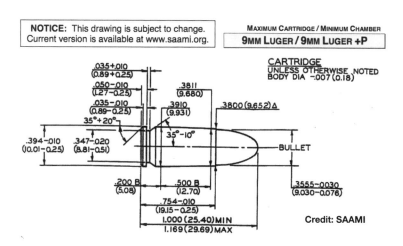

Credit: SAAMI

VELOCITY AND PRESSURE:
VELOCITY & PRESSURE DATA – TRANSDUCER

(N/E = Not Established)

Cartridge	Bullet Weight (gr.)	Velocity (fps)		Transducer Pressure (Solid test barrel, psi/100)[1]		
		Nominal Mean Instrumental @ 15' Vented Bbl.[2]	Nominal Mean Instrumental @ 15' Test Bbl.	Maximum Average Pressure (MAP)	Maximum Probable Lot Mean (MPLM)	Maximum Probable Sample Mean (MPSM)
9mm Luger	88	[3]	1,500	350	361	378
	95		1,330			
	100		1,195			
	105		1,200			
	115		1,135			
			1,210			
	124		1,090			
			1,130			
	135		1,060			
	147		985			
9mm Luger +P	90	[3]	1,375	385	397	415
	101		1,220			
	115		1,100			
			1,235			
	124		1,180			

Credit: SAAMI

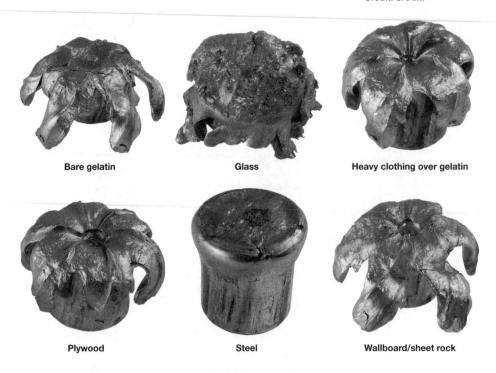

Bare gelatin   Glass   Heavy clothing over gelatin

Plywood   Steel   Wallboard/sheet rock

9mm Luger bullets recovered from a variety of materials after an FBI protocol test.

9MM BALLISTICS (SUBSONIC LOADS)

Bullet	Manufacturer	Muzzle Velocity (fps)	Muzzle Energy (ft-lbs.)
125-grain Lehigh Xtreme Defense Lead-Free	Black Hills	1,050	306
147-grain FMJ	Magtech	990	320
158-grain FMJ	Fiocchi	940	309

9MM BALLISTICS (STANDARD LOADS)

Bullet	Manufacturer	Muzzle Velocity (fps)	Muzzle Energy (ft-lbs.)
115-grain FMJ	Brown Bear	1,180	355
124-grain FMJ	Armscor	1,090	348
147-grain FMJ	Remington	990	320

9MM BALLISTICS (+P LOADS)

Bullet	Manufacturer	Muzzle Velocity (fps)	Muzzle Energy (ft-lbs.)
92-grain HP	G2 Research	1,250	319
115-grain HP	Barnes	1,100	309
124-grain JHP	Hornady	1,200	365
147-grain JHP	Grizzly	1,120	409

9MM BALLISTICS (+P+ LOADS)

Bullet	Manufacturer	Muzzle Velocity (fps)	Muzzle Energy (ft-lbs.)
90-grain Lehigh Xtreme Defense Lead-Free	Underwood	1,550	480
115-grain HP	Magtech	1,328	451
147-grain FMJ	Buffalo Bore	1,300	461

CHAPTER 8

WHY THE 9MM BEATS THE .40 S&W AND .45 ACP

So now that we know a bit about the specifications and data for the 9mm cartridge, what is it that makes it so popular? It does not have stellar, tack-driving accuracy like other pistol calibers, nor does it have the power of other cartridges. It is far from the perfect cartridge but is still the most prevalent worldwide. Even science gives the 9mm low marks compared to larger calibers. It's simple physics. A bigger, heavier bullet carrying more energy means a deeper and larger wound channel. So why is the 9mm king? There are three reasons: Shootability, increased magazine capacity, and ammunition choices.

Before we get into these, let's talk physics and math. A light projectile sheds velocity and energy faster than a heavier one.

More velocity equates to more energy. More energy factors into the amount of penetration, which affects terminal performance. Energy is the benchmark by which we rate a bullet's performance. To sum up this fast physics lesson: all things being equal, a larger, heavier bullet will penetrate deeper than a lighter one.

The move to the 9mm was not an instant success, as the Illinois State Police learned. As mentioned in an earlier chapter, they were one of the first U.S. law enforcement agencies to adopt the 9mm in the Smith & Wesson Model 39. The standard-issue round was either 100- or 115-grain, standard-velocity. The load was mediocre at best as the troopers found out, but when they changed to 115-grain hollowpoint +P+,

Muzzle energy is not the only standard by which to judge calibers. Ammo cost, speed on target, and capacity are top considerations.

those .380-inch bullets leaving the muzzle of their Model 39s at a velocity of 1,300 fps changed the game. The initial 9mm rounds at the time used by law enforcement did not yet reach the nine's full potential.

One of the issues our military experienced with the 9mm was dissatisfaction with the M9 pistol specifically and ammunition in general. It boiled down to a report compiled by the Center for Naval Analyses (CNA) and released in 2006 entitled, Soldier Perspectives on Small Arms in Combat. The report detailed a formal independent review of soldier opinions of their small arms in combat situations. Specifically, the Project Manager, Soldier Weapons (PMSW) wanted to know soldier perspectives on the reliability and durability of the M9 pistol, as well as the M4 and M16 (A2 and A4) rifles, and the M249 light machine gun. These four weapon systems are the standard-issue guns being used by Army soldiers in Iraq and Afghanistan.

Just to level set the results, weapon reliability is defined as "soldier level of confidence that their weapon will fire without a stoppage in the combat environment." Weapon durability is defined as "soldier level of confidence that their weapon will not suffer breakage or failure that necessitates repair before further use." Survey participants included over 2,600 soldiers who had returned from Iraq or Afghanistan and who had engaged in a firefight using the weapons listed. The net result was that soldiers were least satisfied with the M9 compared to the other weapons and "the most frequent recommendations included weapons and ammunition with more stopping power/lethality; higher quality magazines for the M9, M4, and M16; more durable ammo belt links and drum systems for the M249; and reduced size and weight in the M16 and M249."

Call it lethality, stopping power, or knock-down power, but there is no such thing as a caliber with this magic attribute. The truth is a combination of bullet placement and design, and follow-up, are what stop a threat. If a shooter does his job and places the shot accurately the 9mm can stop a threat. Our bodies can take an enormous amount of punishment. Our organs can move around inside us, so what might have been a good hit is not. There are numerous examples of people who are shot in a gunfight and did not realize they were hit until after the fight was over.

It may be ironic that the Mozambique Drill is a technique used with a Rhodesian mercenary, Mike Rousseau, during the Mozambican War of Independence from 1964 to 1974. Rousseau was fighting at the airport at Lourenço Marques, which is now called Maputo. He turned a corner and came face-to-face — about 10 paces — with a FRELIMO guerrilla armed with an AK-47. Armed with a Browning HP35 pistol chambered in 9mm, Rousseau immediately brought up his Hi Power and shot the guerrilla twice in the chest. This was a traditional "double tap" maneuver. According to Rousseau during a conversation with Jeff Cooper, Rousseau hit the guerrilla on either side of the sternum, which is typically sufficient to kill a man. Yet the guerrilla was still advancing, so he tried for a headshot and instead hit the guerrilla through the base of his neck, severing the spinal cord. Jeff Cooper, the founder of the Gunsite Academy shooting school and father of the "modern technique" of pistol shooting, decided to incorporate a drill similar to what Rousseau had experienced. Cooper called it the "Mozambique Drill."

The drill has you fire the first two shots to the center of mass and then a slight pause. The pause allows you to assess the situation and determine if a third shot is needed to the head. The drill has since been renamed

Failure Drill or Failed to Stop Drill due to political correctness. No doubt Cooper is rolling over in his grave over that, since he had no patience for political correctness — only fast, precise shooting.

I've talked to some recent veterans who have combat experience with the M9 and, according to some of them, the reason it has a 15-round magazine is that you need two shots to immobilize an opponent. That is due to the M882 cartridge, the U.S. military load for the 9mm — not the handgun itself. The military has plans to change the 9mm load and may even walk away from the FMJ ball ammo and use a more effective bullet.

With no further ado, here are the reasons the 9mm beats all other cartridges for combat and self-defense.

Shootability

When the 10mm Auto was dropped by the FBI in favor of the .40 S&W, law enforcement agencies nationwide followed suit and shifted to the .40, dropping the 9mm in what seemed like the blink of an eye. Even so, for most LE agencies the breakup with the nine would be short. The .40 S&W had what they wanted: a larger bullet at a higher velocity that created a larger and hence more lethal wound channel. At one time, manufacturers were introducing pistols in .40 S&W first and then following up with the same hand-gun chambered in 9mm. The H&K USP model is an example. Today, the .40 S&W might be considered, but now most handgun manufacturers introduce 9mm first, then .40 S&W and maybe .45 ACP.

The .45 ACP has been in use with our military since WWI and is a proven combat caliber. The problem with it is recoil. Even with full-size, steel receiver pistols like the 1911, the .45 ACP is a handful to control. Pistols chambered in 9mm — from sub-compacts to full-size models — have less recoil and that translates into you shooting the pistol better. Better shooting means better accuracy. Faster follow-up shots are one of the 9mm's greatest benefits.

Increased Magazine Capacity

Additional magazine capacity of the 9mm is a benefit over the .40 S&W and .45 ACP. For example, look at the Smith & Wesson M&P series. The M&P 9 has a capacity of 17+1 rounds. The M&P 40 has a capacity of 15+1, and the M&P 45 has a 10+1 round capacity. The 9mm offers less reloading and more shooting — something to think about if you get into a gunfight. The ability to confront multiple threats with more firepower and not have to take time to reload is a plus. Most who carry do not have spare ammo on them (they should). Concealing a 9mm pistol means more rounds on hand.

CALIBER COMPARISON			
Caliber	Bullet Diameter (inches)	Muzzle Velocity (fps)	Muzzle Energy (ft.-lbs.)
9mm 115-grain FMJ	.355	1,180	355
.40 S&W Auto 180-grain FMJ	.400	985	388
158-grain FMJ	.452	837	356

The typical double-stack 9mm has a capacity of at least 16+1 rounds. The .40 S&W has 15+1, and the .45 ACP 10+1.

Ammunition Choices

Since the 9mm is so popular there are many bullet options loaded by nearly every ammunition manufacturer. From fast 115-grain ammo to slower and heavier 147-grain rounds, the 9mm offers choice. The cost of 9mm ammo is less than .40 S&W and .45 ACP. Plus, it is easy to find 9mm ammo at nearly any store that sells ammunition. That means you can train more often and longer for less cost.

The 9mm was once embraced, tossed aside, and now embraced again. It's not a compromise cartridge — you now have more round capacity with bullets that provide wound cavities pacing those caused by larger cartridges. Times have changed and so has the 9mm.

The 9mm offers a wide assortment of ammunition choices. Small sample of 9mm cartridges available.

CHAPTER 9

CURRENT TRENDS IN 9MM AMMUNITION

The Mechani-Lokt belt used in Remington's Golden Saber Black Belt ammo firmly locks the jacket to the core and offers reliable expansion and consistent penetration.

Major ammunition manufacturers offer numerous bullets designed to perform specific tasks. A hollowpoint bullet that offers controlled expansion may not provide deep penetration. While a full metal jacket (FMJ) bullet may work on paper targets, when training on steel, a frangible projectile might be a better choice. Looking at the spectrum of bullet choices offered in factory loaded ammunition, there are traditional offerings on one end and new bullet designs on the other that push the performance envelope of the 9mm. All the well-established manufacturers — Winchester, Remington, Hornady, Fiocchi, Sellior & Bellot, Aguila, PPU, Federal — produce a variety of 9mm ammo for different shooting requirements including target, competition, plinking, and defense. The current trend is the rise of smaller ammo manufacturers like Underwood, NovX, Liberty, SIG Sauer, and many more. These niche makers are producing cutting-edge defensive ammo that is really making the industry rethink bullet design. Here is a look at some of the

BONDED JACKETED HOLLOWPOINTS			
Bullet Weight (grains)	Manufacturer	Muzzle Velocity (fps)	Muzzle Energy (ft.-lbs.)
115	Double Tap	1,415 (+P load)	511
124	Winchester PDX1 Defender	1,200 (+P load)	396
147	Atomic	900	264

players and trends in 9mm ammunition. Note that velocity and energy are factory data and will vary depending on the barrel length of your pistol.

Bonded Jacketed Hollowpoints (BJHP)

The BJHP bullets are manufactured with a process that bonds the copper jacket to the lead core. This prevents fragmentation and guarantees more retained weight. Typically used with +P ammo, this ensures the jacket stays adhered to the bullet core, especially at high velocity. Some manufacturers that load subsonic ammo also use bonded bullets to ensure less fragmentation while penetrating.

Weight in Grains: 115, 124, 147
Uses: Defense

Bonded Polymer Tip

Bonded polymer tips are manufactured by Nosler and are designed to perform like the company's long-established AccuBond hunting bullets. These bullets are designed with a tapered jacket and specially engineered lead alloy core for predictable expansion and penetration. The polymer tip resists clogging and aides smooth, reliable feeding.

Weight in Grains: 124
Uses: Defense

Full Metal Jacket Flat Nose (FMJ-FN)

Similar to full metal jacket, FMJ-FN bullets use a flat tip rather than the rounded nose of the FMJ. The type features a lead core and copper jacket or copper coating. Depending on the manufacturer, the base of the bullet may or may not be coated or jacketed. The bullets are designed for maximum accuracy — like wadcutter or semi-wadcutter bullets — and will punch cleaner holes through cardboard or paper targets than an FMJ, yet the bullet's nose design ensures reliable feeding. Buffalo Bore loads a +P 147-grain with hardcast lead flat nose and cranks up to 1,100 fps. This is a specialty round for bear country and designed to pen-

BONDED POLYMER TIP			
Bullet Weight (grains)	Manufacturer	Muzzle Velocity (fps)	Muzzle Energy (ft.-lbs.)
124	Nosler	1,200 (+P load)	396

FULL METAL JACKET FLAT NOSE

Bullet Weight (grains)	Manufacturer	Muzzle Velocity (fps)	Muzzle Energy (ft.-lbs.)
115	HPR	1,128	325
125	Winchester Train and Defend	950	295
147	Speer Lawman	985	317
147	Remington UMC	990	320
147	Buffalo Bore	1,100 (+P load)	395

etrate 4 to 6 feet! Winchester Train and Defend is match ammo; Train is designed for training and practice and Defend is used for defense. The rounds have the same ballistics and recoil, so training can be as close to using defensive ammo without the cost.

Weight in Grains: 100, 115, 147

Uses: Target Shooting, Plinking, Training, Defense, Competition

Fluted Bullets

Fluted bullets have three to four flutes carved out of the bullet nose. The flutes are engineered to create a maximum hydraulic displacement and terminal energy transfer into tissue. Lehigh Defense manufactures a variety of fluted bullets for its line of ammo and reloaders. Other manufacturers use Lehigh bullets in their ammo. There

For high-volume training, Blazer is loaded with a 147-grain FMJ-FN projectile. Blazer keeps costs down by using non-reloadable aluminum cases.

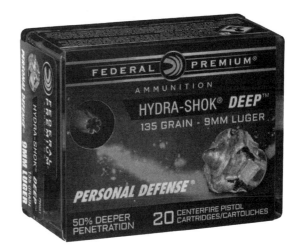

Federal Premium's Hydra-Shok Deep cartridge features a more robust center post and a core design that provides as much as 50 percent deeper penetration than original Hydra-Shok and other hollowpoint bullets. Photo: Federal Premium

are a few types of fluted bullets and each is designed for a different purpose. Lehigh's Xtreme Defense fluted bullets are designed to create a massive wound channel and reduce penetration depth. The bullet has an optimized flute, bullet weight, and velocity to achieve 18 inches of penetration. NovX 9mm ARX Engagement cartridges are loaded with a polycarbonate/copper ARX bullet with a Shell Shock Technologies

FLUTED			
Bullet Weight (grains)	Manufacturer	Muzzle Velocity (fps)	Muzzle Energy (ft.-lbs.)
65	Underwood Xtreme Defender	1,700	417
65	NovX ARX Engagement	1,655	395
65	Polycase Inceptor ARX	1,620 (+P load)	379
90	Lehigh Defense Xtreme Defense	1,450	420
100	Underwood Extreme Penetrator	1,350 (+P+ load)	465
115	Underwood Extreme Penetrator	1,250	400
125	Black Hills Xtreme Defense	1,050 (subsonic load)	295

NovX Engagement Extreme ammo loads a 65-grain fluted copper polymer projectile to create massive wound channels.

stainless steel case. These bullets operate on the principle of aero and fluid dynamics, not hydrostatic shock or mushrooming. The bullet is constructed of a blend of powdered copper and epoxy/polymer resin and is heated under high-pressure injection molding. The 65-grain offering is loaded to +P velocity to provide maximum wound damage with controlled penetration.

Weight in Grains: 65, 90, 115, 125
Uses: Defense

Frangible Bullets

Designed to disintegrate upon hitting a target harder than the bullet is the frangible projectile. Frangibles are molded using powdered copper and a polymer. The majority of frangible ammunition is used for training. Fiocchi Frangible ammunition, for example, is loaded with a SinterFire frangible bullet designed to crumble on impact with hard

PolyCase produces Ruger ARX loads using a 74-grain injection-molded copper/polymer matrix projectile.

FRANGIBLE			
Bullet Weight (grains)	Manufacturer	Muzzle Velocity (fps)	Muzzle Energy (ft.-lbs.)
65	Liberty Ammunition Civil Trainer	1,700	417
65	Polycase Inceptor RNP	1,565 (+P load)	354
80 (#6 shot)	CorBon Glaser Blue Safety Slug	1,500 (+P load)	399
80	CorBon Glaser Silver Safety Slug	1,500 (+P load)	399
80	Ammo Inc. OPS	1,320	329
85	HPR BlackOps	1,259	299
92	G2 Research Telos	1,210	299
100	Hevi Shot Hevi Duty	1,200	320
100	Fiocchi Frangible	1,300	375

NovX Cross Trainer ammo loads a 65-grain RNP copper polymer projectile that breaks up upon impact on hardened steel. It's a good option for training on steel.

A 100-grain SinterFire frangible, lead-free bullet is loaded into Fiocchi frangible ammo. The copper/tin composite projectile features a molded-in taper crimp to ensure reliability and functionality.

surfaces like steel plates so there is no splash back on bystanders.

The Glaser Safety Slug is a pioneer in frangible ammo for personal protection. In a defensive situation, frangible ammo is designed to resist deep penetration of soft tissue while fragmenting upon initial contact into the target. Glaser Slugs use #12 or #6 shot in lieu of a polymer/copper bullet. The Glaser Blue Safety slug penetrates 5 to 7 inches and Glaser Silver to 6 to 8 inches. Ammo Inc. makes a defensive frangible round loaded with a hollowpoint frangible (HPF) bullet designed to work on soft targets. HPR's frangible defense round uses an open tip bullet.

Full Metal Jacket

Perhaps the most common 9mm bullet is the full metal jacket (FMJ). This is the typical military round with a copper jacket covering a lead core. Some FMJ bullets, such as Winchester Super Clean, use a non-lead core made of zinc. NATO ammo is loaded with FMJ bullets and, while this type abides by international laws of warfare, the bullet is better suited to target shooting

and plinking rather than stopping a threat. Yes, the FMJ bullet is used in combat and is up to the task, but other bullet types (namely hollowpoints) are better suited to stopping an attacker. However, as a training round the FMJ shines. Some brands of FMJ ammo are relatively inexpensive, like TulAmmo, which loads the FMJ in a non-reloadable steel case. And while TulAmmo can make inexpensive stuff for blasting, brands like ASYM offer precision ammo for formal target shooting. Most FMJ 9mm bullets have a rounded nose but some weights use a flat nose. Winchester Winclean loads a brass enclosed base (BEB), which is for all intents and purposes an FMJ with a fully enclosed lead core and a brass jacket. This type of ammo is designed for indoor training where lead fumes are an issue.

Weight in Grains: 90, 115, 124, 147

Uses: Training, Plinking

Hollowpoint Bullets

Hollowpoint (HP) bullets are designed to expand upon impact. The traditional HP design received a boost in technology in recent years due to some radically de-

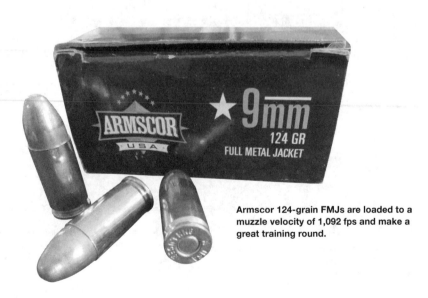

Armscor 124-grain FMJs are loaded to a muzzle velocity of 1,092 fps and make a great training round.

Aguila 124-grain FMJ is manufactured using case crimp to reduce the potential for setback of the projectile. It has decent muzzle velocity, too, at 1,115 fps.

signed bullets by such brands as G2, Liberty, Barnes, Lehigh, and others. Many of these new designs are manufactured from solid copper and contain no lead. Examples include Underwood cartridges loaded with Lehigh Maximum Expansion bullets. These projectiles are made of solid copper with a deep hollowpoint and razor-sharp petals designed to expand to the largest diameter, providing a maximum cutting surface. G2R's R.I.P. or Radically Invasive Projectile is a true high-tech HP. It uses a trocar point that acts like a hole saw to penetrate target material. The thing can inflict nine separate wound channels. As the R.I.P. penetrates, the petals expand and break off to create a wound channel up to 6 inches in diameter. The Civic Duty round is similar to the R.I.P.

bullet and expands, but does not fragment. The Civic Duty expands 2.5 times its initial diameter after contacting a fluid medium like flesh. This round retains 99.9% weight inside the intended target without concern of over-penetration. Liberty Civil Defense ammunition is loaded with a 50-grain lead-free fragmenting HP bullet that travels at high velocity — 2,000 fps — resulting in 12 inches of ballistic gel penetration and a permanent wound cavity greater than 3.5 inches in diameter. Barnes TAC-XP bullets feature all-copper construction and produce very large, deep hollowpoint cavities via consistent expansion and penetration.

Weight in Grains: 50, 70, 92, 94, 95, 105, 115, 135

Uses: Defense

	FULL METAL JACKET		
Bullet Weight (grains)	Manufacturer	Muzzle Velocity (fps)	Muzzle Energy (ft.-lbs.)
90	Winchester Super Clean	1,325	315
115	Winchester White Box	1,325	362
115	Remington UMC	1,145	335
115	Blazer Brass	1,125	325
115	Federal American Eagle	1,160	344
115	SIG Sauer Elite Performance	1,185	359
115	TulAmmo	1,150	338
115	Black Hills	1,150	336
124	Winchester NATO	1,140	358
124	Federal American Eagle	1,120	345
124	MagTech Sport	1,109	339
124	Speer Lawman	1,090	327
124	Federal American Eagle Suppressor	1,030	292
147	DoubleTap	1,135 (+P load)	420
147	Fiocchi Shooting Dynamics	1,050	360
147	Federal American Eagle	1,000	301
147	MagTech Sport	990	320
147	SIG Sauer Elite Performance	985	317
147	Winchester White Box	990	320
147	Remington UMC	990	330
147	Winchester Train Reduce Recoil	950	295
147	ASYM Precision Match	900	264

The author has run a lot of SIG Sauer 115-grain FMJs through many different pistols with the same consistent results.

Speer Lawman loaded with 115-grain FMJ bullets worked well in older 9mm pistols manufactured before hollowpoint ammo became popular.

Sure, this TulAmmo loaded with a 115-grain FMJ smells like Putin's dirty socks when fired, but it is inexpensive and runs great in the author's Glock 17 Gen3.

Winchester White Box loaded with 115-grain FMJ bullets for positive functioning at an affordable price.

Jacketed Hollowpoint

A jacketed hollowpoint (JHP) bullet is the same as a traditional lead HP bullet except the lead core has a copper jacket or coating. Some bullets may have a brass jacket in lieu of copper. The jacket helps prevent leading issues associated with a plain lead bullet and ensures proper feeding in semi-automatic pistols. These bullets are loaded by a number of ammunition manufacturers and are by far the most popular defense bullet made. Typically, JHP bullets are less expensive than some of the newer HP ones. Like HP, JHP are designed to expand when penetrating a target. In the best situation, JHP bullets perform as advertised but debris can be trapped in the hollowpoint cavity preventing full expansion. Thick clothing like denim or leather, glass, plasterboard, wood, and other material that the bullet may need to penetrate before hitting a target can clog the cavity.

Makers like Speer engineered the JHP to provide consistent expansion through all types of barriers. Speer Gold

Dot ammunition is loaded with bonded core bullets. Bonding the jacket to the core means the core and jacket will not separate and the bullet will have better weight retention. Federal Premium Personal Defense ammunition uses an HST bullet that features a tapered jacket profile for reliable feeding, a cannelure that locks the copper jacket to the lead core, patented co-aligned internal and external skiving

HOLLOWPOINT			
Bullet Weight (grains)	Manufacturer	Muzzle Velocity (fps)	Muzzle Energy (ft.-lbs.)
50	Liberty Ammunition Civil Defense	2,000 (+P load)	417
70	Underwood (Lehigh Maximum Expansion bullet)	1,650	354
92	G2 Research R.I.P.	1,250	399
94	Buffalo Bore (Barnes TAC-XP bullet)	1,100	399
95	Underwood (Lehigh Controlled Fracturing bullet)	1,550 (+P+ load)	329
105	Underwood (Lehigh Controlled Fracturing bullet)	1,375 (+P+ load)	299
105	Underwood (Lehigh Maximum Expansion bullet)	1,275 (+P load)	299
105	(Underwood Lehigh Maximum Expansion)	1,175	320
105	Buffalo Bore (Barnes TAC-XPD bullet)	1,175	375
115	Double Tap (Barnes TAC-XPD bullet)	1,400 (+P+ load)	375
115	Gorilla Silverback Defense	1,350 (+P load)	375
115	Black Hills (Barnes TAC-XPD bullet)	1,200	375
115	Barnes TAC-XPD	1,200	375
115	Fiocchi Frangible	1,100	375
124	Prime Hexagon	1,148	375

A 94-grain pure copper petaled-trocar bullet is loaded into G2 Research Civic Duty cartridges. The bullet is designed to deliver an intense energy dump on the target while limiting the depth of penetration.

G2 Research Telos loads a 92-grain controlled fragmenting, 100 percent copper projectile. Unique tooling inside of the hollowpoint cavity allows it to fragment upon entering a gel or liquid target.

A 50-grain lead-free fragmenting HP projectile is used in Liberty Defense Civil Defense ammo. The bullet travels at 2,000 fps and penetrates 12 inches of ballistic gel while creating a permanent wound cavity over 3.5 inches in diameter.

L-Tech Enterprise loads a 124-grain pure copper hollowpoint in a Shell Shock two-piece reloadable steel case.

The G2 Research R.I.P. (Radically Invasive Projectile) features a 92-grain petaled-trocar bullet that penetrates deep into a target and fragments in fluid.

and a deeply tapered hollowpoint that will not clog.

Some manufacturers like IMI load a bullet with a Di-Cut bullet ogive designed for consistent feeding, which helps the bullet expand upon hitting a target. Since there is such popularity with JHP bullets, there is a variety of specialty loads, like Winchester W Defend Reduced Recoil. This load has less felt recoil than a typical JHP-loaded cartridge with the same bullet weight and makes it easier to shoot from small, lightweight, subcompact pistols. Remington Ultimate Defense Compact Handgun is designed for maximum velocity and energy out of a short-barrel pistol. Federal Premium Personal Defense Micro and Speer Gold Dot Short Barrel are optimized for performance in subcompact handguns with 3-inch barrels.

Weight in Grains: 115, 124, 147

Uses: Defense, Hunting

Federal Premium Personal Defense HST ammunition is a benchmark in jacketed hollowpoint ammo. This 147-grain JHP will deliver 13.63 inches of penetration, 0.63 inches of expansion, and 90 percent weight retention through all FBI protocol test barriers.

Jacketed Soft Point

A jacketed soft point (JSP) bullet offers more penetration than a traditional JHP bullet, but with the expansion of a JHP.

Weight in Grains: 95, 124

Uses: Defense, Hunting

Polymer Tip Hollowpoint

The polymer tip hollowpoint takes the JHP to the next level by filling the cavity with a soft polymer designed to deliver reliable and controlled expansion regardless of the target material. Hornady pioneered this design with its FTX bullet and offers variations in a number of its cartridge lines. Hornady FlexLock bullets are designed to deliver barrier-blind performance when shot through common urban barriers, for example. This bullet features Hornady's Flex Tip design to eliminate clogging and aid bullet

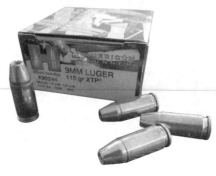

Hornady American Gunner launches Hornady's 115-grain XTP JHP bullet to a muzzle velocity of 1,200 fps. The author has fired bucket loads of these cartridges and can vouch for their accuracy and consistency.

The 147-grain XTP JHP projectile in Hornady Custom offers 310 ft.-lbs. of muzzle energy and a muzzle velocity of 975 fps.

	JACKETED HOLLOWPOINT		
Bullet Weight (grains)	Manufacturer	Muzzle Velocity (fps)	Muzzle Energy (ft.-lbs.)
115	Underwood (Nosler JHP bullet)	1,400 (+P load)	501
115	Remington High Terminal Performance	1,250	399
115	Sellier & Bellot	1,237	391
115	Winchester White Box	1,225	383
115	Speer Gold Dot	1,200	355
115	Silver Bear	1,180	355
115	PMC Bronze	1,160	344
115	Fiocchi (Hornady XTP bullet)	1,160	340
115	Speer Gold Dot Short Barrel	1,150	364
115	IMI	1,150	338
124	Black Hills	1,250 (+P load)	430
124	Speer Gold Dot	1,220 (+P load)	410
124	Hornady American Gunner (XTP bullet)	1,200	396
124	SIG Sauer Elite Performance (V-Crown bullet)	1,165	374
124	Federal Premium Personal Defense (Federal HST bullet)	1,150	365
124	Speer Gold Dot	1,150	364
124	Hornady Custom (XTP bullet)	1,110	339
124	Remington Ultimate Defense Compact Handgun	1,100	333
124	Fiocchi Shooting Dynamics	1,125	333

Bullet Weight (grains)	Manufacturer	Muzzle Velocity (fps)	Muzzle Energy (ft.-lbs.)
147	DoubleTap	1,125 (+P load)	410
147	Winchester Super-X Silvertip	1,010	333
147	Federal Premium Personal Defense Federal HST bullet)	1,000	326
147	Buffalo Bore (Speer Gold Dot bullet)	1,000	326
147	Winchester White Box	990	320
147	MagTech	990	320
147	Hornady Custom (XTP bullet)	975	310
147	Winchester W Defend Reduced Recoil	950	295
150	Federal Premium Personal Defense Micro (Federal HST bullet)	900	270

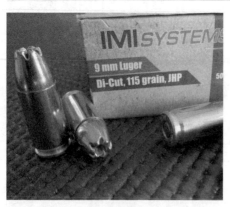

The 115-grain JHP in IMI ammo features a Di-Cut bullet o-give designed for consistent feeding and operation in a wide range of 9mm pistols.

Prime Ammo 124-grain Hexagon JHP is loaded by GECO, a high-tech Swiss munitions manufacturer. It is top-shelf ammo.

SIG Sauer V-Crown loaded with 115-grain JHP achieves a factory muzzle velocity of 1,185 fps and 359 ft.-lbs. of muzzle energy.

Winchester W Defend Reduced Recoil loads a 147-grain JHP for less recoil and is a good choice for lightweight micro 9mm pistols.

expansion, and a large mechanical jacket-to-core InterLock band that works to keep the bullet and core from separating for maximum weight retention, excellent expansion, consistent penetration and terminal performance.

Speer Gold Dot G2 uses a polymer-filled hollowpoint. The G2 features a shallow dish filled with an elastomer that, on impact, is forced into internal fissures of the bullet to start expansion, as opposed to conventional bullet designs, which rely on target media to enter the hollowpoint and create expansion forces. The Federal Premium Guard Dog line features a bullet design with a fully enclosed polymer-filled nose. It is more like an FMJ than a PTHP but performs like a PTHP. The enclosed nose on the Guard Dog prevents the hollow tip from filling with a barrier material, yet upon impact, the tip collapses and expands with consistency.

Weight in Grains: 100, 105, 115, 124, 135

Uses: Defense, Hunting

Lead Round Nose

Lead round nose (LRN) bullets are typically made of lead with no jacket. They are a low-cost alternative for plinking and training, though my choice would be a jacketed bullet for less barrel fouling.

JACKETED SOFT POINT			
Bullet Weight (grains)	Manufacturer	Muzzle Velocity (fps)	Muzzle Energy (ft.-lbs.)
95	MagTech Sport	1,345	380
124	MagTech Sport	1,109	339
124	MagTech Sport	1,109	374

POLYMER TIP HOLLOWPOINT

Bullet Weight (grains)	Manufacturer	Muzzle Velocity (fps)	Muzzle Energy (ft.-lbs.)
100	Hornady Critical Defense Lite (Hornady FTX bullet)	1,125	281
105	Federal Premium Guard Dog	1,230	353
115	Hornady Critical Defense (Hornady FTX bullet)	1,140	332
124	Hornady Critical Duty (Hornady FlexLock bullet)	1,175	380
135	Hornady Critical Duty (Hornady FlexLock bullet)	1,010	306
135	Hornady Critical Duty (Hornady FlexLock bullet)	1,110 (+P load)	396
135	Speer Gold Dot G2	970	307

Hornady's Critical Duty loads feature a 135-grain FlexLock bullet with a polymer tip in the hollowpoint to form consistent expansion while preventing clogging. It is loaded in nickel-plated cases to help prevent corrosion.

LEAD ROUND NOSE			
Bullet Weight (grains)	Manufacturer	Muzzle Velocity (fps)	Muzzle Energy (ft.-lbs.)
124	MagTech Sport	1,109	339
125	Ultramax (remanufactured)	1,060	312

FMJ bullets use a round nose profile as do some frangible projectiles.

Weight in Grains: 124, 125

Uses: Training, Plinking

Total Synthetic Jacket

Total synthetic jacket bullets are similar to FMJ except the bullet is polymer-encapsulated to prevent metal-on-metal contact in the bore, which eliminates copper and lead fouling. Only Federal Premium produces a synthetic jacket bullet and, according to them, the Syntech bullet produces an average of 12 percent less barrel friction and 14 percent less heat.

Weight in Grains: 115

Uses: Training, Plinking

Specialty Ammo

Streak Visual Ammo is a tracer round

Federal American Eagle Syntech loads a 115-grain bullet encased in polymer to prevent metal-on-metal contact in the bore, thus eliminating copper and lead fouling.

LEAD ROUND NOSE			
Bullet Weight (grains)	Manufacturer	Muzzle Velocity (fps)	Muzzle Energy (ft.-lbs.)
115	Federal American Eagle Syntech	1,050	281

that is not incendiary, which means it does not use burning metals to generate light for the trace. Streak uses a non-flammable phosphor material that utilizes the light emitted during the discharging of the pistol to make the projectile glow. The glowing material used is applied only to the aft end of the bullet, making it only visible to the shooter and those within a 30-degree viewing window. Streak rounds are safe to use in environments where traditional tracers are prohibited, such as indoor ranges. In bright sunlight, Streak ammo is difficult to see, but indoor or outside under cloud cover the rounds produce a red or green streak. These rounds are not only fun to shoot since you can see where your bullet will hit, they are useful in helping new shooters get acclimated to firing a pistol, using sights and the relationship to the target downrange.

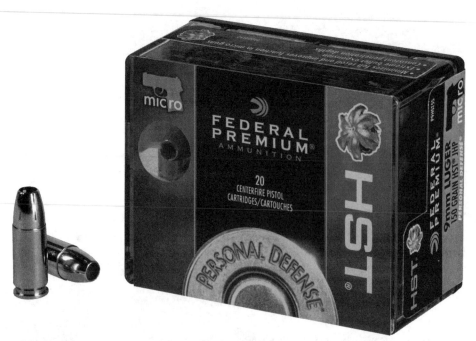

Personal Defense Micro HST cartridges from Federal Premium provide consistent expansion, optimum penetration and superior terminal performance in subcompact, short-barrel semi-auto pistols. The bullet weight and propellant are optimized for efficient cycling and accuracy in subcompact handguns.

CHAPTER 10

ICONIC NINES: GAME-CHANGING 9MMS

Since 1902, when the 9mm cartridge was first produced, there have been literally hundreds of pistols chambered for the cartridge and I would hazard to say thousands of variants of them. Without the right guns supporting the 9mm cartridge, the caliber may not have endured. The argument could be made that the pistols are what made the caliber perform, or it could be flipped and debated that the caliber made these handguns so effective. I'm siding with the latter.

While the fate of some of these pistols has been the display case of a museum, the used rack in a local gun shop, or the back of a collector's gun safe, there is no doubt the relationship between pistol and 9mm cartridge is entwined. Some handgun platforms chambered for the nine found a sweet spot in both performance and usability. These ten pistols are presented in order of introduction from the first to the most current. Sometimes you need to know where you've been to understand how you got to where you are, thus this journey of ten iconic 9mm pistols.

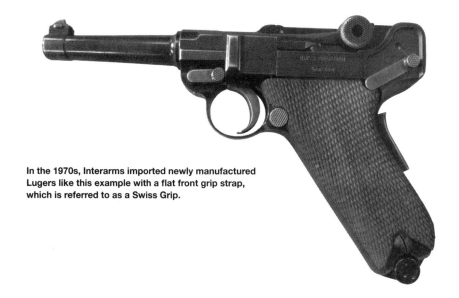

In the 1970s, Interarms imported newly manufactured Lugers like this example with a flat front grip strap, which is referred to as a Swiss Grip.

P.08: The Original 9mm

The Luger P.08 is the original 9mm. It is the first pistol to be chambered in the caliber and one of the first handguns that proved the efficacy of the semi-automatic pistol in combat. Unique and novel, the P.08 is the original game-changer. In fact, it started it all where the 9mm cartridge is concerned.

In 1908, all military organizations and police forces used revolvers as a sidearm. There were a few military organizations that saw the upside of the semi-automatic pistol and, at the time, the Mauser C96 was the top dog being adopted by police forces and armies in Prussia, Austria, Turkey, Italy, and elsewhere. The C96 worked and was adopted into service in 1896, but users knew there had to be something better. The Luger was that "something better." It housed the magazine in the grip of the pistol in lieu of an internal box mag like the C96. More compact, lightweight, accurate and reliable, the P.08 displaced revolvers. When the Luger was chambered in 9mm it far surpassed other combat sidearms of the time and in hindsight created the most popular and enduring caliber used to this day. Obviously, the Luger pistol is no longer considered a viable combat sidearm, but at the time it was cutting edge.

The P.08 holds the distinction as being one of the first successful modern semi-automatic military sidearms with widespread adoption among fighting forces at the turn of 20th century. To a modern shooter the P.08 might seem dated and, compared to a modern, double-stack pistol with a polymer frame and striker-fire mechanism, it is.

As mentioned, some semi-automatic pistols of this era utilized an internal box magazine housed forward of the trigger guard. The Mauser C96 is one example, but there is also the Bergman-Bayard Model 1903. Meanwhile, others such as the FN Browning M1900 and the Luger had mags housed in the grip of the pistol, which is how most modern handguns evolved. In operation the Luger uses a toggle and barrel assembly that moves rearward after a round is fired, then the barrel is stopped by the frame as the toggle continues; the knee joint of the toggle bends to extract the empty cartridge case, pushing a fresh round from the magazine and into the chamber. The trigger is a type of striker-fire mechanism. Like most semi-automatics of the time, the Luger required careful hand fitting of parts, and manufacturing was expensive and time-consuming.

There is sheer beauty in the way the Luger mechanism operates. In hand, the comfortable grip angle makes it a natural pointer. Grasp a Luger and you'll know what is meant by that. Shooters in that era bent their wrist slightly forward when aiming and this put the Luger dead on, as it does with many revolvers. (Modern handgun shooting technique has the shooter lock the wrist, which makes the Luger point high.) The Luger has a grip angle of about 125 degrees and points like a Ruger Mark IV. (As a comparison, the 1911 has a 110-degree grip angle.) The Luger is easy to aim and gets on target fast. And the thing is utterly reliable. When using high-velocity cartridges that produced enough recoil to operate the mechanism, the handgun runs well. Don't listen to those who complain about early 20th-century pistols loaded with 21st-century hollowpoints. Use cartridges loaded with 124-grain full metal jacket bullets and the Luger runs like a Porsche.

The Luger, as originally designed in 1898, was chambered in .30 Luger (7.62x21mm) and produced by Deutsche Waffen-und Munitionsfabriken (DWM) starting in 1900. The Swiss military was the first to adopt it that year. The German

Navy liked it, too, but wanted one with a more powerful round. In 1902, the idea of new, more powerful cartridges began to germinate. The bottleneck .30 Luger was redesigned by resizing the case mouth to hold a larger bullet and the 9x19mm or 9mm Luger/Parabellum round was created. In 1904, the Imperial German Navy adopted the Luger chambered in 9mm with a 5.9-inch barrel and a two-position rear sight. The German Army was also excited about the new pistol, and in 1908 adopted it as the Pistole 08 or P.08.

The P.08 with a 3.9-inch barrel is perhaps the most common variant of the Luger. It served with the German Army during World Wars I and II. Shortly after the German adoption, other countries like Holland, Brazil, Bulgaria, Portugal, Russia, and others followed. The U.S. Army even considered it but adopted the M1911. Today, Lugers are highly prized, even coveted, by some collectors.

In the 1970s Interarms imported new Mauser-built Lugers with a straight grip front strap, known as a "Swiss Grip," and in the more common P.08-style grip. My sample Swiss grip Luger features a grip safety similar to a 1911. It's beautifully made and still sports most of the deep bluing offset with straw-colored controls. The straw coloring is yellowish gold, a color found on the trigger, takedown lever, magazine release, and safety. This modern Luger has a tapered 4-inch barrel. The front blade is dovetailed into the barrel and the rear sight in a fixed notch at the back of the toggle. The sights are fine like an original 1911 or 1911A1 — not what a modern shooter expects. The trigger is wide and smooth and housed in a very small trigger guard that is not glove friendly. The trigger press is just under 6 pounds and not crisp, but it is consistent like some modern striker-fired numbers. The safety lever cannot be operated

by the thumb of the shooting hand. The non-shooting hand is tasked with voting it up for safe and down for fire. The magazine release is located near the thumb of the shooting hand but just out of reach, so the pistol grip needs to be repositioned to press it. The button is angled flush with the grip. Modern shooters expect a large, easy-to-access mag release and with the Luger, this is not the case.

Test and Evaluation: Interarms "Swiss-Style" Mauser Eagle

When it came to testing the Interarms Swiss-style Luger, I found that loading the magazine is similar to a .22 LR pistol. A button on the right side allows you to compress the spring and insert cartridges. It is not the fastest nor easiest magazine to load and getting that last round into the magazine takes effort. Thus, the mags are difficult to fully load fast.

SPECIFICATIONS

MODEL: Interarms "Swiss-Style" Mauser Eagle
DESIGNED: 1898
CALIBER: 9mm
ACTION: Semi-Automatic, Short Recoil-Operated, Toggle-Locked
TRIGGER: Striker-Fire
BARREL LENGTH: 4 in.
OA LENGTH: 8.75 in.
WEIGHT: 30.72 oz. (unloaded)
GRIPS: Checkered Wood
SIGHTS: Fixed, Notch Rear/Dovetailed Blade Front
FINISH: Blued Frame/Barrel, Straw Controls
CAPACITY: 8+1, Single-Stack Magazine

The P.08 Luger features a striker-fire trigger.

With a magazine inserted, the Luger is cocked by grasping the knurled knobs on both sides of the toggle. Hand strength is required, and the motion is counterintuitive to the operation of the slide on a modern pistol.

In hand the P.08 has beautiful balance and points naturally. The grip is angled and aiming it you notice there is not much handgun forward of the trigger guard — the bulk of it is in your hand. While the takedown lever is semi-modern, the manual safety can

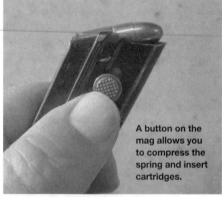

A button on the mag allows you to compress the spring and insert cartridges.

To cock the Luger, grab the knurled knobs and pull upward.

The P.08 Luger has beautiful balance and points naturally.

PERFORMANCE: INTERARMS "SWISS-STYLE" MAUSER EAGLE

9mm Ammo (bullet weight in grains)	Velocity (fps)	Energy (ft.-lbs.)	Best Accuracy (inches)	Average Accuracy (inches)
Hornady American Gunner 115 XTP	1,100	309	2.0	2.5
Aguila 124 FMJ	1,048	302	2.5	2.7
SIG Sauer 115 FMJ	1,048	392	2.8	3.0

only be quickly manipulated with the supporting hand, and that is if you are a right-handed shooter.

The toggle is pulled up and to the rear and takes some effort. It's not as easy as a slide on a modern pistol. The magazine is loaded via a button that retracts the spring, so cartridges can be pushed in slowly. With FMJ I found I like this pistol a lot, even with its archaic idiosyncrasies. Call it obsolete, call it an antique, the Luger should be experienced by every 9mm shooter.

Browning Hi Power: John Browning's Last Pistol Design — Sort Of

The Hi Power pistol is one of the best combat handguns ever designed. You will hear this type of statement often as you read about these iconic nines and that is because combat has evolved since World War I when the 9mm Luger was introduced. As fighting changed so have the tools.

Lightweight, comfortable grip angle, accurate, and chambered in 9mm with a 13-round capacity magazine are among the Hi Power's selling points. First produced in 1935 by FN as the "High Power," it is still being used by military forces in over 50 countries worldwide. (Hi Power is the name Browning has used since 1954 when they started making commercial versions. It's safe to say High Power and P-35 were the pre- and post-WWII names. Brits and Aussies call it an HP.) So why are some American shooters ready to write off the Hi Power? Outside of the U.S., the Hi Power is held in high regard. Ask a grunt from Australia, the UK, Canada, most of South America, in the Mideast, India, and Southeast Asia and you will hear this sentiment expressed *ad nauseam*. Since it was the last pistol designed by John Browning — sort of, but I'll get into that shortly — who designed the 1911, which is held in the highest esteem by Americans, we want to like the Hi Power, but we don't. You'll hear a lot of "buts" when shooters talk about the pistol's characteristics. Some will call them quirks or peculiarities. What could be more American than John Browning?

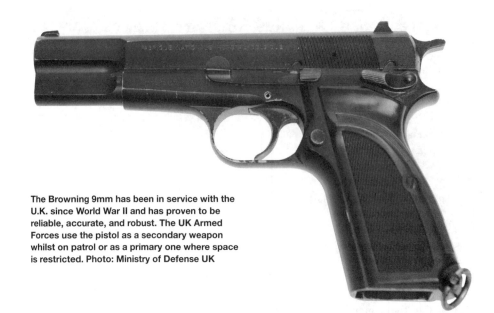

The Browning 9mm has been in service with the U.K. since World War II and has proven to be reliable, accurate, and robust. The UK Armed Forces use the pistol as a secondary weapon whilst on patrol or as a primary one where space is restricted. Photo: Ministry of Defense UK

The author used three types of 9mm ammo: Aguila 124-grain FMJ, Hornady American Gunner 115-grain XTP, and SIG Sauer 115-grain FMJ to test the Hi Power. There were no failures or stoppages.

So why don't American shooters embrace the Hi Power like the 1911? What's not to like? The design is seminal, even innovative, with many features copied by manufacturers today. Perhaps it is because the Hi Power is a French design — again, sort of, but I'll get into it.

I doubt John Browning would recognize the Hi Power as his last pistol design. In the 1920s Browning was done with Winchester and crossed the Atlantic to Fabrique Nationale (FN) in Herstal, Belgium, to design shotguns, machine guns, and pistols. The pistol Browning was working on was chambered in 9mm with a 16-round capacity double-stack magazine, slightly different grip angle than the 1911, a unique barrel linking system, and a pivoting trigger. Metal was shaved from the slide and receiver to make the pistol lightweight and provide balance. Browning also incorporated a striker-fired mechanism. Was he ahead of his time incorporating a striker-fired mechanism? I'm nodding my head, yes and you should be, too.

The French military, however, had a different idea of what the next generation of combat handgun would be and, in the 1920s, embarked on a new pistol design calling it the *Grande Puissance*, which translated means "High Power" — hence the first of many names it would receive. The French spec called for the sidearm to be compact and durable, yet simple to disassemble and reassemble, and have a magazine capacity of at least 10 rounds, a magazine disconnect device, an external hammer, and a positive manual safety. The striker mechanism was scrapped in lieu of a hammer system.

Browning died before the design was finished and FN's Dieudonné Saive picked up where Browning left off. By 1928 the patents on the Colt 1911 had expired and Saive incorporated some of the 1911's features. He also opted for a slide with an integral barrel bushing and built in a magazine disconnect device per the French specs. By 1934, the design was finished and the French military, after years of testing and redesigning, opted out of the Hi Power. Too bad for the French. However, the Belgium military adopted the new pistol calling it the Browning P-35 or P35 (the "35" indicating the year it began service). If this was the first major name change for the Hi Power, the next would come via the Nazi war machine.

By 1940, Germany's preamble to World War II, the Blitzkrieg, had German troops occupying the FN factory. They decided to keep the factory and produce the new pistol designating it Pistole 640(b). German Waffen-SS (among other troops) used the Hi Power during the war. Blueprints for it were smuggled out of occupied Belgium and brought to Canada where they were manufactured by the John Inglis and Company for use by Allied forces during WWII. Here's where more name changes were introduced and the Hi Power gained traction among military forces as a superb fighting pistol. Depending on the country adopting it or where it was made, the Hi Power would be called the HP or BHP. The British call it the L9A1, Pistol No. 2 Mk 1, Pistol No. 2 Mk 1* (yes, with the asterisk), or Mk 1. In Bulgaria, a licensed copy is known as the Arcus 94. In Israel, the licensed version is the Kareen. In Argentina, it is the FM90. RFI manufactures the Hi Power in India and calls it the Pistol Auto 9mm 1A. In the U.S. it's known as the Hi Power — a distinction made by the Browning firearms company when importing the pistols from Belgium.

Pick up a Hi Power and what immediately becomes apparent are the ergonomics. In your hand, the pistol seems almost contemporary. It doesn't feel like a combat pistol that first saw action nearly a century ago. That's the attraction to the Hi Power, and for some, it ends there.

There have been many improvements and variants over the years. Early guns had internal extractors like the 1911, but in 1962 that was changed to a more robust external extractor. As ambidextrous safeties became popular, the Hi Power incorporated them. As shooting tastes changed over the years the Hi Power tried to keep up. A double-action model, called the BDA, was developed to keep up with Wonder Nines in the late 1970s and 1980s. Most Wonder Nines died out fast like one-hit wonder pop bands, and so did the BDA.

What dates the Hi Power is its single-action mechanism. The grip angle is a comfortable 105 degrees. The 1911 has a grip angle of 110 degrees; a Glock 17, 112 degrees. Natural and comfortable are the best ways to describe the angle. The grip itself is thin. Most double-stack

The Hi Power has a small beavertail, which can cause hammer bite for shooters with large hands.

In 1962, an external extractor was incorporated into the design of the Hi Power.

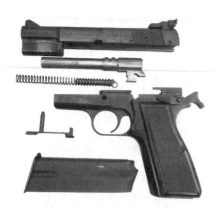

No tools are required to disassemble the Hi Power. It field strips just like a 1911, only faster and simpler.

The barrel slide lockup on the Hi Power is like a 1911; lugs in the barrel lock into slots milled inside the slide.

pistols feel bloated in your hand making them difficult for small shooters to grasp well. The Hi Power packs 13 rounds and it is not that much fatter than a 1911 grip. That 13-round magazine is one trait that made the Hi Power stand out before double-stack mags became the norm. The fact that the Hi Power is made of metal and is as light as a polymer-frame pistol is impressive. It is also much simpler to field strip than a 1911. Those are some of the positives. Here's where the "buts" come in.

The beavertail is small and shooters with large hands can experience hammer bite and there is no simple fix. Modern polymer-frame pistols have modular backstraps, and the grip safety on a 1911 can easily be replaced. Not so easy with the Hi Power. The next "but" and probably the most offensive to shooters is the magazine disconnect safety. With the magazine removed the Hi Power will not fire. Some shooters hate this and have the magazine disconnect removed. Not only does this null and void the warranty (on a new pistol), it also allows an empty magazine to fall free when the mag release button is pressed. We Americans can't stand a combat/defense pistol that doesn't dump the magazine to our feet when we press the magazine release button. The magazine disconnect acts like a brake and holds the mag from falling free. To fix this gripe, a metal spring was added to the magazine body to help it eject freely. Some think this is more of an afterthought than a fix. The last complaint shooters have with the Browning Hi Power is the trigger. It pivots and works with the disconnect. At best there is plenty of take-up and a consistent break, at worst the trigger feels like it is dragging through gravel and crumbles rather than breaks. What we tend to forget is most 1911s made prior to the 1990s had less than perfect triggers, too.

I first became acquainted with the Hi Power when reading the book *Serpico*, about Frank Serpico who joined the NYPD in 1971 and uncovered massive corruption within the department. He armed himself with the 13+1 capacity Hi Power. In the movie, the gun salesman asks Serpico, played by Al Pacino, if he's expecting an army. Serpico replies no, just a division, meaning the corrupt police division. Since reading the book, a few Hi Powers have been through my hands. Recently, a pal of mine let me run his .40 S&W Hi Power and I liked it, but in my opinion, the best ones are chambered in 9mm. (During the rise in popularity of the .40 S&W, Browning offered a variant in that caliber. It has since been dropped from their catalog.) My latest Hi Power is a blued target model made in 1994. The other finish option is a black epoxy coating. What the finish lacks in aesthetics it makes up for in function.

Test and Evaluation: Browning Hi Power

The large target sights on the Hi Power are serrated on the edges facing you so there is no sun glare. Another nice touch: The adjustment directions are clear. The Hi Power never seemed to keep up like the 1911 has with iron sights — another drawback for some shooters. The grips are the iconic flat checkered walnut. Many shooters ditch the factory wood for Pachmayr or Hogue aftermarket grips. The thumb safety is ambidextrous and not as easy to manipulate as those on a 1911.

Well familiar with the Hi Powers, and what I prefer to call their characteristics, I scrounged up two new aftermarket magazines from Mec-Gar. These are 15-round mags that offer two extra rounds while still having a flush fit. There is no spring to help eject the magazine, which is fine by me.

A target model Hi Power with an adjustable rear sight and ramped front sight. Those are Mec-Gar 15-round magazines.

It seemed appropriate to run my Hi Power through the Mozambique Drill, explained earlier, which is actually a part of Hi Power lore. To recap, the drill has you stand in front of targets 5 yards away. At the buzzer, you draw and fire two shots center of mass and one to the head. If you can do it in 4 seconds you're doing good.

I used three types of 9mm ammo: Aguila 124-grain FMJ, Hornady American

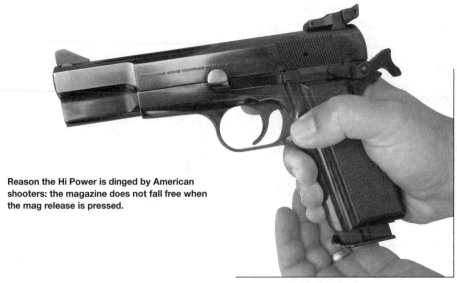

Reason the Hi Power is dinged by American shooters: the magazine does not fall free when the mag release is pressed.

Unlike the 1911, the Hi Power does not use a removable barrel bushing. Notice how the muzzle of the slide is machined to relieve a maximum amount of steel.

Gunner 115-grain XTP, and SIG Sauer 115-grain FMJ, in a good assortment of bullet weights and types. I didn't draw and fire but started at the low-ready position. I began with two fast shots to center of mass followed by a more accurate shot to the head. The Hi Power made me look good and, in fact, jacked my confidence up. Recoil was pleasant, the trigger on my gun a bit gritty, but the center of mass shots were easy to pull off quickly. The headshot took more focus on the trigger.

Moving to accuracy testing I used a rest and a target at 25 yards. Five-shot

PERFORMANCE: BROWNING HI POWER				
9mm Ammo (bullet weight in grains)	Velocity (fps)	Energy (ft.-lbs.)	Best Accuracy (inches)	Average Accuracy (inches)
Hornady American Gunner 115 XTP	1,116	318	1.96	2.48
Aguila 124 FMJ	1,078	320	1.12	1.42
SIG Sauer 115 FMJ	418	392	1.25	1.55

SPECIFICATIONS

MODEL: Browning Hi Power
DESIGNED: 1935
CALIBER: 9mm
ACTION: Semi-Automatic, Short
      Recoil-Operated
TRIGGER: Single-Action Only
BARREL LENGTH: 4.62 in.
OVERALL LENGTH: 7.75 in.
WEIGHT: 32 oz. (unloaded)
GRIPS: Checkered Wood
SIGHTS: Fixed, Notch Rear/Blade Front
FINISH: Blued
CAPACITY: 13+1, Double-Stack Magazine

groups with the Aguila and SIG ammo averaged about 1.5 inches; with the Hornady 2.5 inches. No doubt with a better trigger the groups would be smaller but for a combat/defensive pistol the accuracy was stellar. I found the Hi Power did my bidding with no issues. It ran with no malfunctions. Reliability is built into the DNA of the Hi Power. Magazine reloads needed to be modified since I had to strip out the empty mag. Smoothness and speed would be gained with continued training. I liked the extra capacity of the Mec-Gar mags.

The Hi Power is iconic. Say it's long in the tooth, dated, or even insignificant in this age of polymer pistols. I say long live the Hi Power.

(Right) The P.38 was the first combat pistol to use a combination of features that are now common among modern handguns.

(Left) The P.38 was the first combat pistol equipped with a DA/SA trigger mechanism, which allowed it to be safely carried with a round in the chamber and the hammer down.

Like most European military side arms, the P.38 features a magazine release located on the butt.

Sights are large on the P.38, more like the combat sights on modern pistols.

SPECIFICATIONS

MODEL: Walther P.38 (P1)
DESIGNED: 1938
CALIBER: 9mm
ACTION: Semi-Automatic, Short Recoil-
Operated, Locked Breech
TRIGGER: Single-Action/Double-Action
BARREL LENGTH: 4.9 in.
OVERALL LENGTH: 8.5 in.
WEIGHT: 32 oz. (unloaded)
GRIP: Checkered Plastic
SIGHTS: Fixed, Notch Rear/Blade Front
White Dot
FINISH: Blued
CAPACITY: 8+1, Single-Stack Magazine

Walther P.38: High-Tech Combat Pistol Circa 1938

The P.38 was the replacement for the P.08 Luger, which was costly to produce. At the onset of World War II, the German military required a more cost-effective sidearm. The pistol needed to be mass-produced, reliable, rugged, and suitable for combat. The P.38 was designed for ease of production using stamped and alloy steel with composite grips. It was designed to be affordably manufactured, a trend in all military firearms (the reader should not equate cheaply-made with low quality). Though the P.38 was designed for ease of manufacturing it was cutting edge for the time in 1938. In fact, many modern pistol designs to this day use features that were employed on the P.38.

The operating mechanism features a pivoting and locking bolt with short-recoil action. When the P.38 is fired the barrel and slide move rearward. The barrel does not tilt like in a 1911, SIG, Glock, or Browning-type action. The locking block stops the barrel momentum but allows the slide to go rear-

ward to eject the empty case and cock back the exposed hammer. Twin recoil springs bring the slide forward to chamber a round.

The P.38 was the first combat pistol to use a combination of features that are now common among modern handguns, such as the DA/SA trigger mechanism, which allows the pistol to be safely carried with a round in the chamber and the hammer down. All you need to do is pull the trigger in double action to fire. Subsequent shots are fired single action. The safety lever is located on the left side of the slide and is swept downward to put the gun on safe or pushed forward to fire. When the lever is placed on safe with the hammer cocked, the lever decocks the hammer, another common feature on modern pistols. Another feature is a loaded chamber indicator. On the P.38, a pin protrudes from the top rear of the slide to give you tactile and visual indication a round is in the chamber. It even used an open slide design forward of the breech face, making ejection of empty cases more reliable. The Beretta 92FS and current U.S. Army-issue M9 utilize nearly all of these design characteristics. Since the grips meet to form the backstrap, less metal was required to build the handgun, also making it lightweight. The sights on the P.38 were large and well-defined like one expects on a current combat pistol.

Over one million P.38s were produced by the end of World War II in 1945. Walther, Mauser, and Spreewerke all manufactured the model during the war. After the war, in late 1963, the P.38 was slightly redesigned with an aluminum receiver and named the Model P1. The P1 was adopted by the West German military. During the 1990s, the German military started replacing the P1 and phased it out in 2004.

Test and Evaluation: Walther P1

While I did not have a P.38 to test, I did have a sample of the later P1. My P1 was manufactured in 1981 and imported as surplus in the 1990s. Gone are the ribbed grips and steel frame of wartime P.38s. This P1 has checkered plastic grips and an aluminum frame. In hand, the P1 is thin and easy to aim. The sights are large — much like those a modern shooter expects. The exposed hammer is old school for sure but instantly tells you whether it's cocked. The decocking lever is hard to reach unless you have large hands. I find I use my support hand to operate the safety lever and decock the P1. The pistol is heavier than most current polymer-frame double-stack pistols, and that's not a bad thing since the extra weight helps reduce felt recoil.

Loading the single-stack mag is easy on the thumbs, and witness holes in the side of the magazine alert you to how many cartridges are loaded.

The initial double-action trigger pull is long and heavy yet fairly smooth — what you would expect in a military-style pistol. That trigger clocks in well over 12 pounds

PERFORMANCE: WALTHER P1				
9mm Ammo (bullet weight in grains)	Velocity (fps)	Energy (ft.-lbs.)	Best Accuracy (inches)	Average Accuracy (inches)
Hornady American Gunner 115 XTP	1,100	309	1.6	1.77
Aguila 124 FMJ	1,075	318	2.0	2.75
SIG Sauer 115 FMJ	1,124	323	1.65	1.89

according to my Brownells trigger scale. In single action, the pull weight was 4.9 pounds on average. The balance, accuracy, reliability and safety features of the P.38 and P1 are legendary. Add this one to your bucket list.

Smith & Wesson Model 39: America Discovers the 9mm

After World War II the handgun-shooting public didn't really think much of the 9mm cartridge. We had the .45 ACP and plenty of revolver cartridges, like the .38 Special and .357 Magnum. It was also a time when revolvers were simply more popular than semi-automatics. If you participated in competition shooting during that era, bullseye shooting was the only game in town and it was fired with small-bore .22 rimfire and centerfire pistols. The 1911 in .45 ACP was the pistol to shoot the slow, timed, and rapid stages. Smith & Wesson offered a Model 52 semi-automatic in .38 Special wadcutter, but the .45 ACP ruled the roost and won nearly all the matches.

Part of the reason the 9mm cartridge was unpopular was that no U.S. firearm manufacturers were building handguns in the caliber. You could get a 1911 in 9mm from Colt back then, and you still can to this day, but in most shooter's minds, a 1911 was chambered in .45 ACP — end of story. As action shooting started to take root in the 1970s, the .38 Super played a major role and was very popular due to its light recoil and added round capacity.

The Model 39 (top) was the first American-made DA/SA centerfire semi-automatic in 9mm. The Model 39-2 (bottom) used a shorter extractor. Photos: Smith and Wesson

It wasn't until Smith & Wesson decided to offer the Model 39 to the commercial market that the 9mm started to gain momentum with U.S. shooters.

The Model 39 was originally developed to compete in the U.S. Army service pistol trials of 1954. The Army was looking to replace the .45 ACP 1911 with a lighter sidearm. Colt even developed the Colt Commander model with a shorter barrel and less weight than the 1911A1. The Army's requirements called for a pistol to be chambered for 9mm with a maximum overall length of 7 inches and a weight of no more than 25 ounces.

The Model 39 borrowed features found on the WWII-era Walther P.38, namely the barrel was fixed to the frame, plus it featured a decocking safety lever, and DA/SA trigger. Unlike the P.38 the Model 39 used a conventional slide design with a barrel bushing.

The Commander was Colt's submission, while Smith & Wesson's was the Model 39. The Army ended the search, sticking with the 1911A1 in .45 ACP, so Smith & Wesson had a perfectly functioning 9mm with no customers. Smith & Wesson decided to introduce the Model 39 to the commercial market in 1955.

The Model 39 was the first American-made DA/SA centerfire semi-automatic in 9mm. It weighed 28 ounces, had a 4-inch barrel and an overall length of 7.5 inches. It featured an 8-round single-stack magazine and used a short-recoil mechanism — a modified version of the Browning P-35 (Hi Power) cam-locked breech.

The Model 39 ushered in the widespread use of semi-automatic pistols with U.S. law enforcement agencies and military units. As previously mentioned, the first major police agency to adopt a 9mm semi-auto pistol was the Illinois State Police, the Model 39 in 1967. This was an

SPECIFICATIONS

MODEL: Smith & Wesson Model 39
DESIGNED: 1954
CALIBER: 9mm
ACTION: Semi-Automatic, Short Recoil-Operated, Locked Breech
TRIGGER: Single-Action/Double-Action
BARREL LENGTH: 4.0 in.
OVERALL LENGTH: 7.5 in.
WEIGHT: 28 oz. (unloaded)
GRIPS: Checkered Wood
SIGHTS: Fixed, Notch Rear/Blade Front
FINISH: Blued
CAPACITY: 8+1, Single-Stack Magazine

historic moment for a variety of reasons: a large U.S police agency was adopting a semi-automatic pistol, it was chambered in 9mm, and it introduced autoloading handguns to law enforcement nationwide. You must remember at this time in LE history most uniformed officers were issued 6-shot double-action revolvers chambered in .38 Special or .357 Magnum. Semi-automatic pistols were not even thought of as a police sidearm.

Special Forces at the time were forming, along with the need for specialized weapons. During the Vietnam War, Naval Special Warfare modified the Model 39 with taller sights and attached a suppressor. A slide-lock switch was added to the frame to prevent the slide from operating and the enemy from hearing it operate. This essentially made the pistol a single shot, but it was not the primary weapon of these early frogmen. This set was very successful and effective: with sub-sonic ammunition, the loudest noise from the gun firing was the cycling of the slide. The SEALs called it the Mark 22. Naval Special Warfare also modified the Model 39 with a wider grip frame to accommodate a 14-round magazine. The

Mark 22 was replaced in 1991 by the Mark 23 pistol, a 12-round-capacity .45 ACP made by Heckler & Koch.

The publicity from the Illinois State Police adopting the Model 39 helped create commercial sales among the shooting public for a semi-automatic in 9mm. Smith & Wesson's next big win was their original Wonder Nine, the Model 59.

The Model 59 was very similar to the Model 39 and was likewise chambered in 9mm but featured a double-stack mag with a 14-round capacity and a wider aluminum frame with a straighter grip. The Model 39 was produced from 1955 to 1982 and the Model 59 from 1972 through 1981. Both the Model 39 and Model 59 evolved into the Model 439 and 459, respectively. By the mid-1980s, Smith & Wesson was producing a variety of compact and full-sized 9mm pistols based on the Model 39 and Model 59.

H&K P7: Squeeze Cocker, Gas Operated

If there was ever a pistol revered by Heckler & Koch followers it is the HK P7 — a squeeze-cocker, gas-delayed blowback autoloader. These unique pistols are known for their low barrel axis, slim profile, accuracy, reliability, concealability, and ease of use. What really sets the P7 apart from other 9mms is its operating system and cocking mechanism. While other pistol manufacturers were concentrating on a variation of the Browning system, HK took a different approach.

In 1976, when the P7 was designed to meet the new West German Police pistol requirement, it was nothing less than futuristic. Their specification for the new police pistol required it to be chambered in 9mm, weigh no more than 35 ounces and sized no larger than 7.08 in. x 5.11

In the 1980s the Heckler & Koch P7M8 was a cutting-edge pistol design. Today the iconic handgun has a cult following.

With the front strap cocking lever squeezed, note the pin protruding from the rear of the slide. When not gripped, the pin protracts and the pistol decocks.

in. x 1.33 in. The new pistol was required to be fully ambidextrous, safe to carry with the chamber loaded, quickly drawn and fired instantly, and have a service life of at least 10,000 rounds. The P7 was officially adopted as the PSP (Polizei Selbstlade Pistole or Police Self-loading Pistol). German military special forces embraced it, as did law enforcement agencies and military organizations in Greece and Mexico. In 1981, the P7 was adopted by the New Jersey State Police. A few other agencies like the U.S. Park Police and others adopted it.

The gas-delay blowback action uses the gas from a fired bullet to retard or delay the rearward movement of the slide. A small port in front of the chamber diverts the burning gas into a cylinder and piston located in the receiver. The piston is attached to the slide and keeps the slide forward until the pressure in the cylinder drops. The remaining inertia moves the slide rearward, ejects the empty case, and pushes the next cartridge into the chamber to be fired. The gas-delayed blowback action produces less recoil in a small compact pistol chambered in 9mm. This design allows for a light recoil spring, which means racking the slide takes less effort, making it easier to manipulate. If there is a downside it is apparent after excessive firing. Heat builds up in the cylinder near the trigger and debris from burning gases builds up in the cylinder, requiring more frequent cleaning. Also, reassembly is more complicated due to the piston.

The gas delay works well with the blowback action. Blowback 9mm pistols have been in use since World War I. The issue is, blowback handguns in this caliber use a heavy slide and recoil spring to counteract the force of the fired 9mm

The P7M13 (right) with its 13-round magazine was part of the Wonder Nine era of 9mm pistols. Photo: HK USA

cartridge. The slide cycles fast — the only resistance is the recoil spring and weight of the slide — producing more felt recoil along with a heavier pistol. There can be too many negatives with a 9mm blowback action, especially when the design goal is a compact handgun. That is why most compact 9mm pistol manufacturers use a modified version of the Browning design with a locked breech action and tilting barrel. SIG, Glock, Ruger, Smith & Wesson, and others all use a modified Browning design. However, a gas-delayed blowback action solves the problem.

The barrel is fixed to the receiver, so it does not move when the P7 is fired. This design characteristic makes the P7 inherently more accurate than a locked breech and tilting barrel mechanism. The slide stays on the receiver because of the barrel. There are also no slide rails. The slide is easy to manipulate, unlike some compact locked breech designs that require hand strength to manipulate the slide.

Part of the reason the Heckler & Koch P7 is iconic is not only the gas-delayed blowback system but the squeeze cocking grip and striker-fire single-action trigger. These traits set the HK P7 apart from its contemporaries.

The squeeze cocker grip, which is the front grip strap, is a cocking lever. When you squeeze the grip — as you would normally grip any pistol — about 13 to 15 pounds of force is required to depress the cocking lever, and about one pound to hold it. Once cocked, a pin protrudes from the rear of the slide telling you it's cocked and ready to be fired. The cocking lever moves the striker into battery, so the pistol will fire once the trigger is pressed. This squeeze-cocker feature is the only safety device on the pistol. In the event the firing pin fails to dent the primer of the cartridge and the round does not go off, the cocking

lever is released, and the grip must be squeezed again to fire. The cocking lever also makes it harder to operate the pistol for those with weak hand muscles (like children). The squeeze cocking lever can be a bit odd for an experienced pistol shooter, but it feels quite natural when gripping the pistol.

Field stripping is simple. After removing the magazine, depress the takedown button, retract the slide, and pull up. The slide assembly slides off the barrel. The piston, which pivots on a pin, is attached to the slide. When reassembling, the piston needs to be aligned with the cylinder in the receiver. The process is easy but quite different from the takedown procedure of current locked-breech designs.

The P7M8 variant uses an 8-round single-stack magazine. The P7M13 model employs a double-stack, 13-round mag. This variant is the Wonder Nine P7. Original P7 models used a European-style heel or butt magazine release. HK also offered P7s in the U.S. market with a thumb-operated magazine release. The P7 was produced from 1979 until 2008.

Test and Evaluation: Heckler & Koch P7M8

What you notice first when handling the P7 are its natural pointing ability and excellent balance. The P7 has most of the weight in the butt. The bore axis is low, and the pistol is small. There is not a lot of handgun forward of the trigger guard.

The single-action trigger is relatively crisp and, on my used P7M8, requires a press of about 5 pounds to fire.

Other design features include a fluted chamber similar to an HK G3 rifle. The flutes in the chamber funnel pressure from a fired round to eject the empty case. The P7 does have an extractor, which helps make

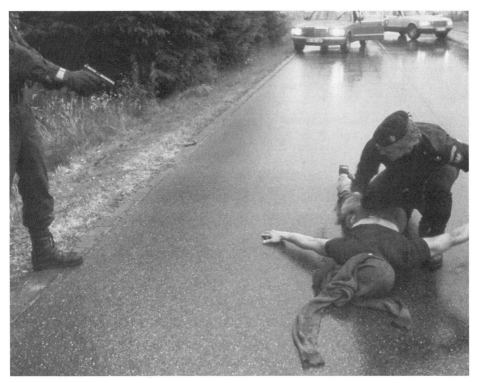

The P7 was used by West German anti-terrorism units. Here operators practice a takedown drill.
Photo: HK USA

the ejection run more smoothly, but if the extractor breaks the P7 will still run. What was also new at the time and relatively

SPECIFICATIONS

MODEL: Heckler & Koch P7M8
DESIGNED: 1976
CALIBER: 9mm
ACTION: Semi-Automatic, Gas-Delayed
    Blowback
TRIGGER: Striker Fire
BARREL LENGTH: 4.1 in.
OVERALL LENGTH: 6.7 in.
WEIGHT: 28 oz. (unloaded)
GRIPS: Textured Polymer
SIGHTS: Fixed, Notch Rear/Blade Front
FINISH: Blued
CAPACITY: 8+1, Single-Stack Magazine

common today is the P7's polygonal rifled barrel. My P7M8 has a European-style magazine release in the butt. The 3-dot sights are large and easy to align.

For the test, I used three different bullet weights and types: Hornady American Gunner with 115-grain XP jacketed hollowpoints, Aguila 124-grain FMJs, and Liberty Ammunition Civil Defense 50-grain hollowpoints. Muzzle velocities varied among the cartridges. The Liberty stuff was the fastest at 1,943 fps, while the Hornady and Aguila clocked at 1,080 and 1,010 fps, respectively. Compared to a compact locked breech pistol firing the same ammunition there was a difference. The felt recoil of the P7 was softer. There were no issues with any of the ammo and the P7 preferred the hot 50-grain Liberty

9mm Ammo (bullet weight in grains)	Velocity (fps)	Energy (ft.-lbs.)	Best Accuracy (inches)	Average Accuracy (inches)
Hornady American Gunner 115 XTP	1,080	298	1.25	1.75
Aguila 124 FMJ	1,010	281	1.14	1.73
Liberty Ammunition Civil Defense 50 HP	1,943	419	1.08	1.56

— my best five-shot group at 25 yards was 1.08 inches.

The P7 is not the lightest of compact pistols thanks to a metal frame, but that extra weight made it a sweet shooting pistol. On average, five-shot groups ranged from 1.5 to 1.7 inches at 25 yards. This old-school pistol still has game.

SIG P6: Progenitor of the Tribe

If you know the difference between a team and a tribe, you know SIG is a tribe. Clint Bruce, former Navy SEAL team leader, coined the term "tribe" and the differences between it and a team. Briefly, a team is committed to a shared goal. There

The SIG P6 is a more compact version of the SIG P220.

are plenty of teams. A tribe is loyal and committed, much like a team, but where the road forks between these two is where a tribe has shared values and identity. That describes the culture at SIG. People and products — think different personalities, statures, skill sets, models of pistols and rifles — all committed to similar values and beliefs with a goal to win. Just look at the SIG lineup of pistols in 9mm from traditional DA/SA, DAO, SA, striker-fire — all are different, and all committed. In my opinion, as well as some collectors and enthusiasts, the P6 was the model that spawned the tribe.

The P6 is related to the P220, which was designed in 1975 as a replacement for the P210 pistol from World War II. The P220 itself was a milestone in 9mm history. It was of German design and Swiss manufacture. SIG acquired J.P. Sauer & Sohn and renamed the company SIG Sauer. The P220 features a modified Browning system. Instead of locking lugs in the barrel mating with recesses inside the slide, the SIG uses an enlarged breech that locks into the ejection port of the slide. This system is used by many manufacturers, including Glock, Ruger, Smith & Wesson, and others. Like many pistol designs after WWII, the SIG was developed for ease of manufacturing. Original P220s had a stamped slide with the internal bushing and muzzle portion welded in place. The SIG had an alloy frame, which today makes it old-school compared to the current trend in polymer-framed pistols.

What also made the SIG stand out from the crowd is its hammer drop safety, what we call the decocker. The lever is located on the left side of the frame and allows you to decock the pistol by pressing it. Though decockers have been incorporated into pistols designs since WWI, SIG made it work. Other safety features include an automatic firing pin block that

West German police pistols incorporate a hook on the hammer. This was a requirement to alert police armorers if the pistol had been dropped on the hammer.

The P6, like other SIG models, uses a locked barrel and slide with an enlarged breech section on the barrel that locks into the ejection port.

is deactivated when the trigger is pressed fully rearward. Again, it's not anything SIG thought up, but they did perfect it. It also incorporates a drop safety. It has a DA/SA trigger, so the first shot is a long press in double action. Subsequent shots are short press single action. The DA/SA trigger may not be the trigger system currently in vogue — that would be striker-fire — but it makes sense to operators whose lives depend on the initial double-action pull, those with no need for a manual safety as on the 1911. The SIG is always ready. Just pull the trigger to make it go bang. Most SIGs still use this mechanism. The P6 is a direct descendant of the

SIG P225. The P225 is a compact version of the full-size P220 that was specifically designed to meet the West German government's new police sidearm standard in the mid-1970s. The idea back then (as it is now) was to create a pistol that was safe, accurate, reliable, inexpensive, and chambered in 9mm. The German government approved pistols for sale to police and designated models with a "P" for police (Polizeri). The P225 was configured to West German standards and called the P6.

The differences between the P225 and P6 are minimal. The P6 has a heavier 24-pound double-action trigger pull, traditional fixed sights, and a spur hammer, and it was stamped on the right side of the slide forward of the ejection port with the "P6" marking. West German agency markings can be found on the right side of the slide and are typically two to three uppercase letters. At the muzzle are date code production stampings in the form of month and year — 2/81, for example, which indicates a pistol proofed in February 1981.

The spur hammer is part of the West German standard. It bends or breaks off if the pistol is dropped on the hammer, thus alerting police armorers. If a pistol was dropped, some internal parts could become fatigued or broken, thus an armorer would need to tear down the handgun and examine the mechanism parts. The 24-pound mainspring provides more resistance during trigger pull, helpful in an especially high-stress situation. The P225 features the standard 19-pound mainspring as in other SIG models. As hollowpoint ammunition became more commonly used, the feed ramp was reshaped to better chamber JHP ammunition.

If the P220 is a good gun, then the P225/P6 is better. It utilizes all the features of the P220 but in a more compact size. The P6 is 6.9 inches long and uses a 3.6-inch barrel; the P220 sports a 4.4-inch barrel. At its widest point, the P225/P6 measures 1.3 inches while the grip is 1.2 inches thick. Unloaded it weighs 30.5 ounces. It feeds from a single-stack 8-round magazine.

Test and Evaluation: SIG Sauer P6

Pick up a SIG P6 and you will experience the excellent grip — not too fat and some palm swell to the checkered

SPECIFICATIONS

MODEL: SIG Sauer P6 (P225)
DESIGNED: 1976
CALIBER: 9mm
ACTION: Semi-Automatic, Short Recoil-
    Operated, Locked Breech
TRIGGER: Single-Action/Double-Action
BARREL LENGTH: 3.9 in.
OVERALL LENGTH: 7.1 in.
WEIGHT: 16.1 oz. (unloaded)
GRIPS: Checkered Polymer
SIGHTS: Fixed, Notch Rear/Blade Front
FINISH: Blued
CAPACITY: 8+1, Single-Stack Magazine

plastic grip. It is compact and points well and tears down like most SIG DA/SA pistols: easy and fast. There is no captured recoil spring on the P6, however. The sights are very modern. They are large and put you in charge. The trigger is the feature that dates the P6. It is a far reach to get to the trigger and takes about 12 pounds of effort to depress in double action. The single-action pull is about half that.

Collectors and users speak with reverence when talking about the P6 and there is a reason for that admiration. It is thin and fits most shooters' hands. It

PERFORMANCE: SIG SAUER P6				
9mm Ammo (bullet weight in grains)	Velocity (fps)	Energy (ft.-lbs.)	Best Accuracy (inches)	Average Accuracy (inches)
Aguila 124 FMJ	1,007	279	1.67	2.1
Federal American Eagle 115 FMJ	1,155	341	2.0	2.5
Hornady American Gunner 115 XTP	1,070	292	2.7	2.9

is compact but performs like a full-size pistol. There is a reason SIG makes the P239 and reintroduced the P225.

CZ 75: Eastern European Sleeper

The CZ 75 could be considered one of the original Wonder Nines. I think of it as a Browning Hi Power with a DA/SA trigger, but it is more than that. From the beginning the CZ 75 has been a sleeper here in the U.S. since it was designed behind the Iron Curtain during the Cold War. It was a secret project in what was then Czechoslovakia but is now the Czech Republic. Stifled and put under wraps by Moscow, which mandated Soviet satellite countries adopt sidearms chambered in 9x18 Makarov, the CZ 75 was not designed for indigenous use but for export. If you lived outside our American bubble in 1975 when the CZ 75 was designed, you would have found what the rest of the world knew all about the CZ 75: It is reliable, accurate, and easy to operate. Since a patent was never filed, CZ 75 clones were manufactured in other countries. CZ at the time couldn't afford to market their products

in the U.S. and that is why the CZ 75 is not as widespread as pistols from other foreign countries. Many countries adopted it while others cranked out clones. Military organizations and police agencies from some 20 different countries use the CZ 75 or an indigenous copy.

The CZ 75 uses a short-recoil, locked breech operating system. Being a Wonder Nine, admission to the club meant it had to have a double-stack magazine with plenty of payload. The CZ 75 holds 15+1 rounds fully loaded. A feature that sets the CZ 75 apart from Smith & Wesson, Beretta, Walther, and other DA/SA pistols is that it can be carried in one of two modes. The first mode is with the hammer fully down so the first shot is fired double action. The second allows it to be carried cocked-and-locked with the hammer cocked fully back and the thumb safety engaged. In this mode, the first shot is fired in single action. Virtually no one else offers both types of carry modes.

A common feature the CZ 75 shares with SIG pistols is the way the slide mates to the receiver. The slide on the CZ 75 and some SIG pistols rides inside the receiver, not on the outside such as those from Walther,

First introduced in 1975, The CZ 75 is one of the original Wonder Nines, featuring a double-stack magazine, all-steel construction, and a DA/SA trigger. Photo: Rock Island Auction Company

Ruger, Colt, Smith & Wesson and others.

CZ clones include the Tanfoglio TZ-75 made in Italy, the BUL from Israel, and others made in China, North Korea, Turkey, Switzerland, and more. The CZ has also spawned numerous variants tweaked for target and action shooting or concealed carry.

What I like about the CZ 75 is the comfortable grip angle and the ergonomic

controls, which are easily manipulated. The double-action trigger pull is long, yet smooth, and single action is good for a service pistol. The all-metal construction helps with felt recoil.

Beretta 92S: Wonder Nine Ground Zero

The Beretta 92S is a second generation 92 that evolved into the 92FS, known to American shooters and military personnel as the M9. The 92S is a lot more of a European gun than the 92FS, which has U.S. influence. The original Model 92 was introduced in 1976 and had a frame-mounted safety like the current Taurus 92 or any 1911. Police and the military in Italy wanted a slide-mounted safety and, in 1977, Beretta introduced the 92S, the second generation 92, and started to sell them to LE agencies around the world. The rest, as they say, is history.

Beretta figured out the correct combination of features on a combat pistol for the time — DA/SA trigger, high-capac-

SPECIFICATIONS

MODEL: CZ 75
DESIGNED: 1975
CALIBER: 9mm
ACTION: Semi-Automatic, Short Recoil-
Operated, Locked Breech
TRIGGER: Single-Action/Double-Action
BARREL LENGTH: 4.7 in.
OVERALL LENGTH: 8.1 in.
WEIGHT: 39.5 oz. (unloaded)
GRIPS: Checkered Polymer
SIGHTS: Fixed, Notch Rear/Blade Front
FINISH: Blued
CAPACITY: 15+1, Double-Stack Magazine

ity magazine, the location of the thumb safety, reliability, inherent accuracy, and light weight due to the alloy aluminum frame. In my opinion, the Beretta 92S was ground zero for the Wonder Nine era. It spawned numerous variants including the 92FS, which Uncle Sam calls the M9.

The 92S differs from the 92FS is in the grip, hammer pin, receiver shape and magazine release, among other details. The 92FS has an enlarged hammer pin to stop the slide from flying off the receiver if it cracks. This was done at the request of the U.S. military after testing the 92S with high-pressure loads. The 92S has the safety lever mounted on the slide, which when rotated up to the fire position exposes a red dot and readies the pistol to fire. Rotate it down to the safe position and the trigger is disengaged but the slide can still be manipulated. The hammer cannot be cocked. With the pistol cocked, rotating the lever to the safe position allows the hammer to safely move forward. The safety is not ambidextrous. The receiver has a rounded trigger guard and the mag release is in the butt. Press and hold the button and the magazine

falls free. If you have ever fired a pistol in snow or tall grass you will understand why the magazine release was located here. Using the support hand to manipulate the magazine release button drops the empty magazine into the palm of the support hand where it can be withdrawn. The magazine release button works like a brake, so you must remove the magazine. This is a European trait of the 92S. Here in the U.S., we are accustomed to dumping empty mags at our feet and, while it free falls, inserting a fresh one. Those unaccustomed to the butt release magazine can be at a loss on how to reload when the slide locks back, but with training and practice one can replace the magazine efficiently. Most mags made for the 92FS are compatible with the 92S, so finding extras — both factory and aftermarket — is simple.

Test and Evaluation: Beretta 92S

The front and rear grip straps on the Beretta 92S are smooth and there is a lanyard loop attached to the butt. The 92S feels rounded in hand, different than the

The Beretta 92S is a lot more European than American shooters like, but with modifications the next generation 92FS proved to be a better design.

Shooters come in all statures and the gripe with some about the Beretta 92 is the girth of the grip.
Photo: DoD

92FS. The plastic grips are checkered on the bottom portion but not the top, something I thought was odd. Field stripping is like any Beretta series 92 pistol — fast and simple.

The example I tested showed signs of holster wear but little actual firing. The bluing was worn, and I would rate the pistol 75 to 80 percent by NRA standards. The slide had no wiggle. It was tight. The trigger measured 11 pounds in DA mode and felt like it. In SA mode there was a lot of take-up and a bit of a mushiness, typical of a service pistol. The sights are small, fixed and without contrasting dots or lines. On a dark background, they could get lost.

All ammunition cycled flawlessly through the 92S. Magazines seated easily. Benchrest accuracy was good, averaging about 2 inches for five rounds at 25 yards. I was able to consistently group five shots into about 1.22 inches with the 124-grain FMJ Aguila ammunition at 25 yards. The Hornady American Gunner ammo with a 115-grain JHP was no slouch either, with average groups measuring 1.8 inches. I did notice the 92S had pleasant recoil. The pistol magazine release took some getting used to and slowed me down when it came to rapid reloads.

The M9 has been in use with the U.S. military for a few generations and is a battle-proven combat weapon.
Photo: DoD

The safety lever on the Beretta 92 is located on the slide. Some operators dislike this since the safety can accidentally be flipped on when the slide is racked.

The circular button is the magazine release catch, which is designed to drop the magazine into the operator's hand rather than free fall.

SPECIFICATIONS

MODEL: Beretta 92S
DESIGNED: 1975
CALIBER: 9mm
ACTION: Semi-Automatic, Open-Slide, Short-Recoil Delayed Locking-Block System
TRIGGER: Single-Action/Double-Action
BARREL LENGTH: 4.9 in.
OVERALL LENGTH: 8.5 in.
WEIGHT: 34 oz. (unloaded)
GRIPS: Checkered Polymer
SIGHTS: Fixed, Notch Rear/Blade Front
FINISH: Blued
CAPACITY: 15+1, Double-Stack Magazine

The 92S is no 92FS, but still provides an excellent example of Beretta's 92 series. Its performance was notable and shooting it provided a step back in time to the Wonder Nine-era of pistols.

Glock G17: Plastic Fantastic

The Glock G17 pistol is the biggest innovation in firearms design in the late 20th century. The pistols are simple to operate, rarely have any problems, and seem to run forever — even if you abuse them. The G17 was a game-changer in the 1980s and it came out of nowhere. Glock was not part of the firearms manufacturing establishment. The company's claim to fame prior to the G17 was small plastic parts molded for the Austrian military.

At the time, Glock seemed to be just another Wonder Nine, but the G17's polymer receiver was the most obvious and significant change over traditional metal frame Wonder Nines. Of course, Glock was not the first to manufacture a polymer-frame pistol — HK had done that years earlier — but Glock did create a combat pistol that was safe and easy to operate. Plus, it was built with minimal parts that could be produced quickly and inexpensively.

The back story is that owner and founder Gaston Glock assembled a brain trust of firearm designers and engineers. Together, they defined a wish list of features and, within a few months, had an operating prototype. Glock was bidding on the Austrian military's RFP for a new sidearm, and while the firearm industry snickered at

U.S. law enforcement embraced the Glock nearly from its introduction. About 65 percent of domestic police agencies are equipped with Glocks today. Photo: Glock USA

him trying to play in their space he ended up winning the contract. To date, Glock has about 65 percent market share of U.S. law enforcement, making it the most-used pistol among police agencies. Numerous countries and agencies around the world have adopted the gun. Glocks are everywhere.

The internal safeties and trigger used in the G17 were coined by Glock as the Safe Action System. Three safeties work automatically and independently and disengage as the trigger is pulled; these automatically reengage when the trigger is released. This makes it safe from accidental discharge if dropped. Since the safeties were built into the design there is no need for external thumb safeties, nor was there reason to add a decocker lever.

The G17 features a locked breech, recoil-operated system with a tilting barrel. The tilting barrel system is similar to the Colt 1911 and Browning Hi Power. The slide and breech block lock up in a Glock a lot like a SIG. The receiver or frame is made of a proprietary polymer and forms the grip. Most manufacturers have copied

SPECIFICATIONS

MODEL: Glock 17 Gen5
DESIGNED: 1982
CALIBER: 9mm
ACTION: Semi-Automatic, Short-Recoil, Locked Breech, Tilting Barrel
TRIGGER: Striker-Fire
BARREL LENGTH: 4.48 in.
OVERALL LENGTH: 7.9 in.
WEIGHT: 25.06 oz. (unloaded)
GRIPS: Textured Polymer
SIGHTS: 3-Dot Fixed, Notch Rear/Blade Front
FINISH: Matte Black
CAPACITY: 17+1, Double-Stack Magazine

this idea. An unloaded G17 weighs 25.06 ounces, 32.12 ounces loaded with 17+1 rounds of 9mm ammunition.

Compare that to a similar-size SIG P226 or Beretta 92FS, which weigh about 37.5 and 34 ounces unloaded, respectively. There was no other pistol at the time that offered the firepower of 17+1 rounds in such a lightweight package.

The original 1st generation G17 with pebbled textured grip. Glock completely changed the way we thought combat pistols should be manufactured and operated. Photo: Glock USA

Since the Glock is made of polymer, which to you and me is plastic, the media touted the pistol as being able to get past airport x-ray machines and metal detectors. What the media failed to understand was that the Glock had plenty of metal parts and could not evade metal detection. The next hurdle Glock endured was questions about durability. Some claimed it was disposable like a plastic cigarette lighter. But the pistols were buried in sand, frozen in ice, dunked in mud, soaked in salt water, dropped from the rooftops of buildings, run over by trucks, and more. Glock not only survived but still operated. It was easy for the Glock to stand out from the other Wonder Nines of the era.

Glock pistols use a striker-fire system, which is another feature copied by other manufacturers. A spring-loaded striker in the slide is cocked as the trigger is pulled to the rear, while the striker is released to fire. The trigger pull of a Glock is odd to experienced operators who are more familiar with DA/SA or single-action only (SAO) triggers.

Is the Glock perfection? (Glock's boastful marketing lines.) No, but it is close.

Kahr K9: Small Size, Big Bite

The reason the Kahr K9 pistol made my top list of iconic 9mm pistols is its size. And although it has been said that size matters, it really does in the case of the K9. This pistol was designed from the onset as a small, concealable, subcompact handgun. It was just the type of pistol used as a backup weapon by law enforcement or civilians who practice concealed carry. While most manufacturers start by designing a full-size pistol and scale it down later for concealed carry, Kahr took the opposite approach. By manufacturing a subcompact Kahr was able

SPECIFICATIONS

MODEL: Kahr K9
DESIGNED: 1993
CALIBER: 9mm
ACTION: Semi-Automatic, Short-Recoil, Locked Breech, Tilting Barrel
TRIGGER: Striker-Fire
BARREL LENGTH: 3.4 in.
OVERALL LENGTH: 6.0 in.
WEIGHT: 25.0 oz. (unloaded)
GRIPS: Textured Polymer
SIGHTS: Bar-Dot Fixed, Notch Rear/ Blade Front
FINISH: Matte Stainless
CAPACITY: 7+1, Single-Stack Magazine

to prove the concept that a 9mm pistol could have the same footprint as a pistol chambered in .380 ACP. Think about that for a second: the K9 is about the size and weight of a Walther PPK, Mauser HSc, Beretta 85 and others — pistols chambered in .380 ACP. Yet, the K9 is chambered in 9mm. Chambering the K9 in 9mm gave it teeth.

This metal-frame pistol uses a recoil-operated, lock breech system along with a double-action-only (DAO) striker-fire

trigger. The girth is slim, almost anti-Wonder Nine, with a 7-round single-stack magazine. The grip is thin and easily grasped by shooters with small hands. It easily conceals. Because of the DAO trigger and passive firing pin block, the K9 is very safe to carry and there are no external manual safeties. They simply are not needed. The K9 can be drawn from concealment and fired instantly with a press of the trigger.

In use, the K9 has a low bore axis, keeping it close to your hand. This translates to less perceived recoil. Kahr built the K9 with an off-set recoil lug to help reduce muzzle flip and felt recoil. If there is any criticism about the K9 it is the weight, though that extra heft helps combat recoil. The solution was to change the receiver material from metal to polymer.

Since the debut of the K9 in 1995, Kahr has introduced a large variety of subcompact 9mms. My personal favorite — as well as my own concealed carry choice — is the CW9. This is the low-budget, no-fancy-slide-machining version with a polymer frame. If you buy a new Kahr, run at least 200 rounds through it to break it in.

The Kahr K Series has proven itself as an excellent concealed carry/backup gun with high-quality and total reliability in a compact, thin package.

CHAPTER 11

WONDER NINES – BIG MAGAZINE CAPACITY, DA/SA TRIGGER, 9MM FUELED

The era of "Wonder Nines" started in the late 1960s and continued through the 1980s. Most did not last due to lack of acceptance from military organizations, law enforcement agencies, and civilian shooters. Many were "me-too" designs trying to grab onto a trend. Some manufacturers moved on — striker-fired pistols were the next trend. What

the Wonder Nine era did accomplish was to usher in the demise of the revolver as a law enforcement weapon. One could question the relevance of revolvers in a world of semi-automatic pistols.

Wonder Nines are defined as semi-automatic pistols chambered in 9mm with a staggered or double-stack magazine, and featuring a DA/SA trigger.

Wonder Nines like this Armalite AR-24 are an amalgamation of traditional 9mm semi-automatic pistol features stuffed with large-capacity mags.

Magazine capacities range from 13 to 15 rounds or more. The typical law enforcement officer back then carried a six-shot revolver chambered in either .38 Special or .357 Magnum. Wonder Nines offered more than twice the firepower and the caliber 9mm was easy to control and accurate. Revolvers seemed as dated as rotary dial telephones.

There were Wonder Nines coming out of nearly every pistol manufacturer. In hindsight, it is interesting to review the ones that flooded the market hoping to snag military contracts, entice law enforcement agencies, and wow civilian shooters. Here is a timeline of the pistols introduced during this era. The production or importation dates are shown in parentheses. Many of them proved to be innovative, complex and expensive to manufacture, thus were very short-lived with limited production dates.

Wonder Nines of the 1980s

The plastic-framed pistol got a little traction with the Heckler & Koch VP 70Z (1970–1984). But it took nearly a decade for it to be considered a real combat sidearm even though it is equipped with a striker-fire trigger, roller-delayed blowback action, and 18-round magazine.

The SIG P220 (1975–present) is an enduring design using the traditional DA/SA trigger but with a decocking lever. The model has since evolved into the P225 and P226. The P226 (1980–present) is still in widespread use with military and law enforcement organizations and is one of few Wonder Nines to withstand the test of time.

Though the CZ 75 (1976–present) began production in 1976, the pistol was initially rare outside of Czechoslovakia, and practically unknown to U.S. shooters (it became more common in the U.S.

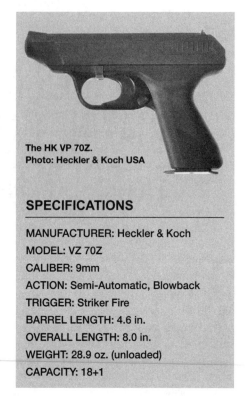

The HK VP 70Z.
Photo: Heckler & Koch USA

SPECIFICATIONS

MANUFACTURER: Heckler & Koch
MODEL: VZ 70Z
CALIBER: 9mm
ACTION: Semi-Automatic, Blowback
TRIGGER: Striker Fire
BARREL LENGTH: 4.6 in.
OVERALL LENGTH: 8.0 in.
WEIGHT: 28.9 oz. (unloaded)
CAPACITY: 18+1

starting in the early 1990s).

What is innovative about it is the slide rides inside the frame like the SIG P210, plus it can be carried cocked and locked, meaning the hammer can be fully cocked back with the safety engaged, similar to a Browning Hi Power or 1911 platform. The CZ 75 has been copied by numerous manufacturers.

Beretta's Model 92 was first designed back in 1975, and in 1977 the manual thumb safety on the receiver was moved to the slide and the pistol was renamed the 92S. With the slide-mounted safety, the Model 92S was adopted by the Italian State Police and Italian Carabinieri. This model offers a smooth DA/SA trigger, 15-round magazine, and a lightweight alloy frame. The Model 92S (1977–1980) is reliable and numerous military organizations have adopted it, including the U.S.

military in 1980. The U.S. military's new handgun test consisted of numerous candidate pistols: Colt SSP, Smith & Wesson 459, Beretta 92SB-F, SIG Sauer P226, Heckler & Koch P9S and VP70, Walther P88, Steyr GB and F, and the Fabrique National High Power, FN Fast Action, FN Double-Action (FN DA) models, and the Star Model M28.

The Model 39 and Model 59 are Smith & Wesson's first generation of DA/SA semi-automatic pistols. In 1981, the second generation appeared with the Model 459 (1981–1988) featuring that trademark S&W look with its squared-off and checkered trigger guard. The Model 459 was innovative at the time since it was a compact 9mm with a high magazine capacity.

The Steyr GB (1981–1988) is a hefty, full-size pistol that uses a gas-delay blowback action, 18-round magazine, fixed barrel, and polygonal rifling.

Astra is one of the oldest and most well-known brands in Spain, first producing firearms starting in 1908. In 1982 the Astra A-80 (1982–1989) was introduced and imported to the U.S. This semi-automatic features a DA/SA trigger, 15-round magazine, and 3.75-inch barrel and includes a decocker lever like a SIG.

Another Spanish firearm manufacturer, Llama, introduced the Omni (1982–1986), an all-steel constructed DA/SA with three safeties, and a 13-round magazine. The Omni is an innovative gun using a Browning 1935-type fixed cam to lock the breech, two-piece ball-jointed firing pin, and dual sear bars for improved trigger pull. The double-stack 13-round magazine is quite unusual, as the first five rounds feed into the action in a single column to reduce the chance of jamming.

Since CZ had issues importing the CZ 75 into the U.S., manufacturers and importers like F.I.E. imported a copy of it from Italy called the TZ-75 (1982–1989). The TZ-75 is basically an inexpensive version of the CZ 75 with some differences in the safety lever configuration.

The P7 M13 (1982–1994) was Heckler & Koch's attempt to glom onto the Wonder Nine craze by incorporating a double-stack, 13-round magazine into their P7 M8 pistol. Like the M8, the M13 uses a gas-delayed blowback system, squeeze cocker grip, and striker-fire trigger.

Smith & Wesson continued with their second-generation pistols, introducing the Model 469 (1983–1988), which is basically a reduced-size Model 459. The Model 469 is an alloy frame pistol designed for concealability and has a 12-round magazine, DA/SA trigger, and bobbed hammer.

Star was another firearm manufacturer in Spain that introduced the Model 28 (1983–1984) in 1983. It features a 15-round magazine, 4.25-inch barrel and DA/SA trigger. Like the SIG, the Model 28 uses a reversed rail/slide system in which the slide rides inside the receiver like a P210, in effect creating a more accurate pistol.

In 1983, a new U.S. military program was started, under the XM9 designation. The Beretta 92 won the second set of tests but bickering and lawsuits ensued from the competing firearm manufacturers. The Army of Brazil awarded a larger contract to Beretta to manufacture the 92.

In 1980, the Brazilian firearm manufacturer Taurus purchased the rights and original Beretta factory and began building the PT-92 (1983–present), a less expensive version of the Beretta 92 and more like the original Model 92 with a frame-mounted manual thumb safety.

SIG P226.
Photo: Rock Island
Auction Company

SPECIFICATIONS

MANUFACTURER: SIG Sauer

MODEL: P226

CALIBER: 9mm

ACTION: Semi-Automatic, Short Recoil,
Tilting Barrel

TRIGGER: DA/SA

BARREL LENGTH: 4.4 in.

OVERALL LENGTH: 7.7 in.

WEIGHT: 34 oz. (unloaded)

CAPACITY: 15 +1

In 1983, SIG debuted the P226 (1983–present), which is basically a P220 with a double-stack, 15-round magazine. The P226 found widespread use among military special operators, the FBI, and other law enforcement agencies. The P226 was the first in a line of many double-stack semi-automatic pistols.

The military XM9 tests included numerous candidate pistols that could be debated as the top Wonder Nines: Colt SSP, Smith & Wesson 459, Beretta 92SB-F, SIG Sauer P226, Heckler & Koch P9S and VP70, Walther P88, Steyr GB and F, and the Fabrique National High Power, FN Fast Action, FN Double-Action (FN DA) models, the Star Model M28, and Ruger P85. The Beretta 92SB-F (1983–1985) was another evolution of the 92SB with

a new combat trigger guard, internally chromed barrel, and matte black Bruniton finish. These modifications were made to make the Beretta more competitive in the military tests. The Beretta clearly won this third set of trials.

1985 was an important year during the Wonder Nine era as the U.S. Army announced the Beretta 92SB-F as the winner of the new handgun trials. All the pistols that competed for the Army contract were, for the most part, strikingly similar. Gun manufacturers were in the "me-too" game of product development. All were chambered in 9mm and each featured a DA/SA trigger mechanism, metal receivers and, depending on the manufacturer, a variety of levers and controls that made the pistol safe to carry. What they also had in common was double-stack mags that offered a higher capacity compared to traditional single stacks. They were all pretty much the same except for the odd duck, the Glock G17.

It was 1985 when Glock began importing the G17 — a polymer-frame striker-fire with a magazine capacity of 17 rounds. Glock entered late onto the Wonder Nine scene but quickly took the lead role and changed the way the military, law enforcement, and civilian shooters defined a combat pistol.

Ruger joined the semi-automatic pistol market in 1985 with the P-series of 9mm pistols. The P85 (1985–2013) was Ruger's first centerfire semi-automatic design built for military and law enforcement markets. It uses a short recoil-operated, locked breech system, like a SIG P220, and a 1911-style tilting barrel. The P-Series features DA/SA or double-action only (DAO) trigger mechanisms and 15-round magazines. The P85 was adopted by a few U.S. law enforcement agencies.

The Astra A-80 evolved into the A-90

(1986–1990) in 1986 and was equipped with updated safety features. Stainless steel pistols were extremely popular in the 1980s and the Smith & Wesson Model 669 (1986–1988) was introduced with full stainless-steel construction. Basically, it was the Model 459 only made of stainless steel and with a 14-round magazine. The Beretta 92SB-F was reported as having a slide failure after firing extensive high-pressure 9mm cartridges that exceeded recommended NATO specifications. Though not the fault of the 92SB-F, Beretta modified the pistol with an enlarged hammer pin to stop the slide from flying off the receiver.

Walther introduced the P88 (1988–1996) for use by military and law enforcement agencies. It features a fully enclosed slide, 15-round magazine, and DA/SA trigger. Though an accurate shooting pistol, the P88 is burdened like many Wonder Nines with metal receivers as being bulky and heavy. The slide stop is awkward to manipulate.

Located in Argentina, Bersa is a manufacturer of small caliber semi-automatic pistols and, in 1989, introduced a full-sized 9mm named the Model 90 (1989–1994). Daewoo, a Korean manufacturer, introduced the 15+1 round capacity K5 (1989–present) built on a metal frame. That pistol was unique due to the "fast action" trigger mechanism characterized by trigger travel like that of a double-action but with a weight that felt like a single action.

The Woundrous 1990s

By 1990, Smith & Wesson was into its third generation of pistols with the Model 5906 (1990–1997). It was introduced with a 4-inch barrel, stainless steel construction, exposed hammer, ambidextrous safety and a 15-round magazine.

The Astra A-100 (1990–1997) was Astra's attempt to refine the A-90 by giving it a larger magazine capacity of 17 rounds. Another interesting handgun appearing around this timeframe was the Star Model 31P. It sported a steel frame, carried 14+1 rounds, and features a decocking lever.

Late in 1990, EEA (European American Armory) began importing a CZ 75 clone manufactured in Italy by Tanfoglio and called the Witness EA 9 (1990–present). The Witness EA 9 series sports a 16-round magazine, DA/SA trigger, and polymer or alloy receiver. These are well-made pistols.

Browning was late to the Wonder Nine party, and in 1991 introduced a DA/SA version of the iconic Hi Power named the BDM or Browning Dual Mode (1991–1997). The BDM features a trigger mode switch on the left-hand side of the slide that allows you to toggle between DA/SA and DAO modes.

More Wonder Nines

FRG in Hungary imported the model R-9 (1992 only), which is essentially a Browning Hi Power knock-off with a DA/SA trigger. Colt's pistol to the Wonder Nine scene was the All American 2000 (1992–1994), which was designed to use either a polymer or aluminum alloy frame, rotary bolt, and locked-breech system with a 15-round magazine. Colt had hoped to recapture the law enforcement market after revolvers were replaced with semi-autos. In a word, the All American was a spectacular failure. Around this same time, Ruger updated the P85 design in 1992 and called it the P89 (1992–2007), adding an ambidextrous safety or decocker depending on the variant. In Hungary, the FEG P9R (1992–2000) looked very much like a Hi Power knockoff but used a DA/SA trigger.

The economy Smith & Wesson Model 915 (1993–1994) with a 4-inch barrel and the 15-round magazine was introduced. Taurus released the PT 908 (1993–1997), a compact pistol. Heckler & Koch needed a replacement for the P7 series and in 1993 introduced the USP (Universal Self-loading Pistol) in .40 S&W — the most popular cartridge with law enforcement at the time.

Smith & Wesson debuted the economy Model 910 (1994–2007), a full-size, alloy frame 9mm with steel slide and a 15-round magazine. Another release in '94 was the Argentine-made Bersa Thunder 9 (1994–present), which is the evolution of the Bersa Model 90. Glock was rolling out new stuff, too, with a compact 9mm called the G19 (1994–present) with a 15-round magazine

and 4.01-inch barrel. The G19 is considered the most popular Glock due to the compact size that doesn't sacrifice magazine capacity.

By the mid-1990s, it could be argued that the Wonder Nine era petered out and a new chapter began. This next period of pistol design is what I like to call the Wonder Nine Lite era, in which manufacturers started to swap metal frames and receivers for polymer ones. This created a lighter pistol. You get the idea: Same great taste, less filling.

In 1995, Heckler & Koch introduced the USP9 (1995–present), and while it isnot as radical a design as its predecessors — the P7 or VP 70Z — it does incorporate a mechanical recoil reduction system. That system uses a recoil spring

HK P7M13.
Photo: Heckler & Koch USA

The Taurus Pt-92.
Photo: Taurus

SPECIFICATIONS

MANUFACTURER: Heckler & Koch

MODEL: P7M13

CALIBER: 9mm

ACTION: Semi-Automatic, Gas-Delayed
    Blowback

TRIGGER: Striker Fire

BARREL LENGTH: 4.1 in.

OVERALL LENGTH: 6.7 in.

WEIGHT: 30 oz. (unloaded)

CAPACITY: 13+1

SPECIFICATIONS

MANUFACTURER: Taurus

MODEL: PT92

CALIBER: 9mm

ACTION: Semi-Automatic, Recoil
    Operated

TRIGGER: DA/SA

BARREL LENGTH: 5 in.

OVERALL LENGTH: 8.5 in.

WEIGHT: 34 oz. (unloaded)

CAPACITY: 17+1

Walther P88
Photo: Rock Island

Smith & Wesson
Model 5908.

SPECIFICATIONS

MANUFACTURER: Walther
MODEL: P88
CALIBER: 9mm
ACTION: Semi-Automatic, Short-Recoil,
Locked Breech, Tilting Barrel
TRIGGER: DA/SA
BARREL LENGTH: 4.0 in.
OVERALL LENGTH: 7.4 in.
WEIGHT: 31.6 oz. (unloaded)
CAPACITY: 15+1

SPECIFICATIONS

MANUFACTURER: Smith & Wesson
MODEL: Model 5906
CALIBER: 9mm
ACTION: Semi-Automatic, Short-Recoil,
Locked Breech, Tilting Barrel
TRIGGER: DA/SA
BARREL LENGTH: 4.0 in.
OVERALL LENGTH: 7.5 in.
WEIGHT: 37.5 oz. (unloaded)
CAPACITY: 15+1

assembly designed to reduce the effect of felt recoil by up to 30 percent. The USP is built with modularity in mind and features a wide selection of trigger/firing modes, including DA/SA with decoding lever and safety, DA/SA with decocking lever and no safety, DAO with safety, etc.

The CZ 100 (1995–present) is another example of the Wonder Nine Lite era. It is CZ's first semi-automatic handgun to use synthetic materials.

Ruger continued to produce the P-series, and in 1995 introduced the P95 (1995–2013), which was similar to the previous P-series models except it uses a new frame/receiver made of fiberglass-reinforced polyurethane. The P95 weighs 4 ounces less than previous models.

The SIG PRO series (1999–present) represented the company's first polymer-frame handguns. These pistols use the traditional DA/SA trigger and were originally developed in .40 S&W. The SP 2009 (1999–2005), chambered in 9mm, was introduced a few years later. The polymer frame makes the pistol lighter and features grip panels, so it can be adjusted to fit most hand sizes. The BUL Cherokee (1999–present) is a polymer-frame full-size pistol based on the CZ 75 design. SIG enhanced their Wonder Nine Lite with the SP2022 first generation (2004–2007) and a second generation SP2022 (2011–present).

FNH USA introduced the FN FNP (2006–present) with ambidextrous decocking levers and a reversible magazine release, and — you guessed right — a polymer frame and traditional DA/SA trigger.

By the late 2000s, many major pistol manufacturers dropped the DA/SA trigger system. The writing was on the wall: Striker-fire pistols were the new norm. Ruger introduced the SR9 (2007–present) and has since released a modular grip striker-fired number called the American (2015-present). The P250 (2007–present) is SIG's entrant into the burgeoning striker-fire market. Unique to the P250 is how you can change its caliber and grip size. It's a truly modular design that uses an internal fire control system that includes the trigger and firing mechanism and is a serialized part of the pistol. Smith & Wesson completely sat out the Wonder

EAA Witness EA 9.

SPECIFICATIONS

MANUFACTURER: EAA (Tanfoglio)

MODEL: Witness EA 9

CALIBER: 9mm

ACTION: Semi-Automatic, Short-Recoil, Locked Breech, Tilting Barrel

TRIGGER: DA/SA

BARREL LENGTH: 4.5 in.

OVERALL LENGTH: 8.1 in.

WEIGHT: 33 oz. (unloaded)

CAPACITY: 17+1

Nine Lite era and instead jumped in with a polymer-frame striker-fire, the Sigma (1994–1996). That one evolved into the SD series, still part of the company's semi-automatic pistol lineup, and — in a sense — is an economical alternative to the M&P (2005–present) models.

There were other 9mms with single-stack magazines introduced during this era that do not strictly abide by the Wonder Nine definition, but nonetheless were part of the many nines developed and produced back then, and even to the present day. The Walther P5 (1977–1993) is like the P.38 but, unlike the WWII pistol, uses a non-tilting barrel and expelled empty cases to the left, rather than the right like all other semi-auto handguns. Taurus introduced the PT 908 (1993–1997), a compact pistol with an 8-round magazine. While S&W produced double-stack 9mms, they also produced single-stack counterparts during this time.

Test and Evaluation: Armalite AR-24

The AR-24 can be considered a Wonder Nine that showed up late. Armalite debuted the AR-24 in 2007 and stopped production in 2013. There are no new high-tech materials or unique mechanisms in this full-size tactical pistol. The AR-24 is not a common polymer-framed piece. Actually, it is based on the popular and combat-proven CZ 75. There's nothing new or fancy about the CZ 75, of course, but it is one of the most-copied pistols in the world and there is a reason for that flattery. The design is excellent and that is where Armalite started — they took an excellent design and enhanced it.

The AR-24 is a short-recoil operated, locked breech pistol that uses the Browning linkless cam locking system like the

The Armalite AR-24 was late to the Wonder Nine party, but is an excellent example of a full-metal frame, DA/SA, and high-capacity 9mm.

Hi Power first built back in 1935. And like the SIG P210 from 1949, the slide rides inside the frame rails rather than on the outside like most pistols. This provides a tight slide-to-slide fit, which contributes to the pistol's accuracy. The standard course back then was to build pistols from forgings that were machined into parts and fitted together. Common features during that timeframe were a rugged steel frame, double-stack magazine, and DA/SA trigger. While some were starting to build polymer-framed guns, eastern European countries continued in traditional old-school pistol making — building steel weapons that could take abuse and give it right back. From its conception, the AR-24 was based on a great design and was only improved upon.

Armalite approached Turkish manufacturer Sarsilmaz — a 120-year-old firm that has provided weapons to the Turkish Ministry of Defense — to produce the AR-24 to Armalite's spec. Sarsilmaz had

SPECIFICATIONS

MODEL: Armalite AR-24
CALIBER: 9mm
ACTION: Semi-Automatic, Short-Recoil, Locked Breech, Tilting Barrel
TRIGGER: DA/SA
BARREL LENGTH: 4.8 in.
OVERALL LENGTH: 8.3 in.
WEIGHT: 35.2 oz. (unloaded)
GRIPS: Checkered Rubber
SIGHTS: 3-Dot, Drift Adjustable Front/Rear
FINISH: Matte Black
CAPACITY: 15+1, Double-Stack Magazine

been building a pistol that served as the starting point for the AR-24.

When I first picked up the AR-24 I was struck by its fine ergonomics. The grip felt full, with generous palm swells.

The rear of the grip has graceful curves like an old glass Coca-Cola bottle. The pad of my index finger fell exactly on the wide, smooth trigger, and with my thumb I could easily sweep the thumb safety on or off. The ergonomics are excellent, like the proverbial extension of your arm when you make ready and fire.

The sculpted slide looks like one from a SIG P210 with rounded edges and fine serrations. The handgun appears rounded and smooth, not blocky. There is an external extractor next to a standard-sized ejection port. The rear slide serrations are fine, unlike the course ones found on most combat handguns today. The 3-dot sights are what I expected on a tactical pistol — large and easy to use. Both sights are fitted into dovetail cuts and the rear can be adjusted for windage using a brass punch and hammer. The front sight can also be adjusted for windage, but a set screw needs to be loosened with a hex wrench before being drifted left or right.

I shoot right-handed and the slide stop falls under the thumb of my support hand while the thumb of my shooting hand lay naturally near the thumb safety on the left side of the frame. The controls are well placed like a Hi Power or 1911 and feel natural in the hand. The edges of the controls have just enough bite, so they are easy to manipulate with or without gloves. They are also just the right size — not overly large and not too small. Both have serrations, so your thumbs do not slip. The thumb safety operates with the hammer fully forward and locks both the slide and hammer from being manipulated. The thumb safety can also be used when the hammer is at half and full cock, so you have the option of carrying the pistol in either mode with the added assurance of the thumb safety. The

hammer is round and serrated, offering a secure gripping surface. A half cock notch acts as an additional safety, stopping the hammer from striking the firing pin if the hammer slips when thumbing it back. Additional safety features include a safety that keeps the firing pin blocked until the trigger is pulled. This ensures no accidental discharge if the pistol is dropped with a round loaded in the chamber.

The magazine release button is under the thumb of a right-handed shooter. It is large and round with serrations that make it easy to use. Press it and the magazine falls free. The trigger guard is large — no problem wearing gloves while using the AR-24 — and the trigger is wide, smooth and comfortably curved for both double- and single-

The rubber checkered grips of the AR-24 have palm swells that allow you to get a sure grip with no gaps.

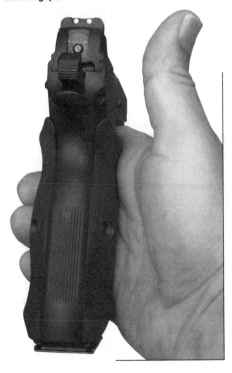

action firing. Fine serrations are found on the front and rear grip strap that aid in gripping when the gun recoils. They provide a sure hold without feeling like they are biting into your hand. There is no accessory rail, which is refreshing. There is an oversized beavertail built into the frame so hammer bite is a non-issue. The frame is contoured and smoothly transitions into the trigger area. The AR-24 has nice lines.

The AR-24's checkered rubber grips with palm swell are some of the nicest feeling factory grips I have held. My hand size is average, and it did feel like the AR-24 was custom contoured to my hand.

Magazines are available in 10- and 15-round configurations. They are simple with a metal floor plate that fits flush with the butt grip. Three witness holes indicate the current capacity of the magazine. A bright red polymer follower is used to indicate the magazine is empty.

The AR-24 uses a traditional SA/DA trigger. The trigger pull is better than military-grade. The double action has a bit of pick-up and there is some slight creep. That double-action pull feels like it takes less effort though, averaging 12 pounds. The trigger setup is good for a tactical pistol. Bullseye matches are not on the AR-24's to-do list, though it would make an excellent IDPA and action shooting contender. The single-action pull averaged 5 pounds, 3 ounces.

The fit and finish are exceptional on the AR-24. A military-grade manganese phosphate and heat-cured epoxy are

Accuracy with the AR-24 was typical of full-size combat-style handguns, about 2-inch groups at 25 yards.

used for corrosion resistance. The metal showed no tool marks inside or out.

I loaded the magazine to capacity and the last round took slightly more effort. The edges of the lips were smooth. The full-size metal frame gives the AR-24 a heft that is unlike any polymer-framed pistol of the same size. That heft relieves recoil and muzzle flip, makes it nearly nonexistent. The hot Hornady Critical Duty +P loads were pleasant to shoot in the pistol. The Armalite chomped through the ammo without a hitch, which is what I expected from a CZ 75-inspired design. At 15 yards, I placed some IDPA-style targets and fired the pistol fast and furious. I'd align the three dots, acquire the target, focus on the front sight and fire, fire, fire. The first shot in double action pushed slightly left of the center of mass, subsequent shots in single action were dead center. By the second magazine, I had begun to speak the same DA trigger language the AR-24 required.

The rear sight is high enough for the slide to be retracted one-handed, which I tested by hooking it onto the edge of my belt and the shooting bench and pushing down to rack the slide. All combat pistols tell the truth at 25 yards. Either the accuracy is there or it's not. Using a rest and shooting single action I was able to punch 2-inch average groups with all the ammo. This pistol speaks the truth and is accurate for tactical situations.

The AR-24 is a traditional combat pistol, from manufacturing and materials to features. What sets this old-school pistol apart are its excellent ergonomics and good looks.

PERFORMANCE: ARMALITE AR-24				
9mm Ammo (bullet weight in grains)	Velocity (fps)	Energy (ft.-lbs.)	Best Accuracy (inches)	Average Accuracy (inches)
Hornady FlexLock 135 JHP +P	1,104	365	2.3	2.5
Black Hills 115 FMJ	1,144	334	1.6	1.8
Winchester Bonded PDX1 147 JHP	946	292	2.3	2.5

Bullet weight measured in grains, velocity in feet per second, and average accuracy in inches for best five-shot groups at 25 yards.

CHAPTER 12

THE STRIKER-FIRE COMETH

With a G19 slide and a G17 receiver, the Glock G19X offers the benefits of a compact pistol along with the 17+1 magazine capacity of a full-size handgun.
Photo: Glock USA

Striker-fired semi-automatic pistols use a spring-loaded firing pin that is partially cocked by the movement of the slide. The trigger continues to cock the firing pin, then releases it to fire the pistol. Striker-fires do this without the use of a protruding hammer. Some models incorporate a safety in the trigger as well as a firing pin safety and drop safety.

By 1986, with the Glock 17 on the scene, many Wonder Nines died off and ceased production. The writing was on the wall. A new generation of combat handgun had evolved, one that used a polymer frame and striker-fire system, and held a whole lot of cartridges. Glock was the game changer. Offering a lightweight, polymer-frame pistol with relentless reliability, ease of use, and three built-in safeties, the Glock was nothing less than revolutionary. It is void of any manual safety or decocking levers. What makes it so unique is that founder and designer Gaston Glock had no idea how to manufacture or design a firearm. He assembled a think tank of firearm engineers who brainstormed what they thought would be the perfect modern combat pistol. The Glock design aesthetics reflect the pragmatic approach: Nothing fancy or flashy, just a better gun, a working tool.

The G17 is manufactured with a polymer or plastic receiver that does not endear it to old-school pistoleros. Not that Glock pioneered a polymer frame nor the striker-fire trigger. Actually, Heckler & Koch had been producing polymer-frame guns with moderate success since 1970 with the VP70, which was the first successful example. The VP70 uses a striker-fire trigger and an 18-round magazine. It ceased production in 1989. When the media heard the Glock pistol was made out of plastic it was assumed it could slip by airport x-ray machines and metal detectors. Obviously, the media did not know how guns are manufactured because the slide, barrel, springs, firing pin, and many other parts are made of metal.

There are variations of the striker firing mechanism and the Glock is a good example. Basically, a spring-loaded firing pin is cocked in two stages before firing. When loaded, the firing pin is in the half-cock position, and as the trigger is pulled the firing pin becomes fully cocked. At the end of the trigger travel, the trigger bar tilts downward by the connector to release the firing pin and fire the cartridge.

It was not that long after Glock was introduced that Smith & Wesson and Ruger stopped producing metal frame, DA/SA pistols and turned their attention to polymer frame striker-fire guns. Smith & Wesson debuted the Sigma series in 1993, which has since been dropped from their line. In Europe, Walther introduced the P99 in 1996 and all of their current full-size and compact 9mms incorporate a polymer frame. The Smith & Wesson M&P series debuted in 2005 and is the company's latest polymer frame, striker fire (a Mod 2 generation began production in 2016). Ruger's answer to the striker-fire crisis is the SR series, introduced in

2005. The Ruger American model, which debuted in 2016, is their latest. In South America, Taurus saw the need for a striker-fire product with a polymer frame and introduced the Millennium series in 2005. Springfield Armory rolled out the XDM in 2006, spawning numerous model variations. Springfield's pistols are based on the Croatian-made SH2000 — a full-size polymer-frame striker-fire. Steyr's version, the M-A1 series, debuted in 2004. Heckler & Koch and Beretta were late to the party. HK debuted the VP9 in 2014, while Beretta released the APX in 2016.

The P-10 is CZ's striker-fired number that debuted in 2017. It uses the same grip angle as the CZ 75 and features a palm swell, deep beavertail, and three interchangeable backstraps to fit a wide variety of hands. If the Wonder Nines ushered in the demise of the revolver as a military and law enforcement weapon, then it can be argued that the striker-fire with polymer frame snuffed out Wonder Nines.

Test and Evaluation: Glock G19 Gen4 MOS

A dramatic change in how concealed carry pistols are equipped has evolved with the G19 Gen4 MOS (Modular Optic System). This Glock allows you to easily mount a small reflex red-dot sight and will no doubt change the way the next generation of concealed carry users defend themselves. Fast target acquisition and easy-to-conceal reflex sights are the next step in high-tech defense and this Glock made the transition from irons to optics seamless.

I put a G19 Gen4 MOS pistol through the day-in and day-out tasks we all do: strapping on a holster, holstering and carrying the gun, then removing it and starting all over the next day.

The Glock G19 Gen4 MOS allows the operator to mount a small reflex red-dot sight. This will no doubt change the way the next generation of concealed carry users defend themselves.

But the carry portion is only part of the story of the optics-ready Glock. The G19 took well to the Leupold DeltaPoint it wore. After a box of cartridges, I was drawing, aiming and hitting targets like I had carried it for years. Will iron sights become backup as they have on AR rifles? I say yes, and Glock has made it easier and infinitely more practical to mount an optic on a concealed carry pistol.

The Glock compact G19 is one of the most popular defense pistols available. It really does not need any introduction. My expectation was the handgun would perform flawlessly, adapt to my hand size, and be extremely reliable. The G19 Gen4 MOS is nearly the same as current G19 pistols except for a cover plate just forward of the rear sight. In MOS configuration, it is only a matter of removing two screws and the cover plate, choosing the MOS adaptor plate that is compatible with your reflex sight, mounting the adaptor plate to

SPECIFICATIONS

MODEL: Glock G19 Gen4 MOS
CALIBER: 9mm
ACTION: Locked Breech, Recoil
Operated
BARREL LENGTH: 4.02 in.
OVERALL LENGTH: 7.28 in.
WEIGHT: 21.16 oz. (empty)
SIGHTS: Fixed, Dot/Outline
TRIGGER: Striker Fire
FINISH: Matte Black
GRIPS: Textured Polymer Modular
Backstraps
CAPACITY: 15+1

the slide, and affixing optic to the adapter plate. It actually takes more time to describe mounting an optic on the Glock than doing it. The MOS adaptor plates are compatible with reflex red-dot sights from a number of manufacturers: Trijicon,

The G19 Gen4 MOS is nearly the same as current Glock 19 pistols except for a cover plate just forward of the rear sight.

Leupold, Meopta, C-More, Doctor, and Insight. The footprint of the adaptor plate on the slide is small, but the actual optic footprint will vary in width and height depending on the manufacturer. They all weigh nearly the same. The Leupold DeltaPoint I mounted sits low on the slide. Its width is 1.2 inches, while the width of the G19 slide is 1.0 inches. An eighth of an inch of the DeltaPoint hangs over each side due to the shape of the sight's widow. It sits at an inch high, while standard Glock sights poke up 1/8-inch.

I've used red-dots for competition shooting, which affords greater speed over traditional iron sights. Plus, there is only one plane to focus on when aiming a red-dot. The three sight planes of traditional open sights — rear, front and target — need to be aligned for shots to hit accurately. It takes practice and training. A reflex sight is far easier to acquire the target, aim, fire, and get back on target. Carrying a concealed pistol equipped with a reflex red-dot sight does not pose a drastic change in the way you carry, but it will change the ease with which you aim.

The iron sights on the G19 are standard height and do not co-witness with the DeltaPoint. Battery life is an issue with

any electronics. Optics are rugged and can take abuse, but there is that voice in the back of your head asking what happens when the batteries die. Here's one thing I found: In a pinch if the battery dies you can use the window of the reflex sight as an extra-large makeshift peep sight in conjunction with the front blade. For close distance, I tried that very thing out to 10 and 15 yards and it worked effectively allowing me to hit a target 18 inches in width or about the width of the average human torso. Battery life should not be an issue barring unforeseen circumstances. Even if dropped in water the DeltaPoint is waterproof. Using any battery-operated accessory requires an additional maintenance task, routinely changing batteries like you do in a flashlight or smoke detector. It becomes second nature and ensures you are not caught unawares.

A Leupold DeltaPoint, which sits low on the slide, was simple to mount on the Glock G19 MOS.

To carry the G19 I used a DGS Arms CDC (Compact Discreet Carry) Kydex IWB (Inside-the-Waistband) holster. I've used this holster to carry a standard G19 in appendix carry. Using a pencil, I marked the holster and used a Dremel tool to cut a slot to allow the handgun with mounted DeltaPoint to be completely holstered. There are now several makers producing holsters for red-dot-equipped handguns.

I found the red-dot did not affect my concealed carry routine. I did need to slightly modify my training when drawing the new Glock from concealment. The taller sights have the potential to snag on concealing garments when drawing if you don't grab that shirttail and yank it

as high as you can (which you should do anyway regardless of your carry gun's sights). I did find the DeltaPoint made a great handle to rack the slide if needed. I admit I used it as a handle a lot to see if the sight would come loose or go out of zero. Nothing doing. I even employed the sight to rack the slide against the edge of the shooting bench, my holster mouth, and with my hand during a reload. Using the sight as a grip means it gets fingerprints. Concealed carry also means lint can build up in the sight window. Part of my new routine became to blow out any lint or debris that would build up using the same canned air I use to clean out my computer keyboard.

From a rest, the author attained surgical accuracy with the Glock. He was using the Hornady American Gunner ammo loaded with 115-grain XTP bullets.

PERFORMANCE: GLOCK G19 GEN4 MOS

9mm Ammo (bullet weight in grains)	Velocity (fps)	Energy (ft.-lbs.)	Best Accuracy (inches)	Average Accuracy (inches)
Hornady American Gunner 115 XTP	1,120	936	1.3	1.5
Winchester Train 147 FMJ	937	287	0.8	1.0
Hornady Critical Defense 135 FlexLock	990	294	1.4	1.7
Winchester Defend 147 JHP	936	286	1.0	1.2

Bullet weight measured in grains, velocity in feet per second, and average accuracy in inches for best five-shot groups at 25 yards.

The real test is making holes in paper. I averaged about 1.7 inches for 5-shot groups using a rest. Firing offhand and finding the red-dot in the sight window took a bit of ramp-up time. By the second magazine, I was drawing and aiming as if I had always used a red-dot on my concealed carry pistol.

Test and Evaluation: Ruger American Pro Duty

We live in a polymer-frame, striker-fire, double-stack world. At first glance, many of these types of pistols look alike but there are features that distinguish them. The Ruger American Pro Duty debuted in 2015 and is a full-size striker-fire handgun with a modular grip. The American comes in a hard case with two stainless steel magazines and three grip inserts to fit different size hands. I suspect that Ruger might have been vying for the U.S. Army's Modular Handgun System (MHS) program (the SIG P320 was ultimately chosen) since many of the pistol's specs sync with the Army's requirements.

My sample wore a matte black finish that was well-executed, and it felt good in the hand with the bore axis lower. It uses a Browning-style locked breech action with a new barrel cam that, according to Ruger, is designed

SPECIFICATIONS

MODEL: Glock G19 Gen4 MOS

CALIBER: 9mm

ACTION: Locked Breech, Recoil Operated

BARREL LENGTH: 4.02 in.

OVERALL LENGTH: 7.28 in.

WEIGHT: 21.16 oz. (empty)

SIGHTS: Fixed, Dot/Outline

TRIGGER: Striker Fire

FINISH: Matte Black

GRIPS: Textured Polymer Modular Backstraps

CAPACITY: 15+1

The Ruger American Pro Duty debuted in 2015 and is a full-size striker-fire handgun with a modular grip.

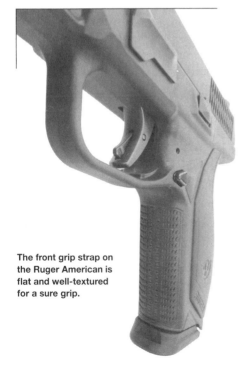

The front grip strap on the Ruger American is flat and well-textured for a sure grip.

to reduce felt recoil by controlling the rearward movement of the slide when a round is fired. It has a solid steel recoil rod with a trapped recoil spring. Recoil was quite manageable. The extra ounces

Genuine Novak sights on the Ruger American offer a low profile and fast acquisition.

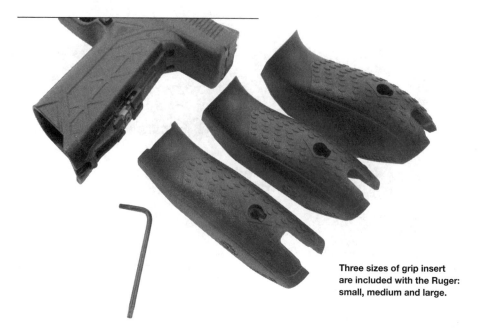

Three sizes of grip insert are included with the Ruger: small, medium and large.

the American weighed compared to other striker-fire pistols damped felt recoil. I like how the American operated. The slide is chiseled at the muzzle, making it easy to holster. Serrations at the rear of the slide are in an X-style pattern and offer lots of texture to get a firm hold. Sights are a Novak LoMount 3-dot system, which is excellent. The rear sight is windage adjustable and the front is dovetailed into the slide. It has a large external extractor and a viewport in the top of the breechblock that allows for visual confirmation of a loaded or empty chamber.

It uses what Ruger calls a pretensioned striker-ignition system. That means the cycling of the slide partially

Note the barrel cam, which is designed to reduce recoil along with a low-mass slide and low bore axis.

PERFORMANCE: RUGER AMERICAN PRO DUTY				
9mm Ammo (bullet weight in grains)	Velocity (fps)	Energy (ft.-lbs.)	Best Accuracy (inches)	Average Accuracy (inches)
Hornady American Gunner 115 XTP	1,077	269	1.91	2.15
Liberty Civil Defense 50 HP	2,075	478	1.80	1.98
SIG Sauer 115 FMJ	1,095	306	1.70	1.89
Aguila 124 FMJ	1,046	301	2.70	2.95

Bullet weight measured in grains, velocity in feet per second, and average accuracy in inches for best five-shot groups at 25 yards.

cocks the striker, which is fully cocked by depressing the trigger. When the slide is cycled, the striker is in the fully cocked position so when the trigger is depressed it instantly releases the sear. This is supposed to create a shorter, crisper trigger pull. The trigger is made of steel and so is the safety lever insert. There is a trigger stop built into the inside of the trigger to stop overtravel.

The slide stop and magazine release are ambidextrous, something most shooters can appreciate. The magazine button was small and triangular in shape. The polymer receiver has an assortment of grip textures. The rear strap has a course diamond texture, the grip insert a fine pebble texture and the front strap a small diamond surface. I found swapping grips a bit of a task until I figured it out. A hole in the rear strap gives access to a Torx screw. (The Torx tool is included with the pistol.) The grip insert on the American allows for a wide range of hand sizes. A rail is built in to accept lights or laser pointers.

Field stripping is simple via the takedown lever. Unload, rotate the lever, and you have five pieces. The magazines have witness holes on the side and they are easy to load even to the last round. The body of the magazines is coated with a nickel-Teflon. The floorplate has a built-in lip so when the mag was inserted it forms the bottom edge of the front strap.

At the range, the American proved to have the accuracy of a defensive firearm. I averaged a little over 2 inches across all ammo. With SIG 115-grain FMJ ammo I shot a best, 5-shot group of 1.70 inches at 25 yards. The American is quite capable. In closer distance and firing for speed, it was easy to control thanks to the low bore axis. Even with a wide assortment of ammo, bullet styles, and weights, the pistol performed without a hitch. There was a fair amount of take-up with the trigger before it broke. But the break was consistent.

The Ruger American is a capable pistol. Accuracy is good, and reliability perfect. The grip inserts were a bit difficult to swap out until I learned the process.

The Smith & Wesson M&P 9 M2.0.

Test and Evaluation: Smith & Wesson M&P 9 M2.0

There are two ways you can look at the new Smith & Wesson M&P 9 M2.0. One is, why fix what isn't broken. The M&P 9 M1.0 works fine, leave it alone, right? Forward-thinking manufacturers know life is not static nor does it occur in a vacuum. Needs evolve and change, so S&W delivered on the change. The company chose to learn, listen, test, adapt, and evolve, and they did it with the M&P 9 M2.0.

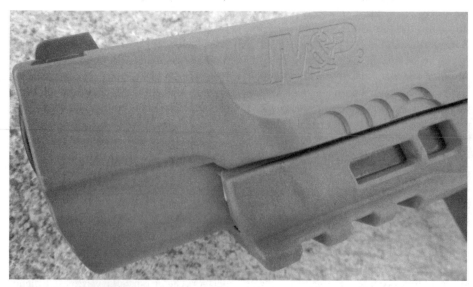

The cutouts reveal one of the major renovations to the M&P series: an extended stainless-steel chassis embedded in the polymer receiver.

I like the M&P series and found these pistols perform. I've witnessed M&Ps endure excessive round counts. As long as magazines are loaded the pistols keep churning up the dirt backstop without taking a break — until they become hot to the touch. The M&P is not fazed by high round counts and does not cave under the torture. In reality, no one will ever shoot 1,000-plus rounds as fast as possible, unless you happened to be like me and try to find a gun's weak spot. I couldn't break the old M&P 9 M1.0.

There are other things I like about the original M&P, which I hoped they would leave well enough alone. One is the grip. The 18-degree grip angle of the first gen M&P was similar to a 1911 and comfortable to shoot. A Glock, in comparison, is about 22 degrees. Smith & Wesson wisely chose to keep the angle at 18 degrees.

The trigger on older models is good, too, but is always the thing that could be improved. Forget about the ease of use and field stripping. The M&P is simple and safe and, yes, a thumb safety is available on older M&P models if that feature is a requirement. The new M2.0 I tested came with the optional ambidextrous thumb safety. I tried the thumb

The M2.0 uses the same trigger as found in the Performance Series M&P pistols.

safety on the test sample just to tick that off the checklist. It is easily manipulated with the thumb of the shooting hand. If I owned this gun, I would probably never use it since the built-in safeties keep it drop safe. Having the safety redundancy in the thumb safety is a good feature nonetheless.

The slide release is the same as on the M1.0 expect now it's ambidextrous. Also, the mag release is reversible, and the button is made of steel.

Some of the M2.0 design changes are obvious. Others not so much. The first thing that I noticed when I pulled the M&P 9 M2.0 out of the case was the aggressively textured grips. It reminded me of medium grit sandpaper but with none of the abrasion. Think Glock RTF2 texture but not as spiny. That texture offers good adhesion without feeling like your palm is being worn down one layer of skin at a time. The M2.0 comes with four grip inserts for petite to large hands. The palm swell grip inserts are sized small, medium, medium-large, and large. What I like about the M&P grips are the palm swells, which enable the pistol to stick to more of your hand with fewer gaps — gaps that are common on handguns with flat grip sides. Another plus with the new M&P is how the front grip strap

SPECIFICATIONS

MODEL: Smith & Wesson M&P 9 M2.0

CALIBER: 9mm

ACTION: Semi-Automatic, Short-Recoil, Locked Breech, Tilting Barrel

TRIGGER: Striker Fire

BARREL LENGTH: 5 in.

OVERALL LENGTH: 8.25 in.

WEIGHT: 26.9 oz. (unloaded)

GRIPS: Textured Polymer, Modular, 3 Sizes

SIGHTS: 3-Dot, Fixed

FINISH: FDE

CAPACITY: 17+1, Double-Stack Magazine

The palm swell grip inserts included with the Smith & Wesson M&P M2.0 are sized small, medium, medium-large, and large.

is void of finger grooves. Sometimes finger grooves fit and sometimes they don't. Some finger groove grip straps feel like they were made especially for you, while others feel like your big brother's hand-me-down clothes.

The next feature that caught my eye was new muzzle-end slide serrations in the trademark S&W scallops. When I compared these to my personal M&P 9 C.O.R.E. Pro Series I could see the stainless-steel slide was profiled a bit differently. That is, relieved of metal to make it lighter.

What was odd and new were cutouts in the polymer frame. These cutouts reveal one of the major renovations to the M&P series: an extended stainless-steel chassis embedded in the polymer receiver. The chassis makes the pistol more rigid to reduce flex and torque when firing. I fired my M&P 9 Pro Series next to the full-size M2.0 and felt the difference in recoil. The M2.0 had less felt recoil.

There are the changes that you can see but there are also upgrades that can be heard and felt. The M2.0 uses a new trigger. The new one is crisper and has a tactile and audible reset. It is the same trigger as found in the Performance Series M&P pistols. The trigger really separates the M&P M2.0 from all the other striker-fired polymer-frame pistols. The trigger is wide, and I felt I had more control with it compared to ones with a safety lever built into the trigger face. It was more consistent.

My test sample was equipped with a 5-inch stainless steel barrel, but it is also available in a 4.25-inch model. Previous 5-inch M&Ps were only available from the Performance Center. The finish was a nicely executed Cerakote FDE.

The high grip on the M&P means the close barrel-to-bore axis translates into more comfortable shooting with faster aim recovery from less muzzle flip. But the truth is in the shooting. I loaded

PERFORMANCE: SMITH & WESSON M&P 9 M2.0

9mm Ammo (bullet weight in grains)	Velocity (fps)	Energy (ft.-lbs.)	Best Accuracy (inches)	Average Accuracy (inches)
Hornady American Gunner 115 XTP	1,100	309	1.18	1.46
SIG Sauer 115 FMJ	1,105	312	1.35	2.06
Aguila 124 FMJ	1,067	314	1.24	1.80
Liberty Civil Defense 50 HP	2,094	491	1.47	1.95

Bullet weight measured in grains, velocity in feet per second, and average accuracy in inches for best five-shot groups at 25 yards.

up both 15-round magazines — the M2.0 comes with two steel mags — with some hot handloads loaded with a 115-grain hollowpoint bullet. A piece of broken clay pigeon on the dirt bank at 25 yards worked as a target. I covered the pigeon with the front sight and squeezed off the first round. Dead bird. Not a target pistol by any means, but the M2.0 will gladly do your bidding. I ran the remainder of that magazine and the other to boot just to get a feel for the rhythm of the pistol's cycle.

Hornady American Gunner with 115-grain XP, Aguila 124-grain FMJ, and Liberty Ammunition Civil Defense 50-grain HP rounded out the ammunition. The M2.0 chewed through all the test ammo, which is what I expected from an M&P. I used a rest to collect accuracy data and the Hornady American Gunner ammo gave me 1.5-inch groups at 25 yards. The Aguila and Liberty were both under 2 inches at 25 yards. Shooting for speed — the best part of a test in my opinion — revealed that the new M2.0 has less felt recoil. The enhanced trigger allowed me to get on target and fire quickly.

The S&W M&P M2.0 has morphed an already excellent platform into one that is easier and more comfortable to shoot. The trigger and sights allow you to shoot this pistol well. The four grip options offer a lot of shooting comfort depending on your hand size. I like this pistol a lot. Change is good.

Test and Evaluation: Springfield Armory XD MOD.2 4" Service Model

My expectation was high for the Springfield Armory XD MOD.2 4" even if this polymer-frame striker-fire does not have a modular grip. Truth is, it fit my average-sized hand like a glove. The multi-textured grip is what Springfield calls Grip Zone, stuff that allows you to have a secure hold. Grip Zone is designed with three different types of textures. Zone 1 texture is located on the front and back straps, Zone 2 is aggressive and is found on the side panels, and Zone 3 is a pebble-like surface that covers the frame. The receiver is molded so your finger falls

Springfield Armory XD MOD.2 4"
Service Model.

The Springfield Armory XD MOD.2 incorporates
a safety lever that must be depressed to pull
the trigger.

The red fiber optic front sight is easy to find when
aiming at a target with a dark background.

naturally by the trigger. The front strap has very shallow finger grooves. In hand, the XD MOD.2 4" feels good, but I'm getting ahead of myself.

The XD MOD.2 4" comes in a hard case with two stainless-steel magazines. My test sample had a gray polymer receiver and a black slide. Fit and finish were excellent, as I expected. The slide is sculpted to reduce weight and provide positive cocking. Course slide serrations are located at the muzzle and rear, so whichever method you prefer a fresh round can be racked with ease. The XD MOD.2 4" requires 18 pounds of effort to rack the slide and cock the weapon. The low-profile 3-dot sights are the best of all three pistols. Though red fiber optic front sights are not traditional, they do allow you to better aim since the red front dot stands out better against a target. The front sight is dovetailed as is the rear, which could be tapped left or right to adjust windage. The rear sight is flush with the rear of the slide providing a maximum sight radius. Plus, the rear sight is serrated to cut sun glare. Also, on the slide's top is a loaded chamber indicator that can be seen and felt. A silver pin protrudes from the rear

A silver pin protrudes from the rear of the slide indicating the Springfield XD MOD.2 is cocked.

Finger grip grooves are shallow on the new Springfield, so they are more user-friendly for different hand sizes.

The business end of the MOD.2 is chamfered to aid in holstering.

SPECIFICATIONS

MODEL: Springfield Armory XD MOD.2 4"
    Service Model
CALIBER: 9mm
ACTION: Semi-Automatic, Short-Recoil,
    Locked Breech, Tilting Barrel
TRIGGER: Striker Fire
BARREL LENGTH: 4 in.
OVERALL LENGTH: 7.3 in.
WEIGHT: 27.5 oz. (unloaded)
GRIPS: Textured Polymer
SIGHTS: 2-Dot Rear, Fiber Optic Front
FINISH: Black Slide/Gray Frame
CAPACITY: 15+1, Double-Stack Magazine

slide cover indicating the pistol is cocked. I like this feature as it instantly told me the handgun was cocked and ready to be fired.

Controls consist of an ambidextrous magazine release button that is good sized and protrudes sufficiently with a raised portioned of the receiver protecting the button from accidental magazine dump. The slide stop is located on the left side as is the takedown lever.

A grip safety adds another level of safety to the striker-fire and I liked the grip safety even if it was redundant to the safety lever built into the trigger. The trigger was very consistent but had a lot of take-up.

At 25 yards, the red fiber optic front sight was an asset. The trigger helped, too. My best group measured 1.32 inches with a 5-shot group using Hornady American Gunner 115-grain XTP ammo. Average accuracy with all ammo was 2.0 inches. For speed shooting, the grip helped me control the XD MOD.2 4".

If missing a modular grip is not a deal breaker, then the XD MOD.2 4" is a gun worth considering. Compact yet feeling like a full-size 9mm, it can be used for everyday

PERFORMANCE: SPRINGFIELD ARMORY XD MOD.2 4" SERVICE MODEL				
9mm Ammo (bullet weight in grains)	Velocity (fps)	Energy (ft.-lbs.)	Best Accuracy (inches)	Average Accuracy (inches)
Hornady American Gunner 115 XTP	1,095	306	1.32	1.49
SIG Sauer 115 FMJ	1,110	315	2.0	2.01
Aguila 124 FMJ	1,077	319	2.09	2.20
Liberty Civil Defense 50 HP	2,095	487	1.7	2.0

Bullet weight measured in grains, velocity in feet per second, and average accuracy in inches for best five-shot groups at 25 yards.

carry. The sights, trigger, grip, and accuracy sold me.

Test and Evaluation: Walther CCP

The Walther CCP uses a gas delay blowback action resulting in a handgun that is easy to operate, small enough to conceal, simple to shoot and light on recoil. Walther calls the system Softcoil Gas Technology.

The CCP is simplified by outfitting it with a striker-fire trigger while merging the trademark ergonomic grip with the gas delay blowback action. It incorporates a thumb magazine release button that is re-

The Walther CCP.

The Walther trademark grip and texture provide nice swells where they are needed on the CCP for a sure grip.

versible. Other than the slide stop, the only other control is a thumb safety. The CCP is perfectly safe to carry with a round in the chamber and the manual thumb safety in fire mode since it uses a firing pin block safety. The thumb safety affords an extra level of safety, but it's not really needed.

In hand the CCP is slim, with the Walther trademark grip and texture providing nice swells where they are needed. The trigger is fairly wide and serrated. With my average-size hands, it is no stretch to reach the trigger. The 3-dot sights are large and useful. Manipulating the slide, you instantly notice how easy it is to rack. The slide serrations both front and aft are course and provide a sure grip.

What is obviously missing is some sort of takedown lever. Since the CCP employs a gas-delayed blowback system the takedown procedure is different than the typical locked breech pistol. Walther provides a takedown tool, but a small, flat blade screwdriver can be used in a pinch. The tool is used to push the latching hook off the counter plate. Once that's accomplished the slide assembly with

piston and recoil spring slide off the fixed barrel. Interesting to note is the CCP does not have slide rails. The slide is aligned with the barrel due to the concentric recoil spring. Reassembly requires aligning the piston with the cylinder. The easiest way to do this is place the pistol on a tabletop with the muzzle pointing to the ceiling. This way you can align the piston and cylinder. When the piston and cylinder are mated together, flip the pistol over so the muzzle is resting

SPECIFICATIONS

MODEL: Walther CCP

CALIBER: 9mm

ACTION: Gas-Delayed Blowback

TRIGGER: Striker Fire

BARREL LENGTH: 3.54 in.

OVERALL LENGTH: 6.41 in.

WEIGHT: 22.33 oz. (empty)

SIGHTS: Fixed Front/Rear

FINISH: Cerakote Black

GRIPS: Textured Polymer

CAPACITY: 8+1

on the tube top and use the disassembly tool or screwdriver to move the locking hook away, push the slide to the receiver and release the locking hook. All this sounds a bit complicated but do it once and it becomes rote. Important: do not oil the piston or cylinder. Oil will just attract more gunk.

At the range, the CCP proved to be soft shooting, though it was easy to tell the handgun went off when firing the hot Liberty ammo versus the Aguila and Hornady. With the Liberty and Hornady, my best five-shot groups at 25 yards from a rest measured 1.12 inches for both ammo types. The best group with the Aguila measured 1.5 inches. The CCP is a sweet shooter with nice, smooth cycling and average shot groups at 1.5 inches. The trigger measures about 5 pounds and is better than what you would expect for a similarly priced pistol. The grip is long enough so it feels like you are shooting a larger handgun. None of that abbreviated grip stuff like in many compact 9mms.

In my opinion, the CCP is a great choice for a concealed carry handgun and has an affordable price to boot.

In the author's hand, the CCP felt large due to the grip, which aids in better control and follow-up shots.

Note the gas piston attached to the front of the CCP's slide. The barrel is fixed.

PERFORMANCE: WALTHER CCP				
9mm Ammo (bullet weight in grains)	Velocity (fps)	Energy (ft.-lbs.)	Best Accuracy (inches)	Average Accuracy (inches)
Hornady American Gunner 115 XTP	1,100	309	1.18	1.46
SIG Sauer 115 FMJ	1,105	312	1.35	2.06
Aguila 124 FMJ	1,067	314	1.24	1.80
Liberty Civil Defense 50 HP	2,094	491	1.47	1.95

Bullet weight measured in grains, velocity in feet per second, and average accuracy in inches for best five-shot groups at 25 yards.

CHAPTER 13

9MM SUBCOMPACTS AND MICRO PISTOLS FOR DEEP CONCEALMENT

It's hard to imagine that it's been just three decades since the use of polymers and high-tech manufacturing redefined the deep concealment handgun. It started when manufactures like Kel-Tec began offering a simple .380 ACP that created a wave of subcompact pistols. Since then, there has been a revolution in subcompact and micro 9mm pistols. The .380 ACP is a fine getaway caliber — use it to surprise your assailant and make your way to your rifle or shotgun. We all know small subcompact handguns are difficult to shoot due to their size, and that the .380 ACP caliber does not have the power of a 9mm (in fact, the .380 ACP is a 9mm Short).

Manufacturers like SCCY, Kel-Tec and Kahr reintroduced shooters to subcompact pistols in 9mm and larger calibers, but it was

The SIG Sauer P365 is a micro-compact 9mm that combines a striker-fired mechanism with a 10+1 round capacity in a highly concealable pistol. Photo: SIG Sauer

the old-school manufacturers like Ruger, Beretta, and Smith & Wesson that made deep concealment 9mms legit and helped change the way users carry concealed.

Looking back, the .380 ACP cartridge was developed for the Colt Model 1908, which 100 years ago was considered a compact pistol. The Model 1908 weighed about 24 ounces, was 7 inches long, and carried 7+1 rounds. Compare that to a Ruger LCP in .380 ACP that weighs 9.4 ounces, has an overall length of 5.16 inches, and holds 6+1 rounds. Sure, there were other smaller pistols manufactured by Beretta, Walther, and others, but those subcompacts were chambered in anemic calibers. They were compact pistols that could literally be carried in a pocket since they weighed about as much as a cell phone. My comfort level, and others, however, is in a larger caliber gun like the 9mm.

Kahr opened shop with the goal of designing and manufacturing reliable, small pistols. Kahr uses a trigger-cocking DAO that is very smooth. The use of stainless steel in the slide, premium Lothar match-grade barrel, and polymer frame make it accurate.

I have tested and carried numerous .380s and like the simplicity of the DAO configuration. Out to 12 yards, I am confident in my ability to hit a target accurately with a laser sight or with irons. I think most armed citizens carry a .380 out of convenience. When temperatures are hot and clothing less bulky, a .380 can be slipped into a pocket and no one is the wiser. They are thin, small, and lightweight — and I like the fact there is no exposed hammer or controls that can snag on clothing. It's better than no gun.

But what I carry most often is a compact 9mm. With an increase in caliber from .380 ACP to 9mm, pistol size

The Glock 26 Gen5 ditches the finger grooves in lieu of a straight grip front strap. With a 10+1 capacity, it is an excellent concealed carry choice. Photo: Glock USA

increases. The compact 9mm I carry is toted in an IWB appendix holster. Some shooters may not need to use a holster, but I am of average stature and a 9mm is heavier. In my pants pocket it would be obvious I'm carrying one without a holster. I also like the fact that a holster keeps my pistol in one consistent place.

An economy 9mm pistol is the Kel-Tec, with its 7-round, single-stack magazine, and DAO action. It is thin and nearly as concealable as the P-3AT. Kel-Tec's P-11 is a super-sized 9mm with an 11-round magazine. The P-11 gives up some concealability with a larger girth but firepower is increased. The SCCY CPX Gen 1 and Gen 2 models are a very economical alternative. CPX-1 models have an ambidextrous manual thumb safety. They feature a 9-pound trigger pull.

Kahr's PM series is an example of a very concealable little handgun that does not compromise on caliber or performance. The PM series mashes together a polymer frame and stainless-steel slide with a buttery smooth trigger. The PM9 is a 9mm that requires minimal maintenance, has an excellent trigger, and sports enough textured surfaces so it does not slip in your hand. The PM9 has a 6+1 capacity with a flush magazine. The CM series — available in 9mm and .40 S&W — offers all the same features as the PM models but with minor cosmetic and manufacturing differences that lower the cost. Traditionalists may like the MK series, which uses a metal frame. Theses nines have more heft than their polymer-framed cousins but that may not be an issue for some users.

The Ruger LC9 is a departure from past 9mm pistols released by the storied gun maker. The LC9 is small and looks like a super-sized LCP. It is 6 inches long and weighs a little over 17 ounces empty. The polymer frame is nicely textured in the right places, so though the pistol is small, during rapid-fire strings you can maintain control. The front and rear grip straps are checkered. Also, there is plenty of surface area on the rear slide serrations for an easy and sure grip. Subcompact and compact pistols can be slightly more difficult to operate than full-sized ones. Retracting the slide on pistols with stiff recoil springs can be difficult because there is less material to grasp. The LC9 is slim and trim thanks to its single-stack magazine and has sights that are similar to a full-size pistol. The trigger breaks at about 6 pounds with a long, smooth pull.

The Smith & Wesson Shield is a compact version of the S&W M&P. These striker-fired handguns are very concealable and slim. The Nano from Beretta is also thin and lightweight due to its polymer frame. It follows Beretta's heritage of fine compact pistols. The Kimber Solo is slim but uses an aluminum frame. The Solo Carry model weighs only 17 ounces empty and employs a single-action striker-fired trigger setup. The XD(M) and XD(S) lines from Springfield Armory have crisp striker-fired triggers and come in compact packages.

These subcompact and compact pistols fill the gap between concealed carry and convenience — superseding the need to carry a full-size handgun.

Test and Evaluation: Kimber Micro 9

Although both the SIG and Kimber use a 1911-style platform, what separates these two micro shooters are aesthetics, controls, and ergonomics. The Kimber Micro 9 Desert Tan (LG) with laser grip and the SIG Emperor Scorpion P938 are both 9mms with barrels that measure 3- and 3.3-inches, respectively, and have a single-stack magazine — clearly designed for concealed carry. These micro 1911s looks similar to the full size, but the systems are quite different.

Scaled down for concealment, the Kimber and SIG are packed with 1911 design elements. Those include the controls, single-action trigger, and grip angle, all adding up to make a truly backup-sized 1911. If you are familiar with the 1911 then the transition to one of the micro 1911s will be seamless. The thumb safety,

The Kimber Micro 9 Two-Tone (DN) is a subcompact single-action 9mm based on the 1911. The large TruGlo sights make it feel like you are aiming a full-size handgun.

slide release, and magazine release are just like those in the 1911 design. These mini 9mms disassemble with ease so maintenance is not a chore.

For speed testing, I performed the Bill Drill at 7 yards, firing a magazine as fast as I could while keeping hits in an 8-inch circle. The intent of this drill is to improve speed without eroding accuracy. It also was an opportunity to run the pistols dry, check for slide lock-back, perform numerous magazine changes, and repeatedly use the slide release as well as test rapid sight alignment and trigger press. I started at the low-ready position. Here's what I found running these micros muzzle to muzzle.

The Kimber, Micro 9 Desert Tan (LG) looks like a shrunken Government 1911 model with its rounded slide top and internal extractor. The fit and finish are well executed and held up during testing. The model was equipped with Crimson Trace laser grips, which in my opinion enhances the shootability of the tiny handgun at close range. The pistol came in a soft case with two magazines, each of which had an extended rubber bumper floorplate that act as a finger rest. The floorplate is rounded on all edges. In fact, the edges of the Micro 9 are rounded making it snag-free for a smooth draw from deep concealment.

I liked the large 3-dot sights. Speaking of sights, those found on both the Kimber and SIG are similar in size to ones used on full-sized guns, which made shooting easier. The Kimber has a left-side thumb safety similar to the setup on a Government 1911A1. It is easy for a right-handed shooter to manipulate the safety with the thumb of their shooting hand, though the SIG provides a bit more safety lever surface area and was slightly easier to manipulate.

A button on the front strap activates the laser grips. Simply grasping the pis-

SPECIFICATIONS

MODEL: Kimber, Micro 9 Desert Tan (LG)
CALIBER: 9mm
ACTION: Short Recoil, Locked Breech
TRIGGER: Single Action
BARREL LENGTH: 3.15 in.
OVERALL LENGTH: 6.1 in.
WEIGHT: 15.6 oz. (unloaded)
GRIPS: Checkered Polymer Crimson Trace Laser Grips
SIGHTS: 3-Dot, Laser Pointer
FINISH: Desert Tan/Matte Black
CAPACITY: 6+1, Single-Stack Magazine

tol activates the laser. I could also loosen my grip and turn it off. I liked the ease of activation and use. A switch on the left grip allowed me to completely turn off the laser. The grips themselves have textured polymer and felt thicker in my hands compared to the SIG. The SIG felt thin and flat. Its mag release button was simple to work and dumped the stainless magazines freely.

The Micro 9 has slightly more hammer surface area for texture than the SIG, so it is a bit easier to cock, though neither were difficult. The Micro 9 has a slightly larger beavertail than the SIG so ham-fisted testers feel more comfortable shooting the Kimber. The trigger is serrated so your trigger finger pad or first knuckle stick to it better during recoil. There is a polymer insert in the rear strap with fine checkering that helps keep a grip on the gun when shooting. Field stripping is easier than a Government 1911 and is the same for both pistols.

In hand, I liked both guns but be aware these lightweight 9mms can produce recoil. That said, the recoil from either was controllable, even pleasant. The Kimber slide required 14 pounds of force to rack and cock, slightly less than the SIG.

PERFORMANCE: KIMBER MICRO 9 DESERT TAN (LG)

9mm Ammo (bullet weight in grains)	Velocity (fps)	Energy (ft.-lbs.)	Best Accuracy (inches)	Average Accuracy (inches)
Armscor 124 FMJ	1,002	276	3.40	3.65
SIG Sauer 115 FMJ	1,006	258	3.3	4.15
Aguila 124 FMJ	1,008	280	3.20	3.95

Bullet weight measured in grains, velocity in feet per second, and average accuracy in inches for best five-shot groups at 25 yards.

Twenty-five yards is pushing the range of these small pistols but, due to the single-action trigger, large sights, and a rest, I was able to shoot five-shot groups that averaged 4 inches. My best group was with Aguila 124-grain FMJ ammo — a 3.2-inch group. In close range, I was able to shoot them fast and accurately. Small pistols require a tight grip. They can easily shift in hand during recoil.

SIG Sauer P938 Emperor Scorpion

The SIG Sauer P938 Emperor Scorpion is striking in appearance with an FDE (flat dark earth) finish and G10 grips. It comes in a hard case with two stainless-steel magazines; one with a finger rest and one without, the latter of which fits flush in the butt. In the case was a SIG polymer OWB (outside-the-waistband) holster. I used the magazine with the floorplate finger rest for most of the testing since I liked this setup the best. The finish was well executed on the SIG — no surprise there. I expected the SIG to run and it

The SIG Sauer P938 Emperor.

PERFORMANCE: SIG P938 EMPEROR SCORPION

9mm Ammo (bullet weight in grains)	Velocity (fps)	Energy (ft.-lbs.)	Best Accuracy (inches)	Average Accuracy (inches)
Armscor 124 FMJ	990	270	3.10	3.45
SIG Sauer 115 FMJ	971	241	3.20	3.45
Aguila 124 FMJ	968	258	3.30	3.60

Bullet weight measured in grains, velocity in feet per second, and average accuracy in inches for best five-shot groups at 25 yards.

did. But first, let's get into what makes the SIG different from the Kimber. The slide of the little SIG is shaped like those found on SIG's other models. That is, blockier and squared off. Sights are large, allowing you to be in charge. This model features Siglite 3-dot night sights. It took about 15 pounds of effort to rack the slide and cock it. I liked the fact the SIG had serrations at the muzzle and rear of the slide. (The Kimber had serrations only at the rear.) I appreciated being able to rack the slide using a variety of methods. I also found the larger sights allowed me to rack the slide

SPECIFICATIONS

MODEL: SIG Sauer P938 Emperor
    Scorpion
CALIBER: 9mm
ACTION: Short Recoil, Locked Breech
TRIGGER: Single Action
BARREL LENGTH: 3.0 in.
OVERALL LENGTH: 6.0 in.
WEIGHT: 16.0 oz. (unloaded)
GRIPS: Piranha G10 with Medallion
SIGHTS: 3-Dot, Siglite Night Sights
FINISH: FDE
CAPACITY: 6+1, Single-Stack Magazine

on the edge of a Kydex holster, tabletop, and nearly any edge. The outside edges of the SIG are sharper and less smooth than the Kimber.

The SIG features an external extractor and an ambidextrous thumb safety that is slightly easier to manipulate than the Kimber. There is a bit more metal to allow me to flick it on and off without drastically changing my grip. The serrated hammer has a bit less surface area to grasp and cock than the Kimber. The beavertail is smaller than the Kimber's, but I did not experience hammer bite. The face of the trigger is serrated, useful when shooting for speed.

The SIG is much flatter and thinner. The rest found on the floorplate is handy — it makes the pistol feel like a larger piece. What set both of these micro nines apart from other striker-fire or DAO 9mm pistols is their relatively large sights. The SIG is a small pistol, but it feels like a large one and is easier to shoot.

Using a rest and shooting out to 25 yards, the SIG was a pleasure to shoot due to its grip, sights and fairly crisp single-action trigger. I was able to put five rounds into a 3.1-inch group with

Armscor 124-grain FMJ ammunition. On average, the handgun grouped 3.5 inches. In terms of accuracy, I would say the SIG and Kimber were comparable. For the speed shooting phase of testing, I favored the toothy texture of the SIG as it stayed adhered to my hand with no discomfort. The front grip strap is checkered, and it has a plastic checkered insert in the rear strap — lots of texture without being raspy to the hand. The Kimber laser grips are slicker to the grasp.

Both pistols performed flawlessly. At close range, the Kimber Micro 9 is accurate and easy to handle. The laser allows faster aiming in dark conditions while the full-size sights make aiming easier. I like all the smoothed edges and the beavertail. The SIG feels thinner and has a better texture than the Kimber. The SIG has large night sights that served me well. Recoil is pleasant but more noticeable with these lightweight micro nines.

Test and Evaluation: Kahr CM9

It has been said that necessity is the mother of invention and that is exactly how Kahr Arms started. Justin Moon was an avid shooter but wanted a truly ultra-compact 9mm pistol that was totally reliable and easily concealable. In 1996, the Kahr K9 debuted and completely changed the way shooters and those who carry concealed define a compact handgun. Moon designed his first compact semi-auto with a stainless-steel frame. Chambering it in 9mm gave it teeth. It was all good, but it was a bit heavy. The next evolution of the design was the PM9, which incorporated a lightweight polymer frame. What more could concealed carriers want? A less expensive pistol maybe? Enter the CM9, a 9mm subcompact pistol that won't take a large bite out of your wallet but performs flawlessly.

The Kahr CM9.

The front grip and rear backstrap of the Kahr CM9 are stippled for a sure grip.

The CM9 is everything the PM9 is except for a few modifications that make it much more affordable. Think of the CM9 as a PM9 stripped of all unnecessary adornment. The CM9 has less machining of the slide, and the roll marks on the slide aren't as refined. The front sight is pinned in place instead of the PM9's dovetailed blade. The controls, namely the slide stop lever, are metal injection molded. Instead of polygonal rifling, the CM9 has conventional cut rifling. It is shipped with one magazine. The aesthetics are the shortcut to cost savings but there are no shortcuts when it comes to the internal mechanism. The CM9's internal parts are the same as the PM9, as is the polymer frame. On the outside,

the CM9 is a bit of a plain-Jane but on the inside, it is a beauty that maintains Kahr's reputation for sweet-shooting pistols. These cost-saving modifications may make the CM9 look slightly different from the PM9, but they lop off some $200 from the price tag. A great shooter at a really good price.

The CM9 uses a Browning-style locked-breech design with a striker-fire mechanism that operates with a passive firing pin safety. The Kahr design is notable for its smooth pull, which feels like a slicked-up DAO revolver. When the trigger is depressed a double-lobed cocking cam rotates and draws the striker to the rear, deactivating the firing pin block. The system is very safe as well as smooth and consistent. Trigger pull averages about 6 pounds, 8 ounces. The smooth, wide trigger no doubt makes the pull feel less.

Kahr pistols are known for their thin girth and lightweight heft and the CM9 is no different. Many times, as the size of the pistol shrinks, the ability to operate and shoot it accurately diminish, too. Some compact 9mm pistols have hard-to-rack slides and some have small controls. The CM9's slide is easy to work. The angled serrations at the rear give good purchase. The sights are made of polymer and are a dot and bar setup. The front sight has a white dot while the rear sports a white vertical bar so when the sights are aligned they form a lowercase "i." It is a fast sighting system to use. The rear sight is dovetailed in place and can be adjusted left or right using a brass punch and hammer or a sight pusher. The external extractor acts as a loaded chamber indicator, slightly protruding when a round or empty case is chambered. The pistol uses a solid recoil rod that no doubt aids accuracy.

The frame of the CM9 offers plenty of texture where it is needed, like the

Small pistols can be difficult to operate due to their size, but the Kahr CM9 is easy. The trigger is smooth and consistent.

front and rear grip straps and the sides of the grip. The coarsely checkered pattern on the front and rear grip straps make the small gun easier to control when firing hot 9mm rounds in rapid fire. The grip sides have a stippled texture that works even when firing with sweaty hands. The oval mag release button is serrated and easily manipulated with the thumb of a right-handed shooter. It protrudes just enough and works consistently, allowing empty magazines to fall free. The grip is short, so most shooters will need to curl their small finger under the magazine. The slide stop is full size, unlike many subcompact pistols that have smaller controls. After the last round is fired the slide locks back giving you a visual clue that it's time to reload. The slide stop — with its serrated surface — is easily manipulated to close the slide on a fresh magazine; or, the slide can be pulled rearward, so it flies forward into battery.

The 6-round magazine is all metal save for the polymer follower. It fits flush with the butt. Witness holes in the magazine body let you know how many cartridges are loaded. Speaking of loading, stuffing the magazine even to full capacity

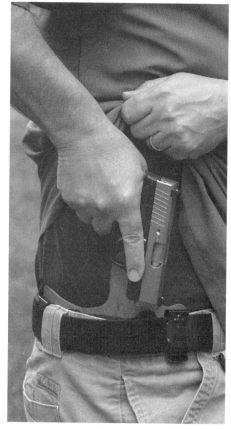

The concealed carry holster the author used with the Kahr CM9 is a Crossbreed MiniTuck IWB (inside-the-waistband) with a forward cant.

The CM9 had very good accuracy for a small value-priced handgun.

Performing a reload with a small pistol can be difficult and requires a slight change in technique.

SPECIFICATIONS

MODEL: Kahr CM9

CALIBER: 9mm

ACTION: Short Recoil, Locked Breech

TRIGGER: Double-Action Only

BARREL LENGTH: 3.0 in.

OVERALL LENGTH: 5.42 in.

WEIGHT: 15.9 oz. (unloaded)

GRIPS: Textured Polymer

SIGHTS: White Bar-Dot Combat

FINISH: Black Frame/Stainless Slide

CAPACITY: 6+1, Single-Stack Magazine

is easy on your thumb. The lips of the magazine are rounded. No cut thumbs.

According to the manual, Kahr recommends you fire at least 200 rounds to ensure it will perform reliably. Not many manufacturers state that in their literature but we all know that any mechanism needs to be broken in. With that in mind, I had an assortment of reloads and factory ammo to run through the CM9. The reloads were — to be honest — not the best-looking cartridges. They were plenty tarnished and had been through the reloading press a few times. The Kahr chewed through them all. It just fired and ejected the brass with no questions asked. I have used these reloads on other 9mms and found other guns choked on them.

For factory ammunition, I had hot Hornady Critical Duty 9mm +P with a 135-grain FlexLock on hand. The FlexLock bullets fill the hollowpoint with a soft rubber that expands the bullet in a variety of media. For standard pressure ammo, I tried Hornady Steel Match with a 115-grain HAP (Hornady Action Pistol) bullet, and some new manufacture Black Hills loaded with a 115-grain FMJ.

PERFORMANCE: KAHR CM9				
9mm Ammo (bullet weight in grains)	Velocity (fps)	Energy (ft.-lbs.)	Best Accuracy (inches)	Average Accuracy (inches)
Hornady Steel Match 115 HAP	922	217	2.12	2.39
Hornady Critical Duty +P 135 FlexLock	909	248	2.22	2.82
Black Hills 115 FMJ	1,028	270	1.67	2.64

Bullet weight measured in grains, velocity in feet per second, and average accuracy in inches for best five-shot groups at 25 yards.

The Black Hills stuff was the fastest out of the CM9 averaging about 1,030 fps; the Hornady loads ranged from 909 fps (Critical Duty) to 922 fps (Steel Match). Shooting for accuracy at 15 yards, I used a rest and squeezed off each round slowly and deliberately. Five-shot groups averaged about 2.5 inches, which was great performance out of such a small-barreled handgun, especially one with a double-action trigger. For rapid-fire testing, I placed a D-1 tombstone-style target at 15 yards. The drill involved me picking up the Kahr from the shooting bench and placing three rounds as fast as I could into the 8-inch ring of the target. By the time the ammo boxes were empty I was quickly tapping the targets consistently in the right spot. The CM9 feels thin, none of that chunky grip you get with other double-stack polymer-framed models. Even with the +P loads, there is little muzzle flip. It is easy to control.

As a concealed carry handgun, the CM9 is easy to hide and a pleasure to carry. It is a quality compact 9mm at an affordable price that makes sense for armed citizens.

Test and Evaluation: Springfield Armory XD Mod.2 - 3" Subcompact

From day one, Springfield Armory's XD series offered ease of use, reliability, a variety of calibers, and accuracy. Since then, the XD series has mutated numerous times and spawned the XD(M) and XD-S models. The XD Mod.2 is a genus of subcompact pistols with enhanced ergonomics, high-capacity payloads, and chambered in 9mm. The Mod.2 pistols have evolved into an even more user-friendly pistol with a grip that offers excellent adhesion — especially important in a subcompact chambered in a powerful caliber. Popular it should be, effective it is as I found out in the 9mm.

The XD ancestry in the Mod.2 is easy to see. It was originally designed as a combat service pistol — large and hand-filling — a brute of a pistol made to be extremely reliable in any conditions it might encounter. It uses a recoil-operated system and is striker fired. XDs are constructed with a polymer frame and steel slide and have a cocking indicator; a pin protrudes from the rear of the slide that offers a tactile and visual indication of being cocked and ready to rock. XDs are known for their excellent and safe USA (Ultra Safe Assurance) trigger system, drop safety and added grip safety. The Mod.2 takes these characteristics of the XD and incorporates them into a more refined platform specifically designed for concealed carry.

Not only does this 3-inch version have a reduced length barrel and grip to make it subcompact as you would expect, but the grip is designed for better control with three different types of textures, what Springfield calls Grip Zone. One might think texture is texture, but serious thought went into the placement of these surface features. Some subcompact handguns lacking grip can shift in your hand during recoil, especially when stoked with 147-grain 9mm loads. This lack of consistent grip makes other pistols difficult to shoot accurately.

The Mod.2 series Grip Zones have three different types of adhesion. Zone 1 texture is located on the front and backstraps, providing a good anti-slip surface. The side panels have Zone 2 texture, which is the most aggressive and, according to Springfield, does the most to keep the pistol under control during recoil. Zone 2 is basically stippling effect, providing a good grip without feeling uncomfortable. The remainder of the frame is covered in Zone 3 texture — the least grippy of textures yet still ... grippy.

The XD-9 Mod.2 has a slimmer frame than the original. To the rear of the trigger on both sides of the frame, the material is relieved so the trigger finger of a left- or right-handed shooter lays more comfortably. The beavertail allows you to get a high hold on the pistol, putting the bore axis closer to your hand, translating to less felt recoil. The rear of the trigger guard is

Springfield Armory striker fires incorporate a grip safety for added peace of mind.

relieved to aid in that higher grip, too. With my average-sized hands, my small finger had just enough grip to stay on the lip of the magazine floorplate, or it could easy curl under the floorplate using the flush-fit magazine. Those flush-fit mags, by the way, are stuffed to the gills with round capacity. The XD-9 Mod.2 holds 13+1 rounds and accomplishes this with a scant height of only 4.75 inches.

Even though the pistol is classified as a subcompact, it features a capacity typically found on full-sized handguns. In addition, it comes with an extended magazine featuring a sleeve over the lower portion of the mag that fits seamlessly with the frame grip to give each pistol a full-size grip. The extended grip is what makes possible the additional three rounds. The trigger guard is

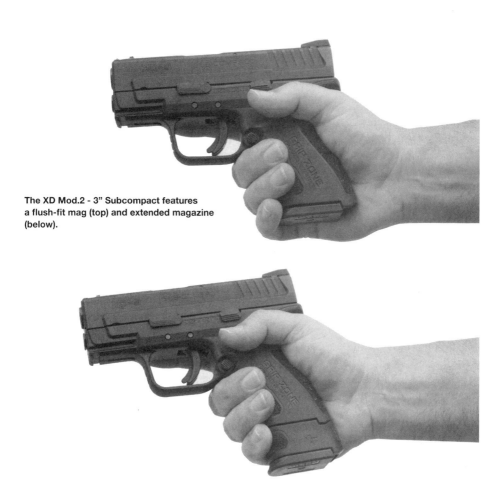

The XD Mod.2 - 3" Subcompact features a flush-fit mag (top) and extended magazine (below).

PERFORMANCE: SPRINGFIELD ARMORY XD MOD.2 - 3" SUB-COMPACT				
9mm Ammo (bullet weight in grains)	Velocity (fps)	Energy (ft.-lbs.)	Best Accuracy (inches)	Average Accuracy (inches)
Hornady Steel Match 115 HAP	1,048	281	1.42	1.62
Atlanta Arms 147 FMJ	816	217	1.42	2.02
Black Hills 115 FMJ	1,099	308	1.02	1.64

Bullet weight measured in grains, velocity in feet per second, and average accuracy in inches for best five-shot groups at 25 yards.

SPECIFICATIONS

MODEL: Springfield Armory XD Mod.2 - 3" Subcompact

CALIBER: 9mm

ACTION: Short Recoil, Locked Breech

TRIGGER: Striker Fire

BARREL LENGTH: 3.0 in.

OVERALL LENGTH: 6.25 in.

WEIGHT: 26 oz. (unloaded, flush-fit magazine)

GRIPS: Textured Polymer

SIGHTS: Fiber Optic Front/ Low-Profile Rear

FINISH: Matte Black

CAPACITY: 13+1 (flush fit), 16+1 (extended)

rounded off at the front and comes equipped with an accessory rail.

The controls are small with minimal footprint, thus more holster friendly and less apt to snag. Total width measures 1.19 inches — much thinner than other XD models. The slide release is aggressively serrated for positive operation. The ambidextrous mag release is serrated and is flush height-wise with the grip panels so accidental magazine drops should not be an issue. Empty mags dump clear of the mag well when the button is engaged.

The slide is slimmed down, is less blocky. The rear cocking serrations are more pronounced, and they make the subcompact easier to operate. There is plenty of useful gripping area. Springfield equips the Mod.2 pistols with an excellent 3-dot system. The low-profile rear sight is flush with the rear of the slide for maximum sight radius. It is smooth and snag-free. The back of the sight is serrated to effectively cut glare. The front sight is a red fiber optic with light gathering ability accentuated during daylight. The operator-facing side is also serrated. At night, the front sight nicely contrasts with the rear white dots. Both sights are dovetailed into the slide. You need a hammer and punch or sight adjusting tool to tweak the rear.

My assumption was the XD-9 Mod.2 might jump around in my grip during recoil. I was wrong. The variety of grip textures resulted in superb adhesion. All I needed to concentrate on was sight alignment and trigger press. I pushed the pistol to its limits, firing it at 25 yards using a rest. The 3-inch barrel is made for concealability and close work. Recoil is less stout in the Mod.2 compared to lighter, smaller handguns. There is some creep to the trigger, which is fine considering it's a defensive pistol. The trigger breaks crisply and consistently, and I was able to get slightly over 1.5-inch groups. The accuracy in part can be attributed to the captive recoil spring and full-length guide rod. I found the XD-9 very pleasant to shoot. No doubt the dual spring, full-length guide rod helped dampen recoil. Using a new Fobus IWB holster I practiced some dry-fire exercises. The Fobus uses either a large or small universal shell and flexible backing to ensure the pistol stays secure when worn. The more I handled the Mod.2, the more I reconsidered limiting my round capacity, as the pistol is nearly the same size as a single-stack handgun.

The XD comes in a hard case that includes an OWB polymer holster and double magazine pouch, plus a handy magazine loader. Out of the box, the Mod.2 offers the concealed carry practitioner a user-friendly and effective system.

The DNA of the Mod.2 3" is pure XD and the pistol easily fills the need for those wanting a concealed carry handgun with no compromise on caliber, magazine capacity and ease of use.

Test and Evaluation: Walther PPS M2

The tactics and equipment on which we depend for self-defense have changed radically over the past 100 years, not to say anything of the rapid sea change that's occurred over just the past decade. Better ammunition, efficient pistol designs, and ultra-precise CNC manufacturing methods give concealed carry holders a wide range of options. The new PPS M2 is a perfect example of Walther's dedication to refinement in a concealed carry handgun.

You might hear some state that the Walther PPS M2 is "new and improved." I hate this expression. It suggests that what came before was "old and lousy," and in no way is that the case with the Walther PPS Classic. In fact, the PPS Classic is a refined, reliable, and accurate personal defense or backup pistol. Thin and flat with flush- and extended-magazine options, plus modular backstraps for a custom fit for most hands, the PPS Classic proved itself to be an excellent single-stack pistol chambered in either 9mm or .40 S&W. Yes, the PPS M2 is new but not just re-skinned with aesthetic changes. This is a new pistol inside and out.

The PPS M2 incorporates the ergonomic Walther grip — like the Walther PPQ style — with a texture that ensures you have a good purchase on the pistol while providing a slight palm swell and shallow finger grooves that give it a big gun feel without the big gun bulk. The polymer frame incorporates a ridge for

The PPS M2 incorporates the ergonomic Walther grip — like the Walther PPQ-style — with a texture that ensures you have a good purchase on the pistol. Photo: Walther USA

With Aguila 147-gr. FMJ bullets the best five-shot group from the Walther PPS M2 measured 0.4 inches.

the trigger finger and the thumb of either a right- or left-handed shooter. This ridge channels your digits toward the trigger during the draw so the grip is smooth and comfortable with your trigger finger extended in the ready position along the frame. The polymer frame omits the modular backstraps and accessory rail of the PPS Classic. I question the addition

of an accessory rail on compact and sub-compact pistols dedicated to deep concealment. I prefer no rail for less bulk and easier holstering.

If the grip design is a new direction for the PPS series, so too is the magazine release. The PPS M2 uses a thumb-operated release. If there is a feature on the PPS Classic that some shooters

Field stripping the Walther PPS M2 is fast and simple.

have a hard time warming up to it is the ambidextrous magazine paddle release built into the rear of the trigger guard. We Americans like our mag releases to be operated by our thumb and Walther has obliged. The checkered button is flush with the edge of the finger channel and is easy to push. In fact, the PPS M2 spits out empty magazines like they were a bad taste in its mouth. Something to note, the Classic and M2 variants of the PPS do not share magazines. Since the PPS M2 now uses a thumb-operated magazine release, Walther engineers have made an undercut at the rear of the trigger guard. This allows you to have a

SPECIFICATIONS

MODEL: Walther PPS M2
CALIBER: 9mm
ACTION: Locked Breech, Recoil Operated
BARREL LENGTH: 3.18 in.
OVERALL LENGTH: 6.3 in.
WEIGHT: 21.1 oz. (empty)
SIGHTS: Fixed 3-Dot
TRIGGER: Striker-Fire
FINISH: Tenifer Black
GRIPS: Textured Polymer
CAPACITY: 6+1, 7+1 and 8+1

PERFORMANCE: WALTHER PPS M2

9mm Ammo (bullet weight in grains)	Velocity (fps)	Energy (ft.-lbs.)	Best Accuracy (inches)	Average Accuracy (inches)
Hornady American Gunner 115 XTP	1,064	289	0.7	1.9
Winchester Train 147 FMJ	919	276	1.3	1.6
Aguila 115 FMJ	1,088	302	0.4	0.7
Winchester Defend 147 JHP	889	289	1.6	2.1

Bullet weight measured in grains, velocity in feet per second, and average accuracy in inches for best five-shot groups at 25 yards.

slightly higher grip on the pistol to better manage recoil and muzzle flip.

Moreover, Walther placed front and rear slide-cocking serrations on the PPS M2. Some subcompact 9mm pistol slides are notoriously difficult to manipulate due to the small size of the pistol and the weight of the recoil spring. Add an oily gun or sweaty hands into the equation and things go south. The large, coarse serrations on the PPS M2 make it easy to operate in a pinch-and-pull or over-the-slide-grasp method. The steel, fixed 3-dot sights are big and bold with large white dots. The sights can easily be removed to upgrade to night sights or the front changed out to a different height, depending on your needs.

The slide rides on steel inserts in the polymer frame. On the right side of the frame, the steel guide is one-piece and nearly three quarters the length of the frame; the left is broken into two sections to accommodate the slide stop lever.

That extended steel guide insert no doubt helps accuracy as do the solid guide rod and dual recoil springs. The dual recoil springs also mitigate felt recoil.

The short 3.18-inch barrel features polygonal rifling. Compared to conventionally rifled barrels of similar length using the same ammo, the PPS M2 eked out a bit more velocity. Looking at my range data, about 10 fps extra — not wildly more, but an edge. A small cutout on the top side of the barrel acts as a loaded chamber viewport.

I spoke with Everett Deger at Walther Arms about the changes to the PPS. "The trigger on the M2 is a new design," he explained. "The new PPS M2 simplifies the trigger and aids in what would be considered a tangible feeling, smoother trigger albeit it isn't necessarily lighter than the previous PPS." The PPS Classic uses a modular backstrap that allows you to change the size of the grip backstraps as well as disable the pistol when the backstrap is removed. But what of the fate of the PPS Classic? "The model will continue to be supported under Walther's Lifetime Warranty, however, [it] will officially be discontinued in the summer of 2016 to make way for the new M2," Deger said.

The trigger is wide, serrated on the edges, and gives the trigger the feel of a full-sized pistol and a lot like the Walther PPQ, but they are different. The factory states the trigger pull of the M2 is 6.1 pounds, yet using my Lyman digital trigger pull gauge I averaged 5.9 pounds. The trigger pull is smooth with a bit of take-up. As you continue the trigger press you'll notice the cocking indicator starts to protrude from the rear of the slide. The rest of the press is clean at the trigger break. Reset is fairly short allowing you to get off a faster follow-up shot if required.

Magazines for the PPS M2 come in three sizes: 6-round flush fit, 7-round extended, and 8-round extended with finger rest. The flush-fit mag keeps the footprint of the M2 compact and extremely manageable for concealed carry. My sample shipped with the 6- and 7-round magazines. I preferred to shoot it with the extended 7-rounder since I could keep my entire hand on the grip for maximum control. Using the flush-fit 6-round magazine I needed to curl my little finger under the floor plate. After my initial range testing, I didn't waste any time and carried the PPS M2 concealed in a Blade-Tech IWB Klipt ambi holster I had on hand. The new Walther fit the Blade-Tech fine after I tweaked the retention screw. Carrying the PPS M2 in appendix carry proved to be comfortable with easy access.

Fielding stripping is simple. Pull down on the takedown lever and the slide moves forward and can be removed from the frame. You don't need muscular fingers to remove the recoil spring and guide rod assembly, either.

I conducted accuracy testing from a rest at 15 yards. In addition, I fired at 5 and 25 yards. I assembled four types of 9mm ammo in a variety of bullet weights. Note the manual advises against using +P ammo in the M2. Winchester Defend and Train is paired ammo; the Train using a 147-grain FMJ bullet and the Defend a 147-grain JHP. Both are loaded to a similar velocity, both rounds will perform similarly. I also tried Aguila 115-grain FMJ and Hornady American Gunner with the 115-grain XTP. I could cover my first three-round Aguila group with my thumb. The 7-round extended mag yields a fuller grip and allows me to get surgical with accuracy. The Aguila five-shot group at 15 yards was nearly one ragged hole. No matter what I fed the PPS M2 I was getting groups that averaged under 2 inches. When I did my part the PPS M2 rewarded me with stellar groups.

During close, rapid-fire drills the M2 was easy to control. At 25 yards my groups opened up, which I expected. Yet I found the M2 had excellent accuracy. There was not even a hint of a malfunction. It chewed on the 9mm ammo and spit it out even when I tried confusing it by firing it with a limp wrist. The enlarged ejection port ensured empties were tossed to the side without incident.

The PPS M2 has evolved into a much-improved concealed carry handgun. Evolution is indeed a good thing.

CHAPTER 14

COCKED AND LOCKED NINES – SINGLE-ACTION 9MMS

The Colt Competition 9mm features a dual recoil spring system that reduces felt recoil. Photo: Colt

When I think single-action pistols, I think of the 1911. It's simply the benchmark in American handgun design. As much as we may think a handgun design adopted back in the year 1911 might seem dated, it just keeps on reinventing itself. I don't necessarily think about the 1911 as being chambered in 9mm, but .45 ACP. The platform, however, is redefining itself in the 9mm chambering. 1911 Commander-size 9mm models have been around since 1950. In fact, the Colt 1911 Commander was one of the first semi-auto pistols mass-produced with an aluminum frame, and the first pistol Colt chambered in 9mm. In recent years, the 1911 chambered in 9mm has been in high demand. Many manufacturers — Ruger, Smith & Wesson, Remington, and many more — are offering the traditional single-stack magazine 1911s in the easier going caliber, while some makers like Armscor produce double-stack 9mm 1911s. One thing's for sure: Chambered in 9mm, the 1911 platform offers lighter recoil, less carry weight, faster follow-up

The Remington 1911R1 Enhanced is one of many 1911s currently being produced in 9mm. Photo: Remington

shots, and more rounds on tap. Plus, the 9mm is cheaper to shoot.

A SA pistol like the 1911 uses what could be debated as the original and simplest of trigger types. SA requires the hammer to be manually cocked. With the hammer cocked back, a press of the trigger releases it to fire. Simple. The earliest of weapons used this type of trigger system — cock the hammer, pull the trigger to fire. Many times, shooters carry their SA pistols cocked and locked, meaning the hammer is cocked back

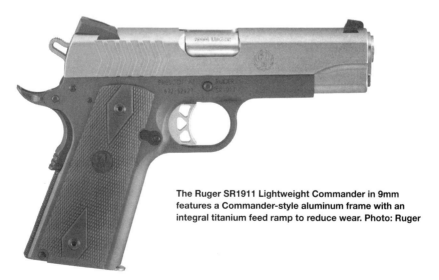

The Ruger SR1911 Lightweight Commander in 9mm features a Commander-style aluminum frame with an integral titanium feed ramp to reduce wear. Photo: Ruger

and the manual thumb safety is engaged. Upon drawing, the safety is swept off to fire.

The two most popular 9mm pistols to use this style trigger are the 1911 and Hi Power. Both are older designs. These iconic pistols are not the only SA 9mms, there are others but most date back to when the cartridge was initially invented. The Mauser '96 Broomhandle, for example, was one of the first successful semi-automatic handguns and employed a SA trigger. During World War II, the '96 was re-chambered in 9mm, as was the Steyr M1912. The M1912 was re-chambered in 9mm when the Austrian Army was absorbed by Germany. The M1912 employs a SA trigger and, like the Mauser Broomhandle, utilizes fixed-box magazines and is loaded via stripper clips. The Polish-manufactured Radom Vis is another one based on the Browning/1911 design and it, too, uses a SA trigger. Fast forward to the 21st century and Smith & Wesson introduced the Model 952 in 2000, which was based on the Smith's Model 52. The Model 952 is chambered in 9mm, had a SA trigger, and was intended to be a target pistol. A long-slide variant of the Model 952 was also introduced, but these two are no longer made. SIG also reintroduced the legendary P210 in 2010 in the P210 Legend Series, which looks very similar to the original P210 but with enhancements — namely a thumb button magazine release as opposed to a heel-style catch release, and beavertail-style backstraps similar to a 1911. Moreover, SIG has produced SAO versions of their DA/SA P226 pistol. The SAO moniker differentiates these from the original DA/SA variants.

While SA semi-automatic pistols are very popular in the 1911 platform, other trigger designs like the DA/SA and striker-fire are more frequently used in 9mm semi-automatic pistols in the 21st century.

Test and Evaluation: Springfield Armory Range Officer

The Range Officer from Springfield Armory is set up like a traditional 1911 with a steel receiver, straight backstrap, and manual thumb safety on the left side of the receiver. What sets this 9mm 1911 apart from others is the fully adjustable

The Springfield Armory Range Officer.

The lightweight aluminum trigger offers a crisp and consistent break.

SPECIFICATIONS

MODEL: Springfield Armory
    Range Officer

CALIBER: 9mm

ACTION: Locked Breech, Recoil
    Operated

TRIGGER: Single Action

BARREL LENGTH: 5.0 in.

OVERALL LENGTH: 8.6 in.

WEIGHT: 41 oz. (empty)

SIGHTS: Fully Adjustable

FINISH: Parkerized

GRIPS: Checkered Double Diamond
    Cocobolo

CAPACITY: 9+1

The rear sight on the Range Officer is serrated to reduce glare.

rear sights, 5-inch stainless-steel match-grade barrel, and lightweight, three-hole aluminum trigger. This 1911 is designed for target shooting, but is just at home as a defensive weapon.

The RO (as it's often called) is a full-size 1911 that is stripped down to run with nothing extra. That is not to say the Range

For better accuracy, the barrel bushing and barrel are hand-fitted.

9mm Ammo (bullet weight in grains)	Velocity (fps)	Energy (ft.-lbs.)	Best Accuracy (inches)	Average Accuracy (inches)
Hornady American Gunner 115 XTP	1,110	315	1.71	1.82
Aguila 124 FMJ	1,086	324	1.5	1.75
SIG Sauer 115 FMJ	1,134	328	1.64	1.7

Bullet weight measured in grains, velocity in feet per second, and average accuracy in inches for best five-shot groups at 25 yards.

Officer is incompetent. This plain-Jane rig features a classic 1911 thumb safety, traditional-size slide release, and mag release just like Uncle Sam specified. The exceptions are the barrel, the swept-up beavertail, and the crisp, SA trigger that all make shooting it a pleasurable and accurate experience. The SA trigger also has a short, smooth pull.

Test and Evaluation: Rock Island TCM TAC Ultra MS HC Combo

The Rock Island TCM TAC Ultra MS HC goes all in with a fist full of firepower in a 1911 high-capacity platform. Not only does the TCM come ready to rumble with a magazine capacity of 17+1 rounds of 9mm fuel, it is tricked out with a match-grade bull barrel, gaping mag well, a crisp and light trigger pull, and adjustable sights that are super easy to acquire and keep on target. When I first picked up the TCM, I thought: Ammo. I'm going to need lots of ammo.

What is cool about the TCM is that it's one of Armscor's combo pistols. You can swap out the barrel and recoil spring and it will shoot .22 TCM, a hyper-velocity .22-caliber round. The guts of the TCM are of the Colt Series 70-type mechanism.

On the slide are coarse, angled serrations at the rear that afford a good purchase with dry or sweaty hands. The top of the slide is domed like a typical 1911A1, but a red fiber optic front sight is dovetailed into the slide. The rear sight is fully adjustable. The rear face of the rear sight is flush with the back of the slide, maximizing sight radius.

The TCM uses a traditional muzzle bushing. The stainless-steel barrel is match-

The Rock Island TCM TAC Ultra MS HC holds 17+1 rounds of 9mm, giving you some serious firepower.

Follow the standard GI 1911A1 instructions to field strip the TCM.

grade with a polished ramp for enhanced reliability. When in battery there is no wiggle in the barrel. A solid guide rod is used to enhance accuracy. The slide is constructed of 4140 hammer-forged steel with a lowered and flared ejection port that puked out empties effortlessly.

The 4140-steel frame is like many wide-body high-capacity 1911s — thicker at the slide rails than a typical single-stack 1911. The grip flares out, so it can accommodate the double-stack magazine. The slide stop is slightly inset into the receiver, which is a telltale clue that this 1911 holds more than a single-stack mag. The slide stop is standard size and gives enough purchase to ride with the thumb of the non-shooting hand for a right-handed shooter. The extended thumb safety is ambidextrous and clicks confidently on and off and is easily manipulated even though the grip is plumper than a single-stack 1911. My average-size hand have no issues with this wide body. The TCM sports an upswept beavertail and good-sized speed bump so even a sloppy draw and grip will ensure the TCM will go bang when the trigger is pressed. The skeletonized hammer has fine serrations, so your thumb won't slip if you should choose to thumb it back. The steel mainspring housing has a fine texture of checkering that is not toothy, so by the end of a match the palm of your shooting hand won't be irritated. The front strap offers the same fine checkering that provides a good grip without too much bite to the skin. The checkered magazine release button pro-

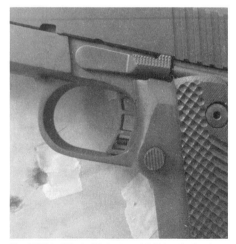
The TCM is fitted with textured G10 tactical grips and is finished with a durable, no-nonsense parkerized coating.

That fat, double-stack magazine has a 17-round capacity.

Standard features include a low-profile rear adjustable 2-dot LPA rear sight, skeletonized hammer, and ambidextrous extended slide safety.

The TCM is fitted with textured G10 tactical grips and is finished with a durable, no-nonsense parkerized coating.

trudes a bit more than a typical 1911, making it easier to press to perform a quick reload. The G10 grips provide a superb grip without irritation during long training sessions.

There is no slide-to-receiver movement on the TCM. This is one tight pistol. At first, it took more effort to rack the slide, something I attributed to the newness of the piece. Once I started to acclimate myself to it the effort to operate the slide became less until I didn't notice any difference.

At the butt is a gaping magazine well that seems to provide suction whenever a loaded magazine is near it. Magazines fly into the magazine well and seat quickly and securely with minimal effort.

The skeletonized trigger has a nice curve to it and the face is textured so your finger sticks even when chewing through rounds at a fast clip. The overtravel can be adjusted via a screw in the trigger face. On average, the trigger breaks cleanly at 4

PERFORMANCE: ROCK ISLAND TCM TAC ULTRA MS HC				
9mm Ammo (bullet weight in grains)	Velocity (fps)	Energy (ft.-lbs.)	Best Accuracy (inches)	Average Accuracy (inches)
Winchester Bonded PDX1 147 JHP	964	303	1.25	1.87
Black Hills 115 FMJ	1,144	334	1.62	1.87
Handload 115 JHP	1,243	395	1.87	2.18

Bullet weight measured in grains, velocity in feet per second, and average accuracy in inches for best five-shot groups at 25 yards.

SPECIFICATIONS

MODEL: Rock Island TCM TAC
    Ultra MS HC
CALIBER: 9mm
ACTION: Locked Breech, Recoil
    Operated
TRIGGER: Single Action
BARREL LENGTH: 4.25 in.
OVERALL LENGTH: 8.0 in.
WEIGHT: 40 oz. (empty)
SIGHTS: Fully Adjustable
FINISH: Parkerized
GRIPS: Textured G10
CAPACITY: 17+1

pounds. There is about 1/8 of an inch take-up, then a crisp break to drop the hammer. The TCM wears a no-nonsense Parkerized finish.

The 17-round double-stack magazine is easy to load, but the last round requires more effort than the first 16. It uses a polymer follower and base pad and sits flush in the butt. Slapping the magazine home I encountered only positive seating, and pressing the magazine release button caused the mags to fall freely from the gun.

For factory ammo I used Winchester Bonded PDX1 loaded with a 147-grain JHP, Black Hills with a 115-grain FMJ, and a reload was assembled using a 115-grain JHP.

"Go big or go home" is an expression that came to mind after the first magazine of Black Hills. Using a rest, the TCM punched a ragged hole in the cardboard at 25 yards. I fired at bullseye targets and plain buff D2-style tombstone targets. I like the tombstone targets as a fresh one, one without bullet holes, offers no specific aiming point. It is up to you to focus on the front sight and determine where the center is located. The red fiber optic on the

TCM did just that. The first few holes in the tombstone provided enough of an aiming point that I poured it on fast. The TCM owned it.

Test and Evaluation: Wilson Combat Sentinel

The saying, "You get what you pay for," is apt when talking about the Wilson Combat 1911 Sentinel. It is not an inexpensive compact pistol. What you pay for are eye-pleasing aesthetics combined with ultra-reliability that proves its worth in superior accuracy. The Sentinel is a well-built top-tier 1911 platform with everything you need in a compact 9mm and more.

Ryan Wilson, Vice President of Wilson Combat, explained the design differences in the Sentinel compared to Wilson's other Combat Compact 1911s. "The frame is shorter than our compact models and so is the slide; it is a half-inch shorter," Wilson said. "The barrel is 3.8 inches long compared to a compact's 4-inch. We also run a flat recoil spring and solid guide rod. The bushing-less cone barrel is hand-fitted to the slide so there is no traditional bushing."

The Sentinel feels small in your hand, so unlike a 1911. The shorter grip is noticeable and happens to be a perfect fit for me. With the magazine inserted into the butt, there is about a quarter of an inch of floorplate extending from the butt. Unlike some small, compact-frame pistols where you have this feeling that your hand needs something more to hang on to, the Sentinel feels secure.

The entire line of Sentinels — there are four models — are only built in 9mm, save one that is a .38 Super. "The reason we built the Sentinel in only 9mm or .38 Super is because of the cycle time," Wilson explained. "In 9mm or .38 Super, the pistols work 100

percent. When you make a compact 1911 and chamber it in .45 ACP the slide moves too fast for the magazine to keep up and feed the rounds to it. It is difficult to get the pistol to work with 100 percent reliability." Wilson Combat won't make a gun that doesn't work 100 percent of the time. They build guns to run on all types of ammo a customer might use. Wilson Combat has complete control over the entire product build, so they can ensure complete reliability. It is all or nothing with these people. No manufacturer can control what type of ammo a shooter will use, and that ranges from inexpensive factory loads to mild reloads or even hot defensive ammo. There are times when the gun and ammo are not a good pairing.

The Sentinel is tight. Not a hint of wiggle between slide and frame. "All our pistols are hand-fitted, there's nothing drop-in about our guns," Wilson said. "All our parts are machined slightly oversized, so everything is hand-fitted with a file and polishing stone to that particular gun. We

have about fifty gunsmiths in-house, some of which have been with us for 30 years." It takes time to hand-fit a pistol and that time ensures it will be reliable and perform when needed. The Sentinel line uses a Series 70-style mechanism. Wilson guns have a steel firing pin with an extra-power firing pin spring.

The edges of the Sentinel are smoothed so there is no fear the gun will snag on clothing when needed quickly. I carried the Sentinel for weeks and found it was fast from the holster during drills. The thumb safety is Wilson Combat's Bullet Proof style that affords plenty of leverage yet is small and smoothed into the frame. The Bullet Proof high ride beavertail grip safety enables you to grip the pistol higher and closer to the bore axis for less muzzle flip and more control. The frame has 30 lines per inch (lpi) high-cut checkering on the front strap and on the abbreviated mainspring housing. The Sentinel's grip doesn't slip even in fast double taps. The magazine

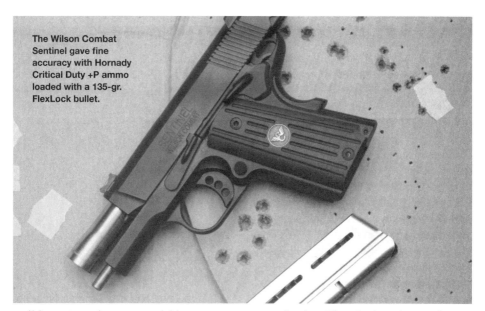

The Wilson Combat Sentinel gave fine accuracy with Hornady Critical Duty +P ammo loaded with a 135-gr. FlexLock bullet.

well is contoured to more quickly accept a reload. The three-hole trigger is long and is finely serrated on the surface for good finger adhesion. The checkered magazine release button is round and jettisoned empty magazines like you would spew out a sip of soured milk.

Grasping and retracting the slide was effortless with the angled slide serrations. You can really appreciate the hand-fitting of the pistol when you work the slide. The top of the slide is domed and front carry cuts at the muzzle taper the end, giving it a distinct look. The Battlesight front sight is dovetailed into the slide and sports a green fiber optic that sucks any available light, projecting itself bright and getting quickly on target. The Battlesight rear has horizontal grooves cut into the shooter-side face to eliminate glare and is shaped like an upper case "U." Loosen two hex screws and the rear sight can be adjusted for windage.

I chose a Black Point Mini Wing IWB holster of minimalist design, which still provides plenty of coverage of the pistol. That holster also has a high sweat guard to protect skin and clothing from chaffing. It is constructed of Kydex with small leather wings where the metal belt clips are attached. The clips are adjustable to fine tune the holster's

The Wilson Combat Sentinel is a well-built top-tier 1911 platform with everything you need in a compact 9mm pistol.

cant. I carried the Sentinel over a number of weeks and it proved to be comfortable and comforting to know it was close at hand.

At the range, the Sentinel met my high expectations. I ran factory FMJ and hollowpoints and even some messy reloads. Factory ammo consisted of Hornady Steel and +P Critical Duty rounds. Both use hollowpoint bullets. For full metal jacket ammo, I ran new Black Hills 115-grain rounds. The Sentinel chewed through it all. For such a small pistol I was surprised how easily it shot accurately, but I shouldn't have been. The trigger broke at a clean, crisp 3.5 pounds. Recoil was reduced in the +P rounds due to the steel frame. It is a small pistol that you will want to train with; you will want to shoot it. In each magazine I was able to shoot two- and three-round clusters that shared the same elongated hole. The Battlesight's deep "U" combined with the fiber optic front sight make for fast target acquisition. A 1911 is only as good as its magazine. The Sentinel's 8-round mag is made of stainless steel. Inside is a

self-lubricating polymer follower on top of a stainless steel wire spring. The floor plate is metal. Easy to load, the slide stays open on the last shot, which is what I expected.

Wilson Combat Sentinels are compact 1911s that are quality-built concealed carry weapons that look flawless and perform strongly.

SPECIFICATIONS

MODEL: Wilson Combat Sentinel
CALIBER: 9mm
ACTION: Locked Breech, Recoil Operated
TRIGGER: Single Action
BARREL LENGTH: 3.6 in.
OVERALL LENGTH: 1.2 in.
WEIGHT: 31.7 oz. (empty)
GRIPS: G10 Slimline
SIGHTS: Battlesight Rear, Fiber-Optic Front
FINISH: Armor-Tuff
CAPACITY: 8+1

PERFORMANCE: WILSON COMBAT SENTINEL

9mm Ammo (bullet weight in grains)	Velocity (fps)	Energy (ft.-lbs.)	Best Accuracy (inches)	Average Accuracy (inches)
Hornady Steel Match 115 HAP	1,093	305	1.12	1.42
Hornady Critical Duty +P 135 FlexLock	1,144	337	1.02	1.42
Black Hills 115 FMJ	1,117	319	0.92	1.62
Handload 90 JHP	1,249	312	0.72	0.87

Bullet weight measured in grains, velocity in feet per second, and average accuracy in inches for best five-shot groups at 25 yards.

CHAPTER 15

SUPER-SIZED HANDGUNS – BRACED PISTOLS

Braced pistols are tactical-looking weapons that have a military ancestry. This is especially noticeable due to the magazine mounted in front of the trigger guard and not in the grip. Exceptions are UZI and MAC-10 semi-automatic pistols. Though these "handguns" look full-auto capable, they are semi-automatic, require two hands to shoot with any degree of accuracy, have high-round capacity magazines compared to typical full-size 9mm handguns, and can be fired with a stabilizing brace.

Initially, there is an awkwardness shooting these pistols since they feel like an SBR (Short Barrel Rifle) yet have no stock for a steady aim. Not only that, they're too heavy to fire in a Weaver, Isosceles or hybrid stance with a two-hand hold like a typical handgun. Adequate range time and proper training are needed to master them.

The upside is that they offer high magazine capacity, decent accuracy, and a lot of shooting fun. Yes, these pistols can make empty brass very quickly. In 9mm, they are well suited for home defense and, as a vehicle weapon, are highly maneuverable. Getting in and out of vehicles takes more effort with a braced pistol than a standard-size one, but the firepower you can pack makes up for that shortcoming.

I like using a sling when shooting these super-size pistols since it gives me more stability. I also use the stabilizing braces, though the handgun does feel like an abbreviated rifle and my nose ends up

The semi-automatic SIG MPX operates from a fully-closed and locked rotating bolt that offers enhanced reliability. The short-stroke gas piston allows the SIG MPX to run all weights and brands of 9mm ammunition.

closer to the pistol's receiver. The stabilizing brace can be used by resting the brace against the side of your cheek. It is not the most stable cheekweld but works when you need to shoot fast at close range. And these big 9mms lend themselves well to optics. A red-dot can dramatically increase your accuracy.

Ammo choices run the gamut of available 9mm cartridges. In my experience, a well-made braced pistol will chew a mix of bullet weights and types from round-nose FMJs to hollowpoints. It doesn't matter with these things once they get into a feeding frenzy. Remember, they're not made for bullseye shooting, but to rapidly squirt lead downrange. A box of 50 rounds can go really fast.

Test and Evaluation: Zenith MKE Z-5RS

The MP5 is an iconic 9mm submachine gun. A full-auto submachine gun, however, is out of most shooters' reach. There is, however, the Zenith MKE Z-5RS. Zenith makes the MP5 delayed roller lock experience attainable, but don't call the MKE Z-5RS a clone, knock-off or wannabe MP5. The Zenith is a licensed version of the iconic Heckler & Koch MP5. Zenith Firearms in Afton, Virginia,

imports a number of HK-licensed delayed roller lock models from MKE (Mechanical and Chemical Industry Corporation) of Turkey.

The Z-5RS is a semi-automatic version of the HK MP5A1 and uses a delayed roller lock action like the HK G3 and the PTR-91 7.62mm NATO rifles. This mechanism is decidedly simple. The MP5 and MKE Z-5RS both employ a delayed rolled block mechanism. Basically, before a cartridge is fired, the bolt carrier and bolt are temporarily locked into the trunnion as rollers engage the locking piece. The bolt remains locked until the bullet leaves the barrel and the pressure drops, at which point the rollers disengage and the bolt carrier moves rearward by the force of the recoil. The MP5 — and hence the Zenith MKE Z-5RS — was originally designed in the early to mid-1960s. Yes, this is an old-school weapon constructed of stamped sheet steel that is welded to form the receiver. It's not as refined aesthetically as most modern designs. You can see hand welds, but the finish is good. The Zenith is heavy and long compared to other braced pistols but has a small profile. It is like a pipe with a pistol grip. In the hard plastic carrying case are a factory cleaning kit, two extra take-down pins, sling, three 30-round steel magazines, and an SB

The Zenith MKE Z-5RS is a licensed semi-automatic version of the iconic HK MP5 9mm submachine gun. If you go old-school, this is the way to go.

Those are 10 rounds through one ragged hole. Yes, the Zenith is capable of surgical accuracy.

Tactical stabilizing brace. The brace is similar to the SIG-style with a hook and loop strap to attach it to your arm. I've tried this setup and it feels like the pistol is a prosthetic. I prefer to use the brace as a cheekweld or against my shoulder.

The upper receiver houses the barrel, operating mechanism, and magazine well. A polymer trigger group snaps into the receiver and a butt cap keeps the pieces together. On the top side is a rear sight drum that has four apertures and is adjustable for windage and elevation. The outer edge of the drum is knurled for a sure grip and to cut glare. The front sight post is enclosed and protected by a ring.

The Zenith uses a non-reciprocating cocking handle located on the left side of the receiver. It is easy to operate.

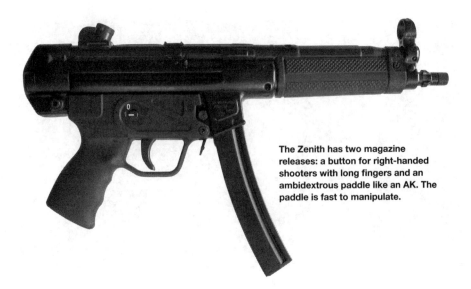

The Zenith has two magazine releases: a button for right-handed shooters with long fingers and an ambidextrous paddle like an AK. The paddle is fast to manipulate.

These are excellent sights in my opinion. The Zenith comes with a Picatinny rail, or aftermarket clamp-style mounts can be purchased to mount a red-dot or reflex optic. The 8.9-inch barrel has a 3-lug quick attachment and a 1/2x28 threaded muzzle. A cap protects the threads. The polymer forend has a coarse texture and is skinny, making it easy to grasp. On the left side is the cocking handle with a rubber knob. It takes a little more effort to cock and lock the bolt back. The Zenith has two magazine releases: a button for right-handed shooters with long fingers

The rotating aperture rear sight and post front are an excellent setup.

PERFORMANCE: ZENITH MKE Z-5RS				
9mm Ammo (bullet weight in grains)	Velocity (fps)	Energy (ft.-lbs.)	Best Accuracy (inches)	Average Accuracy (inches)
Hornady American Gunner 115 XTP	1,193	363	0.38	0.43
Winchester Train 147 FMJ	1,025	343	0.80	0.88
Aguila 115 FMJ	1,214	376	0.40	0.61

Bullet weight measured in grains, velocity in feet per second, and average accuracy in inches for best five-shot groups at 25 yards.

SPECIFICATIONS

MODEL: Zenith MKE Z-5RS
CALIBER: 9mm
ACTION: Roller-Delayed Blowback
TRIGGER: Single Action
BARREL LENGTH: 8.9 in.
OVERALL LENGTH: 17.9 in. (w/o brace), 25.75 in. (w/ brace)
WEIGHT: 6.1 oz. (empty)
SIGHTS: Elevation/Windage Adjustable Rear, Front Protected Post
FINISH: Matte Black
GRIP: Textured Polymer
BRACE: SB Tactical Pistol Stabilizing Brace
CAPACITY: 30+1

and an ambidextrous paddle a lot like an AK. The paddle is faster to manipulate. The magazines are made of steel with a steel follower and floorplate pad and are the easiest magazines I have ever loaded. The mag well is small, though, so extra care is needed to align the two.

The polymer trigger group is a one-piece grip and trigger guard with good ergonomics. The safety selector is located on the left side and is easily operated with the thumb of a right-hand shooter. The status of the safety lever is clearly indicated on both sides of the pistol. The trigger is smooth and has a 5.5-pound pull weight. The trigger and the safety selector can easily be removed from the trigger group housing. In fact, the Zenith came apart easily. There is a reason Zenith provides extra pins. They are easily lost in the field or in a workshop, a limitation to an old-school design.

At 25 yards the Zenith proved to be extremely accurate. I was able to get 10 rounds in a group that measured 0.38 inch using a rest with the Hornady American Gunner ammo. Actually, on the average, all the ammo grouped five shots under one inch. Recoil felt like .22 rimfire — minimal to say the least and the mechanism operated smoothly. Using the brace and firing for speed I could control the MKE Z-5RS with ease. I had no issues with the Zenith. It is easy to understand why the HK MP5 is still in use with many military and LE groups around the world.

If you are an HK MP5 fan, then the Zenith is a great option. The smooth operation, minimal recoil, and accuracy endeared testers to the Zenith.

Test and Evaluation: SIG Sauer MPX-PSB

The MPX-PSB from SIG is based on an AR-15-style platform and uses a closed, fully locked short-stroke, pushrod gas system mechanism. The SIG short-stroke piston harnesses gas from a fired cartridge to operate the piston and push the bolt rearward. AR shooters adapted quickly to the SIG as controls and handling are similar. The MPX-PSB is built with an upper and lower receiver so takedown is just like an AR-15. The quality workmanship is apparent in the SIG and that is what I expected from this manufacturer. The matte black finish is well-executed and there is no wiggle between lower and upper receivers.

In the lower, the bolt, mag releases, and safety selector are ambidextrous and easy to manipulate. The lever and button touch surfaces are finely serrated. It is equipped with SIG's comfortable pistol grip with textured side panels and coarsely serrated front and rear straps. It features a cavernous storage compartment for spare batteries. The magazine well is perfectly flared to suck in the translucent magazine. That magazine, by the way, was easy to load even to the 30th round and has a pebble texture on the sides with serrations on the front and rear edges. That is, not enough to snag in a mag pouch but enough for a sure grip. Plus, it has metal feed lips. I liked the fact that I could see how much was still in the tank through the translucent polymer. The trigger guard is oversized and glove friendly. The rear of the lower has a quick-detach socket and a small rail to attach a brace. The trigger is single stage and breaks at about 7 pounds on average.

The upper offers 14 inches of top rail where the folding front and rear sights attach. The sights deploy and fold without pressing a button. A detent keeps them up or down. There are two rear apertures and the rear is adjustable for windage, while the front is a post adjustable for elevation, which is protected by wings. Since buttons are not required to deploy or stow the sights they can easily fold back if the weapon is

The SIG MPX-PSB's controls are laid out similar to an AR-15, plus they are ambidextrous.

The ejection port is sized for the 9mm cartridge and employs a dust cover.

The folding sights on the SIG MPX-PSB enabled good accuracy. Note the full Picatinny rail offers plenty of optic mounting options.

The pistol can be fired with the brace folded or extended.

accidentally dropped. You also need to be aware that in a tight environment — like getting out of a vehicle or pushing through brush — the sights could accidentally be folded back. Even so, they are easy to use though I'd prefer that they locked in place when stowed and deployed. The KeyMod handguard allows you to mount accessories on five different rails. A hand stop is mounted behind the muzzle. The barrel is free floated and capped off with an A2-style flash hider that can be removed to add your choice of muzzle device. The ejection port is sized to fit a 9mm case and includes a dust cover. The SIG uses an oversized charging handle similar to an AR-15. Cocking the weapon takes some effort just like with any AR pistol. Since your support and firing hands are nearly on top of each other when cocking, there is

With 115-gr. FMJ Aguila ammo the MPX-PSB put five rounds into a 0.54-inch group at 25 yards.

SPECIFICATIONS

MODEL: SIG Sauer MPX-PSB

CALIBER: 9mm

ACTION: Short-Stroke Pushrod Gas System

TRIGGER: Single Action

BARREL LENGTH: 8.0 in.

OVERALL LENGTH: 16.85 in. (w/o brace), 25.75 in. (w/ brace)

WEIGHT: 6.0 oz. (empty)

SIGHTS: Folding, Elevation Adjustable Front/Windage Adjustable Rear

FINISH: Matte Black

GRIP: Textured Polymer, SIG AR-style

BRACE: SIGTAC SBX

CAPACITY: 30+1

Without the brace, the SIG offers even greater ease of maneuverability and use.

ample leverage, making it easy. The MPX-PSB is solidly built and with less bulk.

The MPX-PSB comes well-equipped and includes the folding stabilizing brace, QD sling loop and sling, and one magazine. The SIG was simple to disassemble and clean — just like an AR.

At the range, the SIG showed excellent accuracy. With Aguila 115-grain FMJs my smallest group measured 0.54 inch. The other ammo brands were just slightly larger. On average, the SIG is capable of five-shot groups under one inch.

A red-dot or reflex sight would shrink groups even more, but the irons were easy to use.

I ran the SIG with and without the brace and preferred to use it. One nice feature of the SIG is that the brace can be folded out of the way. The pistol can be fired with the brace folded or extended. Reloads are slick and fast thanks to the rig's generous mag well. The bolt locks back on last round fired so inserting the magazine with your support hand and slapping the bolt release button with your

PERFORMANCE: SIG SAUER MPX-PSB				
9mm Ammo (bullet weight in grains)	Velocity (fps)	Energy (ft.-lbs.)	Best Accuracy (inches)	Average Accuracy (inches)
Hornady American Gunner 115 XTP	1,198	367	0.64	0.96
Winchester Train 147 FMJ	1,012	334	0.85	1.1
Aguila 115 FMJ	1,224	383	0.54	0.87

Bullet weight measured in grains, velocity in feet per second, and average accuracy in inches for best five-shot groups at 25 yards.

support hand thumb is smooth and fluid. Also, the polymer of the magazines seems to be slicker against the metal. All controls work with authority and ease. I ran the SIG hard, firing one- and two-handed, sideways, and even upside down (the gun, not me). Nothing could jam the SIG pistol.

The transition to the MPX-PSB from an AR-15 was smooth and familiar. The SIG is well-built and tight with no wiggle.

Test and Evaluation: CZ Scorpion EVO 3 S1

The Scorpion EVO 3 S1 from CZ has a reputation to live up to. The original Skorpion vz. 61 is a select-fire, blowback-operated pistol chambered in .32 ACP with a cyclic rate of 850 rounds per minute. The Scorpion EVO 3 S1 is an updated semi-automatic version that uses a blowback mechanism, though with a fiber-reinforced polymer receiver in lieu of stamped steel. The receiver of the Scorpion is made of two polymer halves that sandwich together with a trigger group that snaps underneath and a handguard that slides over

the barrel. The barrel is equipped with a CZ flash hider attached via 1/2x28 threads so you can fit either 1/2x28 or 18x1 accessories to the muzzle. The Scorpion has a blocky look that makes it appear heavier and larger than it actually is.

It features an ambidextrous thumb safety and mag release. The safety rotates to either safe or fire mode. Some shooters find the safety selector raps against their knuckle when firing. It is also difficult to flip on/off with the thumb of the shooting hand. HB Industries sells a Right Safety Delete V2 that removes the right-side safety lever. I would invest in this aftermarket product if you want to really run the Scorpion. The magazine release is built into the front of the trigger guard with coarse serrations, thus your trigger finger can easily dump a mag, or you can use the thumb of your supporting hand. The cocking handle can be swapped for either a right- or left-handed shooter. It operates like an HK MP5 — very easily and locks back after the last round. Not a lot of strength is required to cock the pistol or lock it back. With the adjustable

The semi-automatic CZ Scorpion EVO 3 S1 uses a blowback mechanism encased in a fiber-reinforced polymer receiver.

The CZ Scorpion EVO features a hand stop to ensure your support hand does not go past the muzzle. Note the ample rail space.

pistol grip, you can increase or decrease the distance from the backstrap to the trigger face. The grip is relatively smooth on the sides, but the front and rear straps are serrated. The grip butt is flared so your hand does not slide off even in rapid fire. The bolt release is located on the left side in a similar location as an AR-15 bolt release button.

The top side features an 11-inch Picatinny-style rail with steel front and rear sights attached. The front post is adjustable for elevation and protected by wings. A tool comes with the pistol to adjust the front sight. The rear sight has four aperture choices that rotate and click into place and is adjustable for windage with a flat blade screwdriver or a cartridge rim. The shooter-facing side of the sight is serrated to cut glare.

The Picatinny rail allows plenty of options if you want to mount a red-dot or reflex sight. The handguard has rails at the 3, 6 and 9 o'clock positions if you want to mount a tactical light or laser pointer. A hand stop is located at the very end of the handguard as a vital piece of safety gear because your supporting hand can easily slip in front of the muzzle. You can also use the stop to push the pistol toward the target while your shooting hand pulls

back. This is another way to fire more steadily. The trigger has a slight curve and is coarsely serrated. The trigger guard is plenty large, so the EVO can be operated with gloved hands.

The Scorpion is well balanced. I can shoot it one-handed, but fatigue sets in quickly. The ergonomics are good except for the safety selector. The Scorpion is compact and light. An adapter kit that is a buffer tube attaches to a SIG brace. Two 20-round magazines and a bore snake cleaning rod are included. Additional 10- and 30-round magazines are available.

The mags are a translucent polymer, so you can easily see remaining ammo. And they are easy to load. The feed lips of the magazine are polymer and I did not see any significant wear after running the Scorpion.

All ammunition cycled flawlessly through the Scorpion. Magazines seated easily and with authority. The pistol is easy to cock since you can pull back on the cocking lever with your support hand and provide good resistance with the firing hand. I fired the Scorpion with and without a sling and concluded the sling offered a steadier aiming position.

Sights are well-designed and serrated on the shooter-facing side to cut glare.

With Winchester Train ammo using 147-gr. FMJ bullets the Scorpion averaged five-shot 1.05-inch groups at 25 yards.

SPECIFICATIONS

MODEL: CZ Scorpion EVO 3 S1
CALIBER: 9mm
ACTION: Blowback
TRIGGER: Single Action
BARRREL LENGTH: 7.72 in.
OVERALL LENGTH: 16.0 in. (w/o brace), 23.85 in. (w/ brace)
WEIGHT: 5 lbs. (empty)
SIGHTS: Fully Adjustable Aperture/Post
FINISH: Matte Black
GRIP: Smooth Polymer
BRACE: SIG SB
CAPACITY: 20+1

Bench rest accuracy was very good, averaging about one inch for five rounds at 25 yards. I consistently grouped five shots into 0.5 inches with the Hornady American Gunner and Winchester Train ammo. The Scorpion had more felt recoil than the other two pistols due to the simple blowback mechanism. (The CZ's blowback system uses the force of a fired cartridge to throw back the bolt.) Even so, the pistol was easy to adapt to and manipulate. Reloads were fast and smooth. The bolt locked back after the last shot fired. The pistol was easy to shoot with both eyes open. I would prefer a lighter trigger, my sample measured 8.4 pounds, but accuracy was good even with the heavy pull.

In conclusion, recoil was more noticeable due to the blowback mechanism. The ambidextrous safety selector bumped my knuckle when shooting but that is an easy fix. The CZ was easy to cock, and the operating handle was reversible. It is very adaptable for mounting optics, stabilizing braces and other accessories.

PERFORMANCE: CZ SCORPION EVO 3 S1

9mm Ammo (bullet weight in grains)	Velocity (fps)	Energy (ft.-lbs.)	Best Accuracy (inches)	Average Accuracy (inches)
Hornady American Gunner 115 XTP	1,239	392	0.51	1.03
Winchester Train 147 FMJ	1,034	349	0.56	1.05
Aguila 115 FMJ	1,244	395	0.80	1.21

Bullet weight measured in grains, velocity in feet per second, and average accuracy in inches for best five-shot groups at 25 yards.

CHAPTER 16

TRANSITIONAL-TRIGGER NINES – DA/SA MODELS

What is interesting about 9mm pistols is that the handgun design did not start out with one style of trigger mechanism and transition to another over time. Instead, there were all sorts of mechanisms in play. From the beginning, the Luger used a striker-fire trigger system. Not long after, manufacturers rechambered existing SA pistols to 9mm. By World War II, the introduction of the P.38 transformed the 9mm design

again, this time with a DA/SA trigger that would ultimately become the system of choice.

A DA/SA trigger was used in all Wonder Nine and Wonder Nine Lite pistols. Hundreds of handguns and thousands of variants on those designs employed this type of trigger. Today, this transitional system is the second most-used trigger design (striker fire being the first). So, what is it and how

When the U.S. military adopted the M9, there was a complete shift in caliber as well as trigger type. The 1911A1 features a SA one, while the M9 has a DA/SA type.

does it work? A DA/SA trigger combines the double-action capability of a revolver with the single-action function of a semi-automatic pistol. The first shot with a DA/SA has a long double-action pull that feels like a revolver. As the pistol fires and cycles, the trigger converts to a shorter single-action pull. The advantage of a DA/SA trigger means the pistol can be carried with the hammer fully forward (that is, down) on a loaded chamber without the need to use a safety. This provides a level of safety to the user since the double-action pull requires significant effort. A SA trigger with the safety off requires little effort to pull. That is the reason SAs are carried with the hammer cocked and the safety on — known as "cocked and locked."

All you need to do with a DA/SA is pull the trigger to fire. There is no safety that needs to be switched off, as there is with a single action, nor does the hammer need to be manually cocked back. Though, the hammer can be cocked back on a DA/SA to fire the first round in SA mode.

Some manufacturers of DA/SA models, like SIG, Heckler & Koch, and Beretta, employ a decocking lever. After a shot is fired and the hammer fully cocked, you press the decocker lever and the hammer goes from full cock to uncocked status. The pistol can then be fired in DA mode. Other DA/SA pistols use a traditional safety in lieu of a decocker that can be activated in DA or SA mode depending on the pistol design.

DA/SA pistols would soon further evolve, shifting to polymer-frame construction. The Israeli-made BUL Cherokee debuted in 2000 and was a polymer-framed semi-automatic based on the CZ 75. It features an accessory rail, three-dot sights, 17-round magazine, DA/SA trigger, and enlarged trigger guard, frame-mounted thumb safety and half-cock safety. The BUL is used by Israeli security agencies.

In 2005, Beretta launched the PX4 Storm, a full-size 9mm with a polymer frame, traditional DA/SA trigger and 17-round magazine. It uses a rotary barrel system.

It could be debated that the Heckler & Koch P30, which was introduced in 2006, is very effective at combining traditional DA/SA traits with high-tech modularity. The P30 has an exposed hammer like traditional DA/SA pistols but comes in a variety of variants to suit the end user. Variants include a conventional transitional trigger as well as DAO and decocking lever models. The P30's grip is modular with three interchangeable backstrap inserts and three grip panels for small, medium and large hand sizes. The modular grip allows for 27 different configurations.

While striker-fire triggers are the most popular today, there are those shooters who still prefer the DA/SA trigger. You can easily get used to how that first double-action shot requires you to apply pressure to the trigger, pulling through to fire when desired.

The CZ P-07 (2009–2013) was one way CZ modernized the CZ 75. The P-07 is a simplification of the CZ 75's hammer system, plus it has a polymer frame. The cool thing about it is its convertible decocker/safety system, which allows you to carry it cocked and locked like a 1911, or decocked for a double-action first pull of the trigger. The CZ P-09 (2013–present) is a full-size polymer DA/SA pistol with a 19+1 capacity in a flush-fitting magazine. The P-09 includes small, medium and large backstraps to customize the grip to your hand.

The M9 (left), M9A3 (middle), and M9A3 with grip insert (right).

Test and Evaluation: Beretta M9A3

The Beretta M9A3 is everything you would expect in a Beretta M9 series pistol — and more. It is the next Gen M9.

After 30 years of U.S. military use, beginning with conflicts like the invasion of Panama and as recent as the war in Afghanistan, the M9 has proven its worth — and shown its age. It is, after all, a 30-year-old design. The M9A3 is the next generation of M9 fighting pistol that was proposed by Beretta Defense Technologies (BDT) to the Army to equip America's warriors well into the 21st century. However, the Beretta did not make the grade this time around and the SIG P320 won the contract.

When the M9A3 was first proposed to the U.S. Army, I had the opportunity to shoot it and to hear the story of its evolution firsthand on a cold February day in Accokeek, Maryland, at Beretta USA headquarters.

When I speak to veterans about the M9 I can hear it in their stories, see it in their eyes. The M9 is more than a piece of equipment. In some cases, the Beretta saved their lives. That bond was not always there. The M9 earned it one bullet at a time. Change did not come easily. The transition from the venerable M1911A1 to the M9 was wrenching for some in the military, but by 1979 the situation could not be ignored any longer. The M1911A1s in service were worn out. The Joint Service Small Arms Program began searching for a replacement pistol to use the 9x19mm round, which was chosen to comply with the NATO Standardization Agreement (STANAG). The .45 ACP was out. That switch was difficult enough for some in the military to accept, making it easy to see why any pistol chosen — American-made or foreign-produced

The big difference between the M9 and M9A3 is the grip. The M9A3 has a thinner grip similar to the Beretta Vortex.

The M9A3 comes suppressor-ready, and the sights are taller, so you can use them even with a suppressor attached.

— was going to be controversial. The new caliber and Beretta pistol were not without critics or complaints. How could it be otherwise? The M1911A1 at the time had nearly 75 years of service under its belt. The Beretta had to prove its worth even before it was accepted by the military. And it did.

Those who feel the U.S. Army merely settled on the M9 should know that Beretta won three consecutive pistol trials before winning the contract. Prior to the M9 contract, Beretta won the JSAP competition by the Air Force. Test results were contested, and the Beretta was retested in the XM9 trials. Beretta won again, and yet again the results were controversial, so the Beretta was submitted in the 10XM trials. The Beretta excelled in all the trials the military could throw at it while competing against other well-known designs from established companies. After the dust settled, mostly silencing critics, the M9 delivery began. About 600,000 pistols have been delivered to the Department of Defense (DoD) with about 425,000 going to the Army and the rest going to FMS (Foreign Military Sales),

a program in which the DoD either gives or sells M9s to other countries. Many FMS sales have gone to Iraq and Afghanistan.

The first two years of the contract allowed Beretta to supply the U.S. Government with pistols made in Italy. Since 1987, all M9s have been made in Accokeek, Maryland. Beretta USA may have an Italian heritage but the M9 design is owned by the U.S. military and is built by an American workforce — a fact Beretta takes pride in.

Since the U.S. Government owns the M9 design, the DoD is free to make design changes and purchase spare parts from other vendors. Some decisions by the DoD have inadvertently given Beretta grief. For example, the DoD purchased magazines from an outside vendor with a phosphate finish that performed poorly in sandy environments. Beretta got a black eye for it even though the mags were not Beretta-made nor designed. Beretta mags offer a grit-resistant finish that allows gunk and sand to flow through the magazine and not clump up and impede bullet feeding.

Other myths persist, like the M9 having a service life of 5,000 rounds. The original spec 30 years ago called for a service life of 5,000, which was a tremendous step up from the M1911A1. The actual service life of the M9 is about 25,000 rounds.

In September 2012, the Army awarded Beretta USA a five-year ID/IQ (Indefinite Delivery/Indefinite Quantity) contract for up to 100,000 pistols. The Army can order as few or as many, up to 100,000. Of the 100,000, de Plano says, the Army has ordered 20,000 thus far, which means 80,000 can still be delivered. Of the remaining orders, Beretta reasoned, why not improve on the existing design and deliver the M9A3? In addition, around this same time, the Army announced the MHS (Modular Handgun System) program to potentially replace the M9 and the compact M11 pistol. New programs implemented by the Army and other branches of the service are a relatively common occurrence. Some

lead to change while others fizzle out due to lack of funding. This one led to the Army opting for the SIG Sauer P320.

The M9A3 was not an entry for the Army's MHS solicitation, as it would only meet about 80 percent of the draft RFP's requirements. Beretta entered their striker-fire APX into the MHS solicitation. The Army could have taken a dual-prong strategy: improve the M9 while finding a new pistol. In reality, a replacement takes time to implement with design, manufacturing, logistics support, training, ammo procurement, and more slowing the process.

Beretta submitted the M9A3 to the Army as an ECP (Engineering Change Proposal) to the M9. All DoD contractors are required — and in fact, regularly submit — engineering proposals. The DoD also solicited input from the industry on improvements. For instance, the Army recently requested improvements and replacement ideas from the industry for the CSASS semi-automatic sniper rifle

The M9A3 has a smaller grip, making it easier for shooters with average to small hands to grip and control the pistol.

system. The ECP process is part of the Army's tradition of incremental small arms development.

Beretta took the initiative and looked at what could be done to make the M9 better, and began collecting data from a variety of sources. A wish list of sorts was compiled that addressed issues ranging from modularity and durability of the M9 to grip size and ergonomics. The new Beretta M9A3 addressed nearly all of the complaints and the ECP was presented to the U.S. Army Contracting Command on December 10, 2014.

I found the M9A3 pistol had a familiar feel yet fit me better due to the Vertec frame with its straight backstrap and thin grip panels. The Vertec model was offered commercially from 2002 to 2005. The girth of the grip is a complaint of the M9 as it is with many double-stacks. The Vertec addressed the girth issue, making the handgun feel thin. For those with larger hands, the M9A3 comes with a wrap-around grip backstrap, sized like the M9. I fired both versions of the M9A3 grip and liked the wraparound one better. An additional complaint about the earlier M9s concerned magazine capacity. The M9A3 increases capacity to 17+1. The barrel is threaded for use with a suppressor and a thread protector can be replaced from either end. The front sight is removable, so a higher front sight can be configured when the M9A3 is fired with a can (suppressor) or the addition of night sights. An accessory rail was added similar to the USMC's M9A1 variant, opening up laser or light possibilities. The mag release button is oversized, another benefit for shooters with small hands.

To reacclimatize myself with the M9 platform and create a benchmark, I fired it and it wasn't long before the familiarity came back to me: DA/SA trigger, safety lever, the girth of the grip. For testing, I used commercial Hornady Critical Duty

SPECIFICATIONS

MODEL: Beretta M9A3
CALIBER: 9mm
ACTION: Short Recoil
TRIGGER: DA/SA
BARREL LENGTH: 5.1 in.
OVERALL LENGTH: 8.57 in.
WIDTH: 1.5 in., 1.3 in. (at grips)
HEIGHT: 5.4 in.
WEIGHT: 33.3 oz. (empty)
SIGHTS: 3-Dot Tritium, Blade Front/ Notch Rear
SIGHT RADIUS: 6.3 in.
FINISH: Cerakote Flat Dark Earth
CAPACITY: 17+1

135-grain with the Flexlock bullet, which has a factory spec of 1,010 fps. I did not have any mil-spec M882 ball ammo and that is another contention with M9 users — questionable terminal ballistics and accuracy with the stuff. Accuracy is 2.5- to 3 times better out of commercial ammunition compared to M882 with the M9. The original contract testing requirements for the M9 is a 10-shot group with minimum mean radius of 8cm at a range of 50m fired out of a ransom rest. The M9A3 has the same barrel as the M9, so by deduction it should have similar accuracy with M882. With commercial ammo I had no issue shooting the black out of the target at 7 yards. The bullseye was about 4 inches and missing after about 100 rounds, aside from a few errant shots in double-action mode. An AAC Ti-Rant 9mm suppressor was screwed to the barrel muzzle to test balance and performance. Though the sights were normal height, the M9A3 ran exceptionally. Double-action pull is about 9 pounds and smooth. The M9A3 performed flawlessly and is an improvement over the ergonomics of earlier M9s. And it does so with savings to the DoD — no new training, compatibility with existing equipment systems like holsters and magazine pouches, and potentially at a cost less than the current M9. Major components from the M9A3 are 100 percent compatible with the M9; 76 percent of the M9A3 individual parts are interchangeable with the M9.

The M9A3 not only increases the performance of America's battle pistol to the end user — our warriors — but it is a better value for the DoD and us taxpayers. Despite this, on January 30, 2015, the Army rejected Beretta's proposal saying it was beyond the scope of the ECP process. Needless to say, Beretta was obviously disappointed.

The good news for shooters like you and me? A commercial version of the M9A3 was introduced in 2015.

Test and Evaluation: Arex Rex Zero 1

Arex's Rex Zero 1 is a totally new design in an all-metal, 17+1 capacity full-size pistol. Introduced first in Europe at the Eurosatory 2014 Defense Expo, the Rex Zero saw its U.S. release at the 2016 SHOT Show. The Rex 9mm is a classically styled semi-automatic with an exposed hammer-fired and DA/SA trigger.

I previewed the Rex at SHOT in Las Vegas where I fired two sample pistols — one with and one without a suppressor. My interest was piqued. I needed to spend some quality time with the Rex Zero.

The Rex features a locked breech short-recoil system. Basically, it's a modified Browning linkless locking system. The barrel breech block locks into the slide in a similar way to a Glock

The Arex Rex Zero 1 can be carried cocked-and-locked in SAO or DA/SA modes.

The Arex Rex Zero 1 is a full-metal, combat-size pistol vaguely similar to a SIG. The decocking lever doubles as a slide hold open. The lever is easy to operate even with gloved hands.

or SIG. This is a proven system. With its classic DA/SA trigger, the Rex has a long double-action pull, but not so much that shooters with smaller than average hands will have a hard time stroking that first trigger press. The Beretta 92FS is my litmus test for classic DA/SA pistols and the Rex felt more like a Glock 17 or SIG P226. In fact, the Rex Zero looks a lot and acts a bit like a P226, but it brings some added functionality that the SIG lacks. For instance, it has a decocker similar

A full dust cover with Picatinny rail allows for a variety of add-on accessories. Note the one-piece metal guide rod, which aids accuracy.

to the SIG, which allows you to safely decock the hammer from the fully cocked rearward position. The pistol is ready when you need it, simply stroke the DA trigger to fire. The unique feature is a manual thumb safety. This allows it to be carried cocked and locked like a 1911. The thumb safety provides an additional level of user-controlled protection. With the thumb safety engaged the trigger is disconnected, yet the slide can be manipulated to clear the gun. In either DA/SA or SAO modes, the Rex is user-friendly. All the controls, except the decocker/slide stop, are ambidextrous out of the box. Moreover, another safety measure built in is a chamber indicator that gives you a visual and tactile heads up if a round or a case is in the chamber. It includes a firing pin safety that requires the trigger to be fully pulled to the rear to fire.

Arex is obviously positioning the Rex Zero 1 as a suitable military and LE sidearm. It received a letter of conformity from the Minister of Defense in Slovenia by passing all requirements set forth in the STANAG 4512 – D/14 NATO Small Arms Test Manual. The requirement consists of a litany of tortures:

Feed System Safety
Parts Interchangeability
Accuracy and Dispersion
Firing at a Known Distance
Cold Test
High-Temperature Test
Temperature and Humidity
Icing Test
Unlubricated
Accelerated Water Spray Test
Static Sand and Dust Test
Mud
Mechanical Safety
Double Feed Dropping of Weapon from Vehicle

The frame of the Rex is made from T7075-T6 aluminum and wears a hard anodized matte black finish. Serrations are milled into the front and rear grip straps, and give you a good grasp even when shooting for speed. The trigger guard is large and squared off. I tried the Rex Zero using gloves and found its trigger guard accommodating. It incorporates full-length slide rails that promote accuracy. It has a full dust cover and Picatinny rail, too, and the muzzle end of the Rex Zero has a blunt, toothy look.

The slide is machined from solid bar stock with rear and forward cocking serrations that are coarse and easy to grasp when manipulating the slide. High-profile steel 3-dot sights are dovetailed into the top of the slide. Arex cut dovetails so the factory sights can easily be replaced with aftermarket ones. The one-piece barrel is cold hammer forged from solid bar stock. The recoil spring is a traditional coil around a one-piece metal guide rod. Again, a nod to the accuracy of the Rex. Fit and finish are excellent. Even the interior of the slide and receiver are beautifully finished. This is a well-made pistol.

Field stripping is simple, breaking down the Rex into five key components.

Accuracy data was gathered using Hornady American Gunner, Aguila, and SIG V-Crown ammo.

The magazines are made by Arex, not farmed out like with many U.S.- and European-made pistols. The magazines are built with a unique progressive rate spring, meaning it becomes stiffer or more resistant as it is compressed. This ensures cartridges get pushed up when the slide cycles. The mags are easy on the thumbs even when loading the 17th round. The mags have a metal body with clearly marked witness holes for all 17 rounds and are coated inside and out for corrosion resistance. The floor plate is polymer. The magazines are built for easy disassembly and cleaning. The pistol can be field stripped without tools. Just lock back the slide, remove the magazine, flip the takedown lever 90 degrees, carefully release the slide stop while holding the slide, and the slide assembly will pull off the front of the frame.

For testing, I mounted a Viridian X5L green laser and tactical light — a real nice setup for home defense. The light throws 178 lumens on continuous mode and 224 lumens in strobe. The unit has six modes: constant laser, constant laser/constant light, constant laser/strobe light,

pulse laser, pulse laser/constant light, and constant light. Activating the unit is completely ambidextrous. The Rex Zero is so new and there are not many holsters for it, let alone a light compatible one. I did find that the new Comp-Tac QH IWB holster worked well with the handgun.

The QH is a hybrid holster with a modular design that will accommodate multiple firearms in each size. The shell is Kydex so the draw is smooth and slick. The backing is leather. I adjusted the retention screws and found the Rex Zero fit. Since the Rex has a short 4.3-inch barrel it was comfortable to carry behind the hip even while sitting and driving.

The Rex is approved for 9mm +P ammunition so with that in mind I gathered some 115-grain XTP American Gunner from Hornady; Winchester Train and Defend both with a 147-grain bullet that is FMJ or JHP, respectively; and 115-grain FMJ from

The Rex is like a traditional DA/SA, except it has a thumb safety lever so it can be carried cocked and locked.

PERFORMANCE: AREX REX ZERO 1

9mm Ammo (bullet weight in grains)	Velocity (fps)	Energy (ft.-lbs.)	Best Accuracy (inches)	Average Accuracy (inches)
Hornady American Gunner 115 XTP	1,121	321	1.57	1.92
Winchester Train 147 FMJ	1,001	327	1.35	1.53
Winchester Defend 147 JHP	946	292	1.57	1.69
Aguila 115 FMJ	1,145	335	1.17	1.37

Bullet weight measured in grains, velocity in feet per second, and average accuracy in inches for best five-shot groups at 25 yards.

Aguila. The Aguila proved to be the fastest with a muzzle velocity that averaged 1,145 fps. It also eked out the best five-shot groups at 25 yards at 1.17 inches. Average accuracy ranged from 1.37 through 1.92. The Rex liked all ammo and there were no malfunctions. I fired in double action, decocking the pistol after each shot to get a feel for the trigger. Best accuracy came in SA mode using a rest. The slide functioned smoothly and the gun produced soft recoil. I felt I could get back on target fast. This pistol was easy to shoot well and even after burning through a few pounds of ammo it was very comfortable to keep banging away for an extended period of time.

I also found the Rex had zero malfunctions or stoppages — just like other European pistols with notable pedigrees. In fact, the Rex ran and ran, and as much as I tried to confuse this Slovenian-made pistol with either U.S.- and Mexican-made factory ammunition it still fired. Light to heavy bullets, hot to low recoil loads. It chewed through ammo and did it with smooth cycling and soft recoil. Accuracy was good and the large, full sights kept me throwing lead down range with faster follow-up shots. The grip is not chunky like some other metal-framed double-stack pistols. Double-action trigger press is a bit heavy, 12.9 pounds on average, but smooth after the initial take-up. In single action, the trigger breaks cleanly at 5.6 pounds on average after a bit of take-up. The trigger is wide and smooth.

This pistol runs as hard as any of the other more well-known ones from Italy and

SPECIFICATIONS

MODEL: Arex Rex Zero 1
CALIBER: 9mm
ACTION: Short Recoil, Locked Breech
TRIGGER: DA/SA
BARREL LENGTH: 4.3 in.
OVERALL LENGTH: 7.7 in.
WEIGHT: 32 oz. (empty)
GRIPS: Textured Polymer
SIGHTS: Fixed 3-Dot
FINISH: Matte Black
CAPACITY: 17+1

The Springfield XD-E with an extended magazine.

Germany. It makes a fine home defense gun and is an excellent choice for the CCW permit holder who wants a full-size pistol. Reliable and accurate, it yielded the type of consistency I expect and demand in a defensive weapon. It also has an attractive price that is very competitive. The classically designed Rex Zero is economical, rugged, accurate and can unleash a fury of firepower.

Test and Evaluation: Springfield Armory XD-E 3.3

The Springfield Armory XD-E looks like a DA/SA trigger mechanism was placed in an XD-S receiver, then mated to a MOD.2 slide. While most new 9mm pistol introductions are striker-fire models, Springfield Armory took a different route in 2017. The XD-E is a DA/SA model.

Springfield is known for both 1911 and striker-fire pistols, so the XD-E is a departure for them. Pistol trigger designs fall into three major camps: SA, DA/SA and striker-fire. All require different training and operating techniques. With DA/SA the ability to pre-load the trigger is an asset, like pressing back on a double-action revolver trigger. While acquiring the target you can begin pressing the trigger and when on target press through to fire. The initial DA trigger press of a DA/SA can be an asset since it takes longer to press the trigger. In a high-stress situation, this can ensure against a premature shot fired. The switch from DA to SA

The Springfield Armory XD-E features a DA/SA trigger and single-stack magazine, making it slim in hand and easily hidden when carrying concealed.

The Springfield XD-E disassembled.

SPECIFICATIONS

MODEL: Springfield Armory XD-E 3.3
CALIBER: 9mm
ACTION: Short Recoil, Locked Breech
TRIGGER: DA/SA
BARREL LENGTH: 3.3 in.
OVERALL LENGTH: 6.75 in.
WEIGHT: 25 oz. (empty)
GRIPS: Textured Polymer
SIGHTS: Fixed, 2-Dot Rear/Fiber Optic
FINISH: Matte Black
CAPACITY: 8+1 and 9+1

can be confusing for some shooters, but for others, it is not.

The external hammer of the XD-E provides an obvious picture of whether the pistol is cocked or not. What is relatively unique about the XD-E is that it can be carried in DA/SA mode or cocked-and-locked — like a 1911. Due to the smooth trigger press, I'd carry it DA/SA.

An ambidextrous thumb-operated lever acts like a safety when the hammer is cocked. This lever can decock the hammer. The hammer on the Springfield has plenty of texture to grasp and cock with the shooting hand thumb. Compared to other subcompact 9mms that use either a SA trigger or striker-fire, the XD-E is larger in size due to the DA/SA trigger and external hammer. The XD-E is taller in your hand. The trigger geometry in the XD-E is different than a Beretta M9 or SIG P226, but in actual use is easily pressed to fire the handgun. The look of the trigger is a bit deceiving, too, but the reach to it is a comfortable stretch for average-size hands. The DA pull is long and feels like 11 pounds though it is relatively

PERFORMANCE: SPRINGFIELD ARMORY XD-E 3.3				
9mm Ammo (bullet weight in grains)	Velocity (fps)	Energy (ft.-lbs.)	Best Accuracy (inches)	Average Accuracy (inches)
Armscor 124 FMJ	1,010	281	2.70	3.15
SIG Sauer 115 FMJ	1,078	297	2.60	3.05
Aguila 124 FMJ	1,038	297	2.50	3.20

Bullet weight measured in grains, velocity in feet per second, and average accuracy in inches for best five-shot groups at 25 yards.

smooth. In single action, there is some take-up and pull-through required but it breaks consistently.

The slide has similar markings as a MOD.2 without the deep cut sculpting. The red fiber optic front sight is excellent, and the rear is windage adjustable and sits flush with the end of the slide for maximum sight radius. The rear sight is serrated on the back that faces the shooter to cut sun glare. These are excellent sights, easy to acquire the front on target thanks to the red dot. The front sight is dovetailed into place. It takes 15 pounds of effort to rack back the slide and cock the hammer. To me, the grip feels comfortable with textured front and rear straps. The front strap has a subtle finger groove, which fit my second and third fingers. The frame has a Picatinny slot to add a light or laser.

The real tale is in the shooting and I found the XD-E is, in fact, a shooter. My best five-shot group at 25 yards was 2.5 inches with Aguila ammo. When shooting for speed, the larger slide with more surface area makes it faster and easier to grasp and manipulate than smaller handguns. The pistol runs well. Accuracy is good, and the trigger breaks consistently. 1 would not hesitate to use the pistol to defend my home.

Test and Evaluation: SIG P226 Nitron

It is obvious that the SIG P226 Nitron is heir to the SIG P6. The pistols have similar controls — slide stop, decocker, takedown lever, magazine release. The Nitron version uses a far more ergonomic grip than the P6 and earlier P226 models that feature a two-piece grip. The Nitron has a one-piece grip that snaps onto the receiver. It sports subtle palm swells that do the gripping and fit the palm of your hand like a glove.

As a DA/SA, the trigger has a long press in DA and then after the round is fired transitions to SA. Double-action pull weight measures about 12 pounds; SA is about 7 pounds. The trigger is the thing

The SIG P226 operates with a locked-breech short-recoil system, uses a DA/SA trigger, and incorporates a decocking lever on the left side of the frame just above the magazine release button.

SPECIFICATIONS

SPECIFICATIONS
MODEL: SIG Sauer P226 Nitron
CALIBER: 9mm
ACTION: Short Recoil, Locked Breech
TRIGGER: DA/SA
BARREL LENGTH: 4.4 in.
OVERALL LENGTH: 7.7 in.
WEIGHT: 34 oz. (empty)
GRIPS: E2 Textured Polymer
SIGHTS: White 3-Dot, Siglite Night Sights
FINISH: Nitron Matte Black
CAPACITY: 15+1

The P226 is in service with numerous law enforcement agencies and military organizations worldwide.

with this SIG. While in use it feels much lighter. Unique to the P226 is a decocking lever with which you can decock the hammer — go from full cock to DA ready.

At the range, I found the P226 would do my bidding if I did my part. The 3-dot sights are large and offer a great sight picture. The SIG P226 is a benchmark in DA/SA pistols. No wonder law enforcement and military forces around the world count on SIG.

PERFORMANCE: SIG SAUER P226 NITRON

9mm Ammo (bullet weight in grains)	Velocity (fps)	Energy (ft.-lbs.)	Best Accuracy (inches)	Average Accuracy (inches)
Hornady American Gunner 115 XTP	1,120	320	1.57	1.83
SIG Sauer 115 FMJ	1,106	312	2.51	2.65
Aguila 124 FMJ	1,142	333	1.8	2.0
Aguila 124 FMJ	947	293	1.7	2.21

Bullet weight measured in grains, velocity in feet per second, and average accuracy in inches for best five-shot groups at 25 yards.

CHAPTER 17

ROTARY BARREL NINES

The Grand Power K100, the larger cousin of the smaller P1, uses a unique rotary barrel system. Photo: Grand Power

Locked-breech, rotary-barrel pistols enhance accuracy and reduce recoil due to their unique operating systems. Some manufacturers use the system to make their pistols stand out from the pack. The design has been around for a long time and recently manufacturers are reviving the idea. That makes sense, for it affords better recoil control than the traditional tilted-barrel setup.

Here's how it works. As a round is fired, the slide and barrel move rearward before the barrels turns about 30 degrees counterclockwise to unlock. The barrel has a curved slot milled into it, and it rotates inside the slide on a lug protruding from the center block. As the barrel moves back under recoil, the slot in the barrel engages the lug to rotate it. The center block also holds the recoil spring in place inside the slide. The effect of the rotating barrel means the barrel is always fixed, which, in theory, aids accuracy, and the smooth rearward movement means less muzzle flip and lighter felt recoil. Here are a few noteworthy rotary-barrel 9mm pistols.

The Beretta PX4 Storm runs the same short-recoil, rotating barrel action as the Model 8000 Cougar and the same trigger and safety system as the Beretta 92 series. The Storm is built of a lightweight polymer frame with interchangeable backstraps so it can be customized to fit all hand sizes. The Storm has withstood

The Beretta PX4 Storm.
Photo: Beretta USA

a torture test of well over 150,000 rounds with zero parts failing. Another member of the rotary club is the Grand Power K100. Grand Power pistols are manufactured in Slovakia and have a rotating-barrel arrangement. The K100 is a full-sized, polymer-framed pistol with a traditional DA/SA (DA/SA) trigger system. All of its controls are oversized and ambidextrous for fast, easy manipulations. The backstrap is modular so a perfect grip is easy to attain. Think of this Grand Power P1 as a more compact version of the K100. It has all of the same features of the K100 but

The Cougar has a unique rotating barrel system where the slide and barrel move rearward before the barrel turns about 30 degrees counterclockwise to unlock.

is lighter and smaller for easier concealment with a 3.7-inch barrel and an overall
length of 7.4 inches. It still retains a 15+1
capacity.

Test and Evaluation:
Stoeger Cougar

The Stoeger Cougar is one slick
piece of hardware, and that's partially because it did not take the same design path
as other semi-automatic pistols. It is indeed a unique, enduring and reliable design that stands on its own. You see, most
semi-autos use a short-recoil, locked-
breech system in which the slide and barrel lock and recoil together after a shot is
fired, traveling rearward before the barrel
disengages from the slide and tilt upward
on a link or lugs as the slide continues
rearward. Nearly all modern pistols use
this system — 1911, Glock, SIG, CZ, Hi
Power, Smith & Wesson M&P, Ruger,
some Walther. The Cougar, however, has
a rotating barrel system.

The rotating barrel system has been
around for quite a while, and the Stoeger
Cougar, in particular, has a direct blood-
line to Beretta. The Turkish-made Cougar's Italian background began in the
mid-1990s when Beretta debuted the
Model 8000 Cougar, a pistol that offered
better concealability than Beretta's venerable 92 series of pistols. As the popularity of polymer-framed handguns gained
momentum, the Model 8000 evolved into

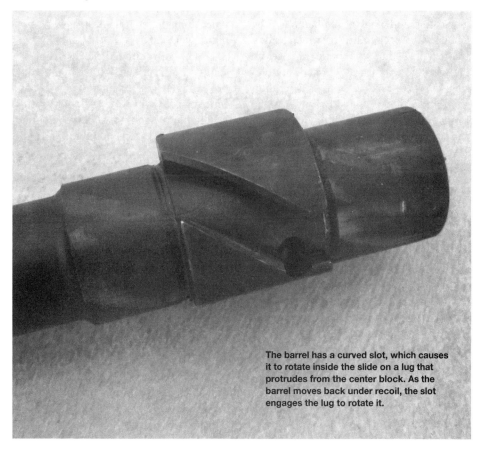

The barrel has a curved slot, which causes
it to rotate inside the slide on a lug that
protrudes from the center block. As the
barrel moves back under recoil, the slot
engages the lug to rotate it.

Beretta's polymer-framed PX4 Storm series, which uses features and parts from both the Model 8000 Cougar and the 92. Of course, Stoeger is owned by Beretta, which shipped the Model 8000 machinery to Turkey for production. The Stoeger Cougar is nearly identical to the Beretta Model 8000 Cougar except for the grip panels and the markings on the slide and frame. This is a well-made pistol worthy of the Beretta lineage. Stoeger has dropped the pistol from its lineup, but these cats can still be found on the used gun market.

The Stoeger Cougar Compact I got my hands on for testing has a shorter grip than the Beretta 8000 and the standard Stoeger Cougar. This rotary barrel 9mm features a traditional DA/SA trigger system with an exposed hammer. The Cougar Compact has a light metal alloy frame with a slim, ergonomic grip despite the fact that it houses 13-round, double-stack magazines. The grip is straighter and thinner than, say, the Beretta 92. The Cougar Compact's grip fit my hand well, and the magazine floorplate makes for a good finger rest to support your small finger. There is no accessory rail, which gives the Cougar a sleek look and suits its concealed carry mission.

Lightweight at 28.8 ounces unloaded, yet substantial enough for soft shooting and easy handling, the Cougar Compact is perfect for self-defense. On my test pistol, the smooth DA trigger pull measured 12 pounds on average. The SA pull clocked in at about 5 pounds on average, and the trigger was crisp in both DA and SA modes.

I also liked its second-strike capability, meaning you can pull the trigger a second time if the firing pin falls on a faulty cartridge primer. The trigger guard has the curved look of a Beretta 92, and the front and backstraps have vertical serrations. Those serrations, along with the checkered polymer grip panels, give the Cougar Compact plenty of traction when unleashing 9mm rounds in a variety of bullet weights.

The Bruniton-finished slide is sculpted to relieve extra metal while providing a chiseled look that is smooth. Since the exterior is snag-free, this thing is suitable for concealed carry undergarments without worrying about shirttails and jackets. The hammer on the Cougar is exposed, but it is low profile, knurled and rounded. It's also easy to cock if needed. The slide serrations are toothy enough to provide a good grip. Racking the slide does not take an arm wrestler's strength, thanks to the rotating barrel. It is very smooth. Since the slide serrations are close to the ambidextrous safety, flicking the safety up to fire or down for safe is a simple habit to learn. The safety is similar to that of Beretta 92F/92FS pistols. There is also an automatic firing pin safety; the trigger must be completely pulled rearward for the firing pin block to move out of the way and allow the firing pin to move forward. On the topside, the pistol's three-dot sights

SPECIFICATIONS

MODEL: Stoeger Cougar
CALIBER: 9mm
ACTION: Short Recoil, Rotary Barrel
TRIGGER: DA/SA
BARREL LENGTH: 3.27 in.
OVERALL LENGTH: 6.8 in.
WEIGHT: 27.2 oz. (empty)
GRIPS: Textured Polymer
SIGHTS: White 3-Dot
FINISH: Matte Black
CAPACITY: 15+1

present a clear sight picture without being too tall or prone to snagging.

Other controls consist of the slide release and mag release. The slide release has enough of a footprint to make it easy to operate without sticking out too much. The polymer magazine release button is reversible if you need to change it. The Cougar fieldstrips like a Beretta 92, which is to say that it's incredibly simple. You simply press the button on the right side of the frame and rotate the takedown lever on the left side. The slide can then be pulled off the front of the frame. The magazine is made of steel with a polymer base pad and it has witness holes to let you see how many rounds are left. I found the magazine easy on the thumbs when loading, even to the very last round.

I let the Cougar Compact run with ammo from Hornady, Federal, and Winchester in a variety of bullet weights and types. As mentioned, the pistol's felt recoil is different. I had another similar-sized 9mm pistol with a tilting barrel on hand just to see if there was substance to the claim. The Cougar Compact recoiled straight back, and though all pistols have some muzzle flip, the Cougar had less. I could get on target quickly and, even though the gun is compact, it gave the feel and control of a full-sized pistol.

At 25 yards, my five-shot groups averaged about 2.5 inches while using a rest. The Cougar Compact particularly liked the 135-grain FlexLock bullets in the Hornady Critical Defense ammo. My best group with this ammo was 1.45 inches. I like that I could stage the double-action trigger and break it just when my sight picture resolved. The handgun ran exceptionally well.

Though the Cougar has been discontinued, it is a 9mm pistol worth investigating to experience the rotary barrel. If you can find one, the Stoeger Cougar Compact will offer a lot of firepower when your claws need to come out.

PERFORMANCE: STOEGER COUGAR				
9mm Ammo (bullet weight in grains)	Velocity (fps)	Energy (ft.-lbs.)	Best Accuracy (inches)	Average Accuracy (inches)
Hornady American Gunner 115 XTP	1,077	296	2.25	2.5
Winchester Train 147 FMJ	942	290	1.85	2.5
Hornady Critical Defense 135 FlexLock	1,007	305	1.45	1.85
Handload 115 FMJ	1,211	375	2.35	2.5

Bullet weight measured in grains, velocity in feet per second, and average accuracy in inches for best five-shot groups at 25 yards.

CHAPTER 18

REVOLVER-INSPIRED DAO 9MMS

What makes a semi-automatic handgun most like a revolver? Answer: A DAO trigger. A DAO semi-auto pistol is designed without a sear so the hammer or striker is not held back after a shot is fired and the slide cycles. The trigger pull cocks and drops the hammer with each pull. There is no SA mode like with a DA/SA trigger. The plus side of DAO? The trigger pull is consistent, and the system very safe. The downside? The pull can be long and require more force to press the trigger compared to other types.

Some designs, like those in the SCCY CPX series, feature a constant hammer fire via the DAO trigger. That is, the hammer strikes the firing pin every time it is pulled. SA or striker-fire pistols require the hammer to be thumbed back or the slide to be retracted, respectively, to reset the trigger and firing pin mechanism. In the CPX series of pistols, if a cartridge does not fire after the trigger is pulled, it can be pressed again to restrike the primer of the cartridge. This design feature does not require you to rack the slide in the case of a misfire.

The Walther PPX is an excellent example of a DAO polymer-frame 9mm pistol.

The subcompact SIG P290 is another example of a subcompact pistol with a DAO trigger. I think of it as a minimalist gun since it is purely simple in operation, and simple is good. The design features a lightweight polymer frame with a steel barrel and slide and the gun weighs 20.5 ounces empty. A press of the DAO trigger drops the hammer each time it is pulled. The pull is about 9 pounds according to the factory, but feels less as it so smooth.

The Kel Tec PF-9 is a simple and reliable 9mm carry pistol as well. It is thin — about 7/8 of an inch thick — and is slightly less than 6 inches in length. It weighs about 13 ounces empty or 18-1/2 ounces fully loaded with eight cartridges packed with 147-grain bullets. There is no manual safety on the PF-9. The DAO trigger works in conjunction with an automatic hammer block safety to avoid an accidental discharge should the pistol be dropped

on a hard surface. Edges on the PF-9 are rounded so it is smooth and snag-free.

The DAO trigger not only makes these types of pistols safer, it also means you need to be fully committed to pulling the trigger since it requires more effort than an SA or striker-fire.

Test and Evaluation: Walther PPX

The Walther PPX takes proven design elements — short recoil, locked breech action — and employs modern manufacturing techniques such as polymer-molded frames and low-profile three-dot combat sights, Picatinny rails, and more. Though the PPX has been replaced with the Creed, it is an excellent example of a DAO polymer-frame 9mm pistol.

Aggressive looks, enhanced features, and an attractive price gel with this pistol. At first glance, the PPX has a radical look. The ergonomic grip looks differ-

The SCCY CPX series features a constant hammer fire via the DAO trigger. Photo: SCCY

ent than most duty pistols, but the shape is comfortable to hold and helps to naturally point it on target. The frame is polymer with a non-slip cross-directional grip surface. It has a bit of a palm swell that feels secure in your hand without feeling overly large. The PPX does a great job of stuffing 16 rounds of 9mm into the grip without it feeling like you are holding a liter-sized bottle of soda.

The slide offers a lot of surface area to grasp without it looking or acting too blocky. The top edges along the length of the slide are chamfered so getting your full palm against the frame is no issue. The old-school pinch-and-pull method to manipulate the slide is effortless. Front and rear slide serrations are large and offer a sure grip. Together, the frame and slide make the PPX look big and beastly, but in actual use, it feels smaller and livelier.

The PPX uses a short-recoil, locked-breech action like Walther's PPQ and P99 to name two models. SIG, Glock, and other manufacturers employ the same type of action.

Three automatic safeties are built into the PPX: trigger, firing pin and disconnector. The safeties prevent accidental discharge if the PPX is dropped, and make it well-suited for safe carry. A loaded chamber viewport — a small notch — is cut into the breechblock, giving you a quick status check of the chamber to see if a live round or empty case is in the chamber.

A hammer is used to strike the firing pin to discharge the pistol. To ready the handgun, the slide is pulled to the rear and released to chamber a cartridge. As the trigger is pulled rearward the hammer protrudes slightly from a recess in the rear of the slide. The trigger releases the hammer, rotating it forward to fire, then the slide moves rearward to begin the firing process again. The slide needs to be retracted to reset the trigger.

The front of the grip has slight finger grooves that actually work for most hand sizes and at the very bottom flare out almost acting like a funnel to ensure fingers stay in place on the front grip.

The front of the trigger guard is squared off and ridged for a secure grip when using a two-hand hold. Plus, the rear of the trigger guard is notched so your index finger and other digits can ride a bit higher. Not only that, but the slide-stop and take-down lever are inset into the frame. They are smooth and snag-free, yet present enough surface area to be used bare-handed or gloved.

I did notice rather early on in testing that the magazines — two are provided with the PPX — are easily swallowed by the mag well in the grip. It is like a black hole that pulls magazines in when they get near it. The mags slip into the mag well with ease and are effortless to seat even when fully loaded. Babying the magazine into place with a push locks it into the grip as does a slap of the palm. Upon pressing the magazine release, mags eject rapidly and free fall into the awaiting palm of your non-shooting hand. The PPX's magazine release is more traditional than those on some of Walther's other pistols — models in which the release is integrated into the rear of the trigger guard.

The PPX is designed for standard and +P 9mm ammunition. I had an assortment of ammo consisting of Hornady's 115-grain HAP (Hornady Action Pistol) Steel Match. This is Hornady's steel cartridge case ammo that is well suited for training, practice, and action shooting competition. For a self-defense load, I used Hornady's 9mm +P 135-grain FTX Critical Duty. This stuff uses Hornady's proprietary FlexLock bullet, a hollowpoint filled with a flexible polymer. The polymer ensures the hollowpoint doesn't clog with whatever type of matter it is fired into — glass, wood, flesh, etc. My

PERFORMANCE: WALTHER PPX				
9mm Ammo (bullet weight in grains)	Velocity (fps)	Energy (ft.-lbs.)	Best Accuracy (inches)	Average Accuracy (inches)
Hornady Steel Match 115 JHP	1,123	322	2.0	4.0
Black Hills 115 FMJ	1,140	332	3.75	5.25
Hornady Critical Duty 135 FlexLock JHP	1,118	375	2.75	4.62

Bullet weight measured in grains, velocity in feet per second, and average accuracy in inches for best five-shot groups at 25 yards.

third choice was Black Hills 115-grain Full Metal Jacket.

The magazine body is steel with a polymer follower and floorplate. I tried to confuse the PPX from the onset by fully loading the magazine with all the different cartridges. Loading the 16th round was nearly as easy as the first one. The magazine lips are smooth and easy on the thumb.

I did not feel like I had to reach to engage the trigger nor did I have to adjust my pull to compensate for a short reach. The trigger is faintly grooved. The factory spec puts the trigger pull at 6.6 pounds, but the PPX tested at 5.7 pounds average.

At 15 yards, I let rip with the PPX firing as fast as I could to see and feel how it reacted to the mix of 115-grain and 135-grain ammo. I easily kept all rounds on the D1 tombstone-style target. The PPX performed well, chewing through the ammo and spitting out empties as fast as I could press the trigger. Using a two-hand hold, weak hand, sideways and upside down I couldn't make the new Walther choke. Even with the +P 135-grain Hornady ammo, the pistol is pleasant to shoot with minimal muzzle

jump. Using a rest I tested for accuracy at 25 yards and, though the pistol is not designed for accuracy per se, it did provide combat-worthy groups. The combat sights are fast on target with the large white dots.

I enjoyed shooting the PPX at close range concentrating on the front sight and ripping through magazines. I quickly became accustomed to the trigger pull and reset. In the end, my paper target was in tatters and I was out of 9mm ammo. No jams were encountered. The PPX lives up to the Walther reputation.

SPECIFICATIONS

MODEL: Walther PPX
CALIBER: 9mm
ACTION: Pre-Cocked
TRIGGER: DAO
BARREL LENGTH: 4 in.
OVERALL LENGTH: 7.3 in.
WEIGHT: 27.2 oz. (empty)
GRIPS: Textured Polymer
SIGHTS: 3-Dot
FINISH: Matte Black
CAPACITY: 16+1

CHAPTER 19

NINES THAT GOT GAME – COMPETITION 9MMS

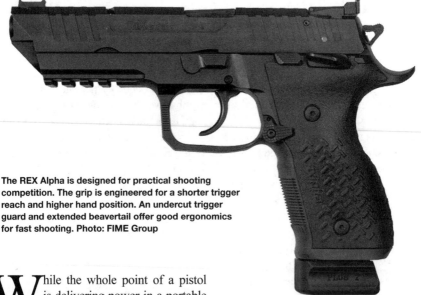

The **REX Alpha** is designed for practical shooting competition. The grip is engineered for a shorter trigger reach and higher hand position. An undercut trigger guard and extended beavertail offer good ergonomics for fast shooting. Photo: FIME Group

While the whole point of a pistol is delivering power in a portable package, there is something to be said for wringing out the most velocity and accuracy possible. And one of the easiest ways to accomplish that on an auto pistol is to lengthen the barrel and slide. The result is a handgun with more velocity, longer sight radius, and a really intimidating look. The long-slide concept has been applied to numerous striker-fire pistols, offering shooters several options. Here are some of the best long-slide 9mm pistols currently available on the market.

Springfield Armory XDM 5.25

The Springfield Armory XDM 5.25 is bred for competition. Not only does the longer barrel, extended sight radius and bright fiber-optic front sight endear it to better accuracy, but its striker-fire system offers a crisp trigger that nearly mimics a SA pull. The accuracy of the XDM 5.25 is further enhanced by a one-piece, full-length guide rod.

The Springfield Armory XDM 5.25.

SPECIFICATIONS

MODEL: Springfield Armory XDM 5.25

CALIBER: 9mm

BARREL LENGTH: 5.25 in.

OVERALL LENGTH: 8.2 in.

WEIGHT: 29 oz. (empty)

GRIPS: Polymer

SIGHTS: Fiber-Optic Front,
         Adjustable Rear

ACTION: Striker-Fired

FINISH: Matte Black

CAPACITY: 19+1

FNS-9 Longslide

In research and development testing, FNH USA put over 400,000 rounds through its FNS Longslide series pistols, so you can be sure that they are pretty reliable. Like its military/law enforcement brethren, the FNS-9 Longslide is built for speed with a striker-fire system, ambidextrous controls, 5-inch barrel and three-dot sights. You can customize the polymer grip frame to fit your hand with interchangeable backstraps.

Glock 17L

The G17L is the first Glock pistol introduced with a long slide and a 6.02-inch barrel. Designed for competition and target shooting, the G17L uses a slotted slide, which has been relieved for less felt recoil. It comes equipped with an adjustable rear sight and a 4.5-pound trigger for maximized accuracy. It has a surface-hardening treatment that is corrosion and wear-resistant.

STI Eagle

The Eagle was the pistol that helped build STI's reputation and prove the performance of the double-stack, steel frame 2011 platform. The 6-inch-barreled version features the 2011 frame with a short dust cover. The robust handgun comes from the factory with a flared magazine well, extended beavertail, skeletonized trigger, ambidextrous thumb safety, and a 15-round mag.

The 6-inch-barreled STI Eagle.

SPECIFICATIONS

MODEL: STI Eagle

CALIBER: 9mm

BARREL LENGTH: 6 in.

OVERALL LENGTH: 9.5 in.

WEIGHT: 41 oz. (empty)

GRIPS: Polymer

SIGHTS: Fiber-Optic Front, Adjustable
         Rear

ACTION: Single Action

FINISH: Matte Black

CAPACITY: 15+1

For competition shooters, the Glock 34 Gen5 MOS offers a Marksman rifled barrel, flared magazine well and the ability to mount a reflex sight.

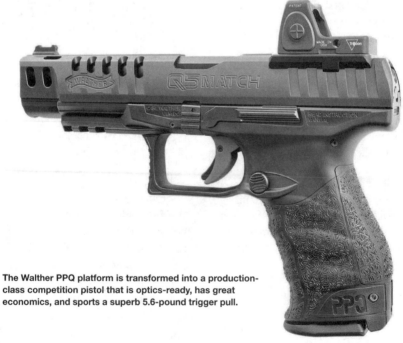

The Walther PPQ platform is transformed into a production-class competition pistol that is optics-ready, has great economics, and sports a superb 5.6-pound trigger pull.

Smith & Wesson Performance Center Model 929 is an 8-Shot 9mm revolver for competition shooters.

Test and Evaluation: Smith & Wesson Performance Center M929

The Smith & Wesson Model 929 is a 9mm revolver bred for competition. When it comes to serious revolver competition shooting, the type you will find at Bianchi Cup, U.S. Practical Shooting Association (USPSA), International Practical Shooting Confederation (IPSC), International Confederation of Revolver Enthusiasts (ICORE) and Steel Challenge, the top dog has been the S&W Model 625 .45 ACP in the revolver major division, while the S&W Model 627 in .38 Special/.357 Magnum is popular in revolver minor. The Model 929 is a 9mm competition machine designed to compete in revolver minor.

The Smith & Wesson Performance Center Model 929's ejector is cut for use with moon clips. The chambers are chamfered.

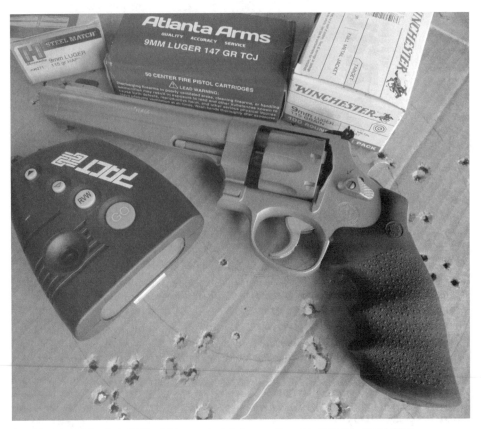

On a black target the Model 929's sights were lost, but on cardboard or steel they worked fine.

A USPSA Revolver Division is an 8-shot minor category, which mirrors Single Stack Division somewhat. Competitors in Revolver Division can choose to shoot major power factor (PF), in which case they must reload after six shots, or minor PF, in which case they must reload after eight shots. Some competitors opt for more rounds before the reload, trading points for non-A hits for time saved reloading. This is just one of the sweet spots that became apparent right off the bat for the S&W Model 929 revolver.

Without getting too deep into the weeds of competitive revolver shooting, a bit of background will help put this revolver into perspective. With USPSA competition, target arrays or groups are limited to eight rounds required per group, with course design making room for reloads and movement. With a 6-shot revolver, this requires extra reloading, unless the course is set up to be 6-shot neutral. In addition, having to reload after six shots compels the competitors to do a lot more strategic planning regarding which targets to shoot and where to shoot them from. With an 8-shot revolver, there is more freedom to engage targets on an "as and when visible" basis, without worrying too much about additional reloads. So, you can see an advantage to an 8-shot revolver depending on your strategy.

The Model 929 is an all-stainless steel N-Frame revolver designed from

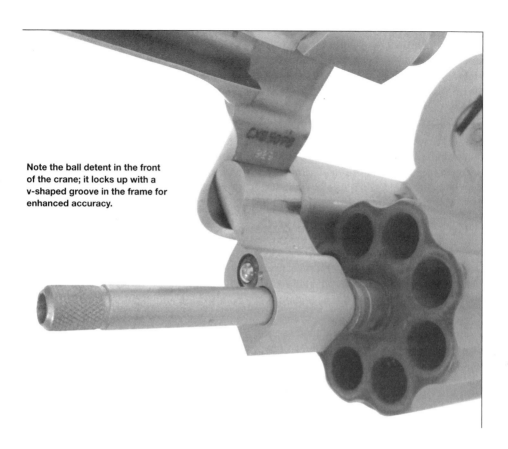

Note the ball detent in the front of the crane; it locks up with a v-shaped groove in the frame for enhanced accuracy.

the grip up for action pistol competition, and it comes with the Jerry Miculek signature. For the record, Miculek made a 1,000-yard shot with the 929 on an episode of *Shootout Lane*.

The 929 features a 6.5-inch barrel with a full-length, tapered underlug to reduce the effects of felt recoil and a compensator to minimize muzzle flip. The compensator can quickly and easily be removed and replaced with a false muzzle. This is a feature I like since some divisions do not allow compensators. On top of the barrel is an adjustable rear sight with a plain, matte black notch. The front Patridge sight is also matte black. On a black target, these sights do get lost. On cardboard and

SPECIFICATIONS

MODEL: Smith & Wesson Model 929
CALIBER: 9mm
ACTION: Revolver
TRIGGER: SA/Double-Action
BARREL LENGTH: 6.5 in.
OVERALL LENGTH: 12.25 in.
WEIGHT: 44.2 oz. (empty)
GRIPS: Textured Synthetic, Finger Grooves
SIGHTS: Patridge Blade Front/Adjustable Notch Rear
FINISH: Stainless Steel
CAPACITY: 8

painted steel, they show up much better. The front sight is pinned so it can be replaced with one more suited to the user. Under the rear sight, the 929 is drilled and tapped so a reflex or red-dot sight can be mounted. Again, depending on the division and type of competition, the ability to mount an optic can be a plus. The finish of the frame and barrel is a matte stainless with no glare when used in bright sunlight.

The 8-shot cylinder is constructed of lightweight titanium. The ejector is cut for use with moon clips and all the chambers are chamfered. The moon clips are easy to load and unload without the use of a tool. They do not bend as easily as with .45 ACP clips I have used in the past. The crane has a ball detent that snaps into a V-shaped groove in the frame. This setup locks up the 929 tight and is a common gunsmithing modification for competition revolvers. The cylinder latch is the type cut for use with a speedloader, and since the 929 uses moon clips it is out of the way and does not impede a fast reload. It takes slightly longer to load this 8-shot 9mm compared to a 6-shot .45 ACP wheelgun, chiefly because the holes in the cylinder of a .45 are larger with more space in between chambers.

Both the trigger and hammer are chrome plated. The hammer is teardrop shaped and offers plenty of traction to thumb cock the 929. The smooth-faced trigger includes a trigger stop, which I liked, especially on a competition revolver. The 929 has a nice trigger, what we expect from the Performance Center. In DA mode, the pull seems less than what it measures, at 10.7 pounds.

At the range with an assortment of ammo from Hornady, Winchester, and Atlanta Arms, I started shooting for accuracy using a rest and found the 929 prefers the 147-grain Atlanta Arms ammo, which gave us the smallest five-shot group of the test at 0.25 inch at 15 yards. A target revolver the 929 certainly is, but for fast-paced action shooting. So, I moved onto shooting fast at tombstone-style NRA D-1 targets set up on P3 target stands from CTK Precision. My drill was to shoot eight rounds, reload and shoot two more rounds all while trying to keep hits in the 8-inch A-ring while shooting as fast as I could. I found the 929 smooth to shoot with little felt recoil even with the heavy 147-grain Atlanta Arms ammo. The 115-grain ammo from Winchester and Hornady was much easier for all shooters to fire fast and accurately. I assume that if this was to be used in competition the shooter would reload ammo with lightweight bullets to help reduce felt recoil and muzzle rise. The comp provided less muzzle rise in fast DA shooting. The hang-up I encountered was the reload. Since the 9mm rounds in the moon clip are small, and there are eight of them, it took some time to align them with the chambers. I eventually got the hang of it and our overall time decreased. Those cartridges that had tapered bullets loaded a smidgen faster until we got our game on.

The grips are definitely too large for some shooters. They could not get a consistent grip, which slowed them down. Removing the finger grooves would provide a better universal grip. The trigger is excellent with no stacking, smooth and consistent throughout the pull.

Overall, the revolver performs like a champ. It is fast on target, smooth in DA, and has enough heft to dampen recoil.

The S&W 929 is a unique revolver for action shooting competition or plinking. It has all the bells and whistles one expects from the S&W Performance Center.

CHAPTER 20

OPTICS-READY 9MM HANDGUNS

These optics-ready striker-fire pistols — Smith & Wesson M&P9 Performance Center Ported (right) and Glock G17 Gen4 MOS (left) — offer more practical game out of the box than traditional iron-sighted handguns.

If there is one new trend taking the handgun industry by storm it is optics-ready pistols. These handguns come from the factory with built-in mounts for installing reflex-style red-dot sights. The Glock G17 Gen4 MOS debuted in 2016, Kahr, SIG, and the Canik from Century Arms soon followed. At the 2018 SHOT Show, Kimber joined the fray with 9mm 1911s so-equipped. Custom gun makers have been crafting pistols with reflex sights for years,

and back in 2012 both Smith & Wesson and FN launched optics-ready models. While Picatinny rails emerged as a standard feature and laser pointers began being offered on many variants, the integral optics mount has taken a while to arrive but is now the next evolution of the handgun.

We have seen this same scenario play out with AR rifles. It's hard to imagine today, but optics-equipped ARs were once an anomaly; now, they're the norm. Adding an optic adds two things to a pistol immediately: faster aiming and ... higher cost. Reflex sights can add anywhere from $240 to $600 depending on the sight. You may also need to purchase a new holster to accommodate the optics and taller iron sights. While the cost may seem excessive for a handgun, no one thinks twice about taking the plunge on rifles.

There is no doubt that red-dot reflex sights allow you to aim faster and more easily compared to irons. With a reflex, you can aim with both eyes open. Small reflex sights work like big ones: You peer through a glass lens onto which a reticle is projected via a light-emitting diode. The sight provides an unlimited field of view, as there is no magnification and no tube, thus tunnel vision is not encountered. Nor is there need to align three planes — front sight, rear sight, and target — as with iron sights. Simply place the red-dot on the target and fire away. During testing, I found that taller iron sights that co-witnessed with the red-dot were preferred. Doing so brings peace of mind, eliminates that dreaded anticipation that the optic will fail or the battery will die when you need it most. A proper maintenance schedule can alleviate this concern. As the footprint of reflex optics has shrunk, they lend themselves to mounting on modern pistol designs with flat slide tops, allowing for plenty of surface area to better mount the sight. As when mounting an optic on a rifle, specific mounts are required.

I've exercised a few factory optics-ready pistols like the Glock G17 Gen4 MOS and Smith & Wesson M&P9 Performance Center Ported model. The Glock and S&W are 9mm striker-fire pistols that are popular and reliable platforms. I was looking for ease of installation, accuracy, simplicity of use, and durability. And that's exactly what I got.

For reflex sights, I used an older Leupold DeltaPoint (which has been discontinued and replaced with the DeltaPoint Pro).

In addition, a Burris FastFire III and Meopta MeoRed were used in the evaluation. The MeoRed was specifically designed for use on handguns with cutout slides, as well as AR platforms and shotguns. Made from aircraft-grade aluminum alloy, the Meopta is waterproof and shockproof and comes with an integrated MIL-STD 1913 rail and adapter plate mounts, but I used the mount that came with the pistol. It features a 3 MOA red-dot reticle with adjustable brightness levels. To turn the unit off, press the button and hold. There is also an auto-off function that turns it off after three hours of continuous use if the function button has not been touched. The MeoRed is powered by one CR2032 battery for up to 300 hours of run time and features a low battery indicator that signals when the juice is running low. The battery compartment is on the right side of the sight and can be accessed without taking the unit off the gun. It is secured with two screws to ensure constant battery contact during recoil. I was impressed by the auto turn-off feature and the ability to change the battery without removing the sight from the adapter plate.

The Glock and S&W came from the factory with a cover plate attached to the top of the slide just forward of the rear sight. A hex wrench is used to remove the cover plate, which is replaced with a brand/model-specific mounting plate that corresponds to your chosen reflex sight. All included the tools to mount the optics and, as I found out, some provided more mounting options than others. All mount somewhat differently.

You can mount the reflex and keep the iron sights on the slide. The S&W features taller iron sights that co-witness with the red-dot — very handy. Glock iron sights are standard size and cannot be used when a red-dot is attached. Mounting the optics is straightforward with only two screws. Sights can be installed in under five minutes using the tools the manufacturers provide.

Once installed, I began a torture test by dropping each red-dot-equipped pistol from waist height to the ground and found no issues. Durability is one of the reasons shooters might be hesitant to mount an optic on a pistol. Will the optic break or malfunction if accidentally dropped? I also dropped them after initial range testing sessions to see if zero would be knocked off and found that did not happen, either. In addition, I used the reflex sights for purposes not intended, such as a makeshift cocking lever. That's not something I would normally do, but it may be needed in a pinch. And it worked just fine.

Test and Evaluation: Glock G17 Gen4 MOS

The Glock G17 Gen4 MOS (Modular Optic System) comes in a polymer carrying case with three magazines, four grip adapters with a tool, and a mounting plate kit consisting of four adapter plates, screws, wrench, and instructions. The adapter plate allows mounting of reflex red-dot sights including the Trijicon RMR, Leupold DeltaPoint, Me-

The adapter plate on the Glock G17 MOS is first mounted to the slide, then the optic is mounted to the plate.

opta, C-More, Doctor, EOTech, and Insight. There are seven different sight options.

The G17 Gen4 MOS has a small cover plate just forward of the rear sight, which is removed from the slide. I used the plate that corresponded to the Meopta and screwed it to the slide, then attached the Meopta to the plate adapter. As mentioned, the standard sights do not co-witness with the optic. The Gen4 series has a Rough Textured Frame (RTF) surface and interchangeable backstraps to enhance grip, which it did without being too aggressive. Without a grip strap installed on the G17, the frame is a short-trigger-reach frame, or SF for "short frame." Four additional backstraps are included, two with a beavertail and two without. The backstraps increase the trigger reach distance. Gen4 pistols feature a user-configurable, ambidextrous magazine release button. Gen3 mags will work in Gen4 pistols if set up for a right-handed shooter but will not if the mag release is configured for left-handed folks. Gen4 pistols have an improved dual recoil spring designed to reduce felt recoil. I did notice that recoil was less with the Gen4 assembly. Another enhancement has been made to the trigger via a new disconnector. A pronounced dot, or dimple, is punched into the disconnector. This connector made the trigger break cleaner and much more predictably. The trigger press still requires about 5.5 pounds of pressure.

At the range, I was more accurate and faster on target compared to iron sights using the Meopta. Accuracy was well under 2 inches at 25 yards using a rest. In fact, with Winchester Train 147-grain FMJ ammo, I shot my smallest group, which measured 0.8 inch. On average, this ammo produced 0.9-inch groups. That's impressive accuracy.

I did need ramp-up time to acquire the dot in the reflex sight for all pistols tested since I am more familiar with iron sights, but once I was over that hump I found that

PERFORMANCE: GLOCK G17 GEN4 MOS

9mm Ammo (bullet weight in grains)	Velocity (fps)	Energy (ft.-lbs.)	Best Accuracy (inches)	Average Accuracy (inches)
Hornady American Gunner 115 XTP JHP	1,120	320	1.3	1.5
Hornady Critical Defense 135 FlexLock JHP	1,010	306	1.4	1.7
Atlanta Arms 147 FMJ	982	315	0.8	0.9
Atlanta Arms 147 FMJ	936	286	1.0	1.2

Bullet weight measured in grains, velocity in feet per second, and average accuracy in inches for best five-shot groups at 25 yards.

I could shoot faster and more accurately with a reflex sight. The transition from irons to optics requires you to aim differently. I needed to slightly lower the muzzle to acquire the red-dot within the sight's window.

The G17 Gen4 MOS performs really well. There's no doubt about it, the reflex sight-equipped Glock can definitely perform defense duty or be run in competition.

SPECIFICATIONS

MODEL: Glock G17 Gen4 MOS
CALIBER: 9mm
ACTION: Locked Breech
TRIGGER: Striker Fire
BARREL LENGTH: 4.4 in.
OVERALL LENGTH: 7.9 in.
WEIGHT: 25.0 oz. (empty)
GRIPS: Textured Polymer, Modular Inserts
SIGHTS: Fixed, Dot Front/Outline Rear; Optics Ready
FINISH: Matte Black
CAPACITY: 17+1

The Glock's iron sights are useless when the reflex optic is mounted.

Test and Evaluation:
Smith & Wesson M&P9
Performance Center Ported

The Smith & Wesson M&P9 Performance Center Ported semi-auto is designed to compete out of the box in action shooting events. It comes in a hard case with one steel magazine, three grip adapters, and tool, and S&W's C.O.R.E. (Competition Optics Ready Equipment) adapter plates, screws and wrenches for up to six reflex sight options. I mounted the Leupold DeltaPoint on this souped-up rig and found the installation straightforward and easy. Installation goes like this: First, find the corresponding plate, place it on the slide, then use the two screws to sandwich the plate between the optic and slide. Determine which adapter plate works with your sight (options include Trijicon RMR, Leupold DeltaPoint, C-More STS, Doctor, or Insight MRDS). The M&P9 comes with tall 3-dot steel sights that can be co-witnessed with the red-dot and are dovetailed into the slide.

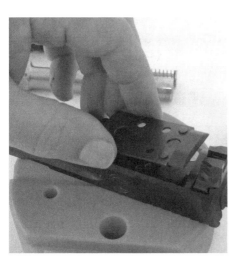

The adapter plate is placed on the M&P9 slide, then the Leupold DeltaPoint rests on top of it. Installation is pretty simple.

This is how the shooter views the reflex red-dot, in this case, the Leupold DeltaPoint. Note that the M&P9's iron sights can be viewed through the sight, a plus in the author's opinion.

The handgun features two oblong barrel ports that align with the two forwardmost ports on the slide. There are eight slots milled into the top of the slide to reduce weight and vent gas. The stainless-steel barrel has a unique viewport so you can see if a round or case is in the chamber. The recoil spring in the M&P9 is a flat coil spring with a steel one-piece recoil guide rod.

The frame has three grip inserts that adjust the trigger reach span as well as provide a bit of a palm swell with a toothy texture. That texture improves grip but does not abrade the skin. I like the palm swell and chose to use the small grip module. The M&P9 stores the grip tool in the butt heal, keeping it handy so it won't get lost. The trigger is enhanced on this model with a Performance Center sear that provides on average a crisp 4.5-pound trigger press. Trigger reset is fast and is equipped with an overtravel adjustment screw. The grip module needs to be removed to adjust the stop with the supplied hex wrench, which is also stored in the butt. The feel of the flat face of the trigger is superb and breaks cleanly.

At the range, the M&P9 has a nice

Three grip adapters are included with the M&P9 that not only adjust trigger reach but also provide a palm swell.

SPECIFICATIONS

MODEL: Smith & Wesson M&P9
        Performance Center Ported
CALIBER: 9mm
ACTION: Locked Breech
TRIGGER: Striker Fire
BARREL LENGTH: 5.0 in.
OVERALL LENGTH: 8.5 in.
WEIGHT: 24.1 oz. (empty)
GRIPS: Textured Polymer, 3 modular
        inserts
SIGHTS: Fixed, 2-Dot; Optics Ready
FINISH: Matte Black
CAPACITY: 17+1

balance and low bore axis, sits low in your hand. I ran it on paper at 25 yards and obtained surgical accuracy. With Hornady American Gunner pushing 115-grain XTP bullets I averaged 0.9-inch five-shot groups. The Winchester Train ammo averaged 1.0 inches. I attributed this accuracy to the enhanced Performance Center trigger. In rapid fire, the M&P9 has slightly less muzzle flip due to the ported barrels. I was likewise impressed with the Delta-Point and the redundancy of the irons.

All in all, the Performance Center M&P9 provides six reflex sight-mounting options, has tall sights, and enhanced features.

PERFORMANCE: SMITH & WESSON M&P9

9mm Ammo (bullet weight in grains)	Velocity (fps)	Energy (ft.-lbs.)	Best Accuracy (inches)	Average Accuracy (inches)
Hornady American Gunner 115 XTP JHP	1,120	320	0.8	0.9
Hornady Critical Defense 135 FlexLock JHP	1,138	388	1.5	1.8
Atlanta Arms 147 FMJ	984	372	0.9	1.0
Atlanta Arms 147 FMJ	973	366	1.0	1.5

Bullet weight measured in grains, velocity in feet per second, and average accuracy in inches for best five-shot groups at 25 yards.

CHAPTER 21

WHEELGUN NINES – 9MM REVOLVERS

As odd a pairing as it may seem, the marriage between the reliable revolver and ever-popular 9mm cartridge makes sense. Indeed, the ability to use the same ammunition in a semi-auto and revolver that may be on hand makes it simply convenient.

The fact is, revolvers were originally designed to fire rimmed cartridges like the .38 Special or .357 Magnum and were later retrofitted to shoot the semi-automatic 9mm cartridge. Chambering a revolver in 9mm is not new.

When you think snubnose revolvers, however, you typically think .38 Special, but since the mid-20th century, revolver manufacturers have been building short-barreled wheelguns chambered for 9mm pistol ammunition. The Smith & Wesson Model 940, Ruger SP101, and Charter Arms Pitbull are three 9mm revolvers that come to mind. The 9mm fired from compact semi-automatic pistols has an edge over .38 Special revolvers due to more capacity, but when you step up to 9mm revolvers the playing field is leveled.

Ruger's New Model BlackHawk Convertible is a traditional western-style handgun chambered in .357 Magnum, but it comes with a spare cylinder chambered in 9mm. The ability to fire .357 Magnum, .38 Special, and 9mm make it very flexible. Just remember that the revolver's bore is rifled for .357 Magnum/.38 Special and not 9mm,

The ejector rod on the Ruger LCR 9mm pushes empties to the very edge of the chamber; a gravity assist is needed to completely eject them.

This Smith & Wesson Model 547 is chambered in 9mm. It requires moon clips.
Photo: Rock Island Auction Company

so the accuracy when firing 9mm may not be ideal.

Revolvers are simple compared to semi-automatics. And simple is good. For instance, if you pull the trigger of a revolver and it fails to fire, you can pull the trigger again. If the trigger in a semi-auto is pulled and it does not fire you must go through a procedure to get the pistol back online (save for those with second-shot capability as discussed earlier). Drop a magazine in the snow, mud, or tall grass and a semi-automatic is out of action. By contrast, the cylinder holds the revolver's cartridges and it's attached to the frame. Nothing to drop, nothing to lose. Revolvers also don't leave empties rolling around on the floor. The complication with revolvers arises when they are chambered in rimless cartridges.

Today's ballistic technology has turned the once underperforming 9mm into a better round. I have performed numerous tests comparing 9mm and .38 Special ammunition from short-barrel handguns, and the .38 Special runs bullets with weights from 110 to 158 grains at muzzle velocities of 900 fps to 1,000 fps. The typical 9mm uses bullet weights from 115 to 147 grains at speeds of

910 fps to 1,100 fps. So, there is a very slight advantage in the 9mm over the .38 Special. A .357 Magnum snubbie, however, is a completely different story in both muzzle velocity and felt recoil as compared to the 9mm. The nine offers less recoil so you get back on target faster. Availability of 9mm ammo is typically good to excellent in places ranging from mom-and-pop stores to big-box outlets, and it's inexpensive — generally less than .38 Special.

The ability to swap ammo between a semi-auto — including +P — and a revolver makes sense, you have only one type of cartridge to purchase. Also, the slide on smaller semi-auto pistols can be difficult for some users to manipulate due to stiff recoil springs. These are some of the reasons revolvers are excellent defensive options. Though some may groan when they see a 9mm revolver, claiming they are as unnatural as three-wheel motorcycles, they need to put their prejudices aside and find out how they perform.

So how does a rimless 9mm cartridge fit into a revolver's cylinder? Won't the round fall right out of the chamber? Most revolvers chambered in 9mm have a stepped chamber that catches the cartridge on the case mouth. The trick is ejecting the spent brass. Some manufacturers — the Charter Arms Pitbull comes to mind — use a retention spring built into the ejector that fits under the cartridge's rim. Other manufacturers like Smith & Wesson, Ruger, and Taurus use moon clips. Moon clips are the standard convention when chambering semi-automatic cartridges in revolvers, and have been since 1917 when .45 ACP was chambered in S&W and Colt's large-frame revolvers. Moon clips make revolvers fast to reload — nearly as fast as a mag change in a semi-auto. But carrying a spare moon clip in your pocket can lead to bent clips, making them inoperable. Not that that is a show stopper, just an idiosyncrasy of moon clips in general. The solution is, don't put a moon clip in your rear pants pocket and sit down. In fact, I have dropped loaded moon clips onto a concrete floor from waist height to see if the cartridges would fall out or if the clips would bend. Cartridges can pop out of the clip, but there was no sign of bending.

One thing to note: moon clips are not compatible with other manufacturers' revolvers. For example, the moon clips from a Taurus 9mm revolver will not fit a Ruger wheelgun in 9mm. If a clip is unavailable, single cartridges can be loaded into the chambers and fired, since the 9mm case headspaces on a step in the chambers. Unfortunately, this workaround requires each case to be pushed out with a pencil, pen or similar skinny object after firing.

Since 9mm revolvers are typically lightweight, bullets might begin to pull out of cases due to the sharp recoil from the peppy cartridge. This is typically an issue with lead bullets but can happen with jacketed bullets, too. As an example, the overall length (OAL) of a cartridge handloaded with a 115-grain bullet measured 1.07

inches. I loaded the bullet along with four other cartridges into a moon clip and fired four rounds, then measured the fifth round to see if the bullet was working its way out of the case. I noted the OAL had changed to 1.11 inches — the bullet had worked its way out of the case by 0.04 inch.

Not that that was a major concern as there is a lot of space in the chamber from the tip of a cartridge to the front of the cylinder — about .5 inch with 147-grain FMJ bullets. With lighter bullets, that space is slightly more. Even if the crimp begins to fail and the bullet works its way out of the case, the cylinder will still rotate without fear of binding on a dislodged bullet. File this under a good reason to test fire your actual defensive ammo in your revolver.

Test and Evaluation: Charter Arms Pitbull

The Charter Arms Pitbull is a 9mm revolver that makes the complicated simple. The Pitbull foregoes the moon clip method with a different design. The extractor, or ejector of the revolver, incorporates a spring-loaded lip of steel that makes full contact with the rim of the rimless 9mm cartridge. This allows the insertion and retention of the cartridge in each chamber of the cylinder. The simple system allows you to quickly eject the empties. There is no need for any half- or full-moon clips. The chambers of the cylinder are stepped so the case mouth of the 9mm bottoms out or headspaces on the step and does not fall through the chamber.

The Pitbull, like all Charter Arms revolvers, is strong, lightweight, and reliable. Charter Arms has been perfecting economical and reliable compact revolvers for decades. They and Ruger are the only major U.S. manufacturers of DA revolvers that use a one-piece frame. (Smith & Wesson and Taurus DA revolvers have a side plate that, once removed, allows access to the mechanism.) The mechanism for the Charter Arms revolver is accessed after removing the trigger guard. A one-piece frame makes Charter's revolvers strong. The Pitbull uses the same frame as its iconic cousin, the .44 Special Bulldog. And since the frame and cylinder are nearly the same as on the Bulldog, the shorter 9mm's bullet travels about 7/8ths of an inch from the cartridge to the forcing cone where it encounters the barrel rifling.

Like other Charter Arms revolvers, the ejector rod is housed in a shroud that blends nicely with the gun's lines. Pushing the cylinder latch with my thumb the cylinder swung smoothly out. The ejector rod is long enough to fully push out the empties. The cylinder snaps back into the frame with a confident sound. The serrated hammer affords a sure grip cocking and decocking the revolver. The firing system employs a transfer bar, which will not allow it to fire even if it is dropped on the hammer. The firing pin is built into the frame. The hammer pounds the transfer bar, slamming the firing pin into the primer of the cartridge.

The checkered black rubber grip does a nice job of filling the space behind the trigger guard. The grip surrounds the frame. There is no backstrap peeking through the grip to slam into your palms when shooting hot loads. The finger grips, too, are comfortable for my hand. The texture feels secure without feeling sticky like some rubber grips. The grip and the smooth-surface trigger work together to produce a clean, DA trigger pull. The overall finish of the Pitbull is matte stainless, which is generally uniform. I had to look for them but a few areas could have used a bit more polishing (like under the hammer). But I'm not complaining.

A revolver in 9mm makes sense since the cartridge is popular as a home defense and concealed carry round. You may already own a 9mm autoloader but you may need a compact carry gun or something for the bedroom nightstand. With the Pitbull, there is no need to buy different ammo. This little revolver will chew through anything you feed your 9mm Glock, Beretta, SIG or Smith & Wesson M&P. The revolver, by its very nature, is a weapon that needs minimal training to be used effectively in a dire situation. Training should be at the forefront of any shooter's mind but the basic simplicity of the revolver allows you to concentrate on

The Charter Arms Pitbull revolver is compatible with 9mm ammo without the need for a moon clip.

Firing the 9mm Pitbull in double action at 15 yards, it was easy to keep all five rounds in the black.

The Charter Arms Pitbull does not use moon clips but a spring-loaded lip of steel that makes full contact under the rim of the 9mm cartridge.

the threat and not on safeties, decockers and other levers.

From a coat pocket or deep concealment, the Pitbull can be quickly brought into action. The sights do not snag. The ramp front and the groove rear sights are large, making target acquisition easy. The Pitbull is no target pistol, nor does it pretend to be. Like its name implies it's a small, ferocious package that's made to be used up close and personal.

At 15 yards and using a rest, I was able to consistently group six holes within 4 to 5 inches. Shooting SA the trigger broke clean and crisp at 4 pounds, 6 ounces. DA pull was just over 12 pounds. I'm no Josey Wales, but I was able to shoot quickly and accurately using a two-hand hold after a few cylinders full of ammo. The 124-grain Speer Short Barrel ammo had nearly the same muzzle velocity as the 115-grain Winchester Super X. The recoil of the Speer ammo was more pronounced than either of the Winchester loads. The Pitbull is a comfortable gun to shoot. In fact, I used up some old reloads to break it in. I had no difficulty ejecting the empties, but after about 200 rounds of mixed fodder — factory and reloads — the

residue built up in the cylinders and a couple cartridges stuck. The Pitbull is not designed for sustained fire. The stuck cases were easily knocked free when I tapped the cylinder on the wood bench.

Charter Arms has made a revolver that coexists perfectly with the 9mm round. The Pitbull is simple to use, easy on the wallet, and readily chews through 9mm ammo with good, consistent groups.

Test and Evaluation: Taurus Model 905

The Taurus Model 905 is a traditional snubnose revolver constructed of stainless steel and wears a non-glare matte finish. The metalwork is well-executed. The caliber marking is found on the bottom side of the barrel lug and is marked "9mm Para," with no indication of whether it's safe to fire +P or +P+ loads. A look through the manual indicated Taurus revolvers can handle +P loads but not +P+. It also states using +P loads "…may affect the useful life of the firearm…"

The hammer and trigger have a brighter finish. The trigger is smooth and the hammer spur well-checkered for thumb

PERFORMANCE: CHARTER ARMS PITBULL				
9mm Ammo (bullet weight in grains)	Velocity (fps)	Energy (ft.-lbs.)	Best Accuracy (inches)	Average Accuracy (inches)
Winchester Super X 115 Silvertip HP	1,100	309	2.75	4.25
Speer Gold Dot Short Barrel 124 GDHP	1,090	327	3.25	3.62
Winchester White Box 115 JHP	876	251	2.0	3.0

Bullet weight measured in grains, velocity in feet per second, and average accuracy in inches for best five-shot groups at 25 yards.

SPECIFICATIONS

MODEL: Charter Arms Pitbull
CALIBER: 9mm
BARREL LENGTH: 2.2 in.
OVERALL LENGTH: 6.75 in.
WEIGHT: 22 oz. (empty)
GRIPS: Checkered Neoprene
SIGHTS: Fixed, Ramp Front/Groove Rear
ACTION: SA/DA
FINISH: Matte Stainless
CAPACITY: 6

cocking and SA shooting. The cylinder locks up in the rear and a detent at the top of the crane snaps into a notch in the frame. The ejector rod is housed in a full-length barrel shroud. The cylinder latch is low profile so it is not in the way when loading the moon clips. The cylinder locks up tight with the crane and frame.

Sights consist of a serrated ramp front sight blade machined into the barrel. A groove along the top strap serves as the rear sight with a U-shaped notch at the rear that contrasts the front blade from the rear sight.

The sights are nothing to write home about but are serviceable. The muzzle is crowned.

The 905 sports a rubber grip, which has finger grooves, left- and right-hand palm swells and texture on the sides and backstrap. A ridge on each side of the grip for right- or left-handed shooters positions the second finger almost level with the bottom of the trigger guard. The grips are nicely done and do a good job of filling up space behind the trigger guard. A roll pin punch and hammer are required to remove the grip from the Taurus.

The tenacious 905 has a transfer bar system, making it safe to carry with all five chambers loaded. A security system can be engaged via a key in the rear of the hammer that locks the works, disabling the revolver when stored.

The Taurus 905 has the ability to be fired both single and double action, but of course, SA fire was an advantage during accuracy testing (the Taurus had a DA trigger pull weight of about 14 pounds). I experienced a bit of stacking in DA mode, meaning there was increasing finger pressure required the farther you pressed. In the speed drill, firing five shots as fast as

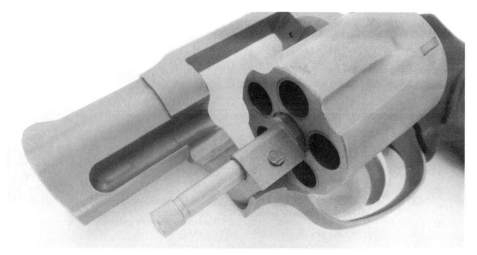

The Taurus Model 905 has a detent built into the crane that locks the cylinder in the front.

possible at a target 7 yards away the Taurus was very controllable.

Full moon clips are easy to load into the chambers, and empties come out smoothly. Unlike .45 ACP moon clips, these do not need a case removal tool. Instead, they come off easily using your fingers. Some are even loose, so if carried in a pocket a cartridge may fall out

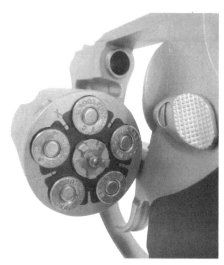

Since 9mm cartridges are so short and tapered, loading the 905 is fast when using moon clips.

during normal everyday carry. I'd make sure the spare moon clip has a good purchase on the cartridges and carry the clips in a spare ammo carrier like you would a speedloader. They do bend easily so acquiring more clips is a good idea as they will not last the life of the revolver, unlike a magazine. The 905 can be loaded with 9mm cartridges without the moon clip but empty cases need to be manually ejected with a rod. This feature is a good failsafe, but I wouldn't want to be in a situation where I needed to poke out those empties in a gunfight, all the more reason to carry extra moon clips.

At the range, the 905 is easy to control even with the snappy Winchester NATO 124-grain cartridges. The grip controls and spreads recoil effectively across the palm of the hand. In bright daylight, the front sight is difficult to see for accuracy work, but at close range it is adequate. After about 200 rounds, I noticed the 905 was more difficult to load due to fouling. I also had to be sure the cartridges were set fully into the chambers. Otherwise, the case rim would catch on the side of the frame

The sights on the Model 905 are serviceable but the author would have liked the front blade to stand out more.

This is how empties are ejected when a moon clip is not used.

and prevent the cylinder from closing. Revolvers are not designed for long, extended shooting sessions. Give yours a thorough cleaning after each use.

The Model 905 is a sturdy revolver with grips that are comfortable without adding bulk. The trigger pull is heavy but serviceable in DA but it had the ability to be fired SA. The 905 was faster to reload than a traditional .38 Special and performed well.

Test and Evaluation: Ruger LCR 9mm

The LCR (Light Compact Revolver) from Ruger is a different breed of snubnose, one that uses polymer, aluminum and steel construction. A polymer fire control housing is the grip and trigger guard portion of the revolver while the frame assembly is aluminum with a stainless-steel sleeved barrel in the frame. The cylinder is stainless steel, too, and is traditionally fluted, unlike the radically fluted cylinder

PERFORMANCE: TAURUS MODEL 905				
9mm Ammo (bullet weight in grains)	Velocity (fps)	Energy (ft.-lbs.)	Best Accuracy (inches)	Average Accuracy (inches)
Winchester NATO 124 FMJ	1,079	321	0.75	1.24
Federal American Eagle 124 FMJ	992	251	1.76	2.11
Atlanta Arms 147 FMJ	808	213	1.17	1.42

Bullet weight measured in grains, velocity in feet per second, and average accuracy in inches for best five-shot groups at 25 yards.

SPECIFICATIONS

MODEL: Taurus Model 905
CALIBER: 9mm
BARREL LENGTH: 2.0 in.
OVERALL LENGTH: 6.5 in.
WEIGHT: 22.2 oz. (empty)
GRIPS: Textured Rubber
SIGHTS: Fixed, Ramp Front/Groove Rear
ACTION: DA/SA
FINISH: Matte Stainless
CAPACITY: 5

of the LCR .38 Special +P model. The Ruger was 5 ounces lighter than other 9mm revolvers tested. That's significant — especially for a daily carry gun — but it's still 3.7 ounces heavier than the LCR .38 Special model. The LCR features a transfer bar safety system that enables the hammer to hit the firing pin only when the trigger is pulled all the way to the rear. It is safe to carry fully loaded.

The matte finish is nicely executed on the polymer/steel portions. The trigger is smooth and feels much lighter than 10.5 pounds due to the friction-reducing cam-fire system. The cylinder latch on the LCR is squeezed rather than pushed forward like on the Taurus or S&W. Manipulating the latch is solid and precise. The end of the ejector rod engages a pin in the shroud, locking it up in the front via the ejector in the rear. Lockup is tight and there is little play side to side or front to rear. The sights are fixed. The ramped front sight blade is pinned in place and replaceable or can be modified for a certain load. The front sight also has a white strip so it is easier to acquire. The rear sight is a groove along the top strap that seamlessly blends into the arched portion of the frame covering the hammer.

The Hogue Tamer grip has a pebbled texture on the sides, palm swells for both left- and right-hand shooters, and finger grooves. There is a section of squishy blue rubber on the inside of the grip to absorb recoil. The grip feels good in the hand but is slightly larger than grips of other snubbies. That trait could make the LCR print or hinder a draw from a pants pocket holster. The rubber-to-metal fit of the grips is

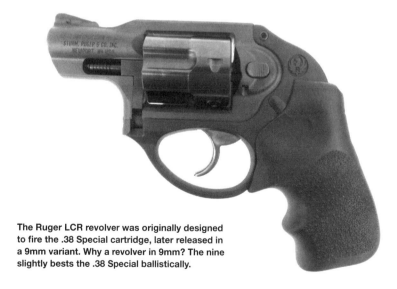

The Ruger LCR revolver was originally designed to fire the .38 Special cartridge, later released in a 9mm variant. Why a revolver in 9mm? The nine slightly bests the .38 Special ballistically.

You can grip the LCR higher, so recoil is directed into the web and palm of your hand. Why a revolver in 9mm? The 9mm slightly bests the .38 Special in the ballistics department.

SPECIFICATIONS

MODEL: Ruger LCR
CALIBER: 9mm
BARREL LENGTH: 1.87 in.
OVERALL LENGTH: 6.5 in.
WEIGHT: 17.2 oz. (empty)
GRIPS: Textured Rubber
SIGHTS: Fixed, Ramp Front/Groove Rear
ACTION: Double Action Only
FINISH: Matte Black
CAPACITY: 5

excellent. Overall, the Ruger has a smooth outside surface.

The ejector rod pushes empties to the very edge of the chamber; a gravity assist is needed to completely eject them. The LCR will fire 9mm cartridges without moon clips but will not eject the empty case. Like the other test subjects discussed, a pencil or some other long, skinny object is needed to eject empties.

As noted, the LCR is lighter than the other wheelguns tested. A higher grip is possible, placing the center line of the bore closer to your hand, which has the effect of reducing felt recoil and muzzle flip. In rapid fire, the LCR is quite effective. In extended fire I had no issues reloading or closing the cylinder.

The more time I spent with the LCR the more I came to appreciate the smooth trigger and grip design — attributes that make this non-traditional revolver easy to shoot and manipulate. The LCR has a buttery smooth trigger and the grip design stands out from traditional snubnose revolvers.

PERFORMANCE: RUGER LCR				
9mm Ammo (bullet weight in grains)	Velocity (fps)	Energy (ft.-lbs.)	Best Accuracy (inches)	Average Accuracy (inches)
Winchester NATO 124 FMJ	1,077	319	0.97	1.54
Federal American Eagle 124 FMJ	996	253	1.74	2.19
Atlanta Arms 147 FMJ	811	215	0.94	1.13

Bullet weight measured in grains, velocity in feet per second, and average accuracy in inches for best five-shot groups at 25 yards.

CHAPTER 22

9MM ARS: PISTOL-CALIBER FIREPOWER

Since the days of John Dillinger, law enforcement agencies have turned to the submachine gun as an effective tool to combat the most egregious lawbreakers. Though the use of compact 5.56mm ARs in personal defense weapon (PDW) variants have to a certain extent replaced pistol-caliber carbines and submachine guns, many present-day agencies across the country still rely on compact pistol-caliber long arms. When short-range work is needed, like across a room, these pistol-caliber 9mms offer more controlled fire for better downrange accuracy. A carbine chambered in a pistol caliber translates to less recoil and muzzle blast and more bullets sent to the intended target.

The 9mm has been chambered in other semi-automatic carbines over the years. The Marlin Camp Carbine (1985–1999) used a simple blowback mechanism with a detachable magazine. It was fed from Smith & Wesson Model 59-series type magazines. Ruger produced the

Police Carbine (1996–2006) to use magazines in Ruger P-series pistols. Both examples are fitted with 16-inch barrels, a sufficient length to pull more muzzle velocity and energy from the 9mm round. The Beretta CX4 Storm (2003–present) is like the Marlin and Ruger but its magazine fits into the pistol grip rather than in front of the trigger like most magazine-fed rifles. The CX4 Storm was designed to be used in conjunction with Beretta's 9mm semi-auto pistols. Ruger released the PC Carbine in 2018. It features interchangeable magazine wells compatible with Ruger and Glock mags. This handy carbine houses a beefed up 10/22 blowback action. The PC Carbine offers easy takedown; the barrel/forend assembly separates from the action for ease of transportation and storage.

An AR chambered in the ubiquitous and inexpensive 9mm gives you the familiarity of the AR platform with less recoil. AR-style 9mms have been in circulation since the 1980s, since the development of the Colt submachine gun and, later, semi-auto versions for the commercial market. It made sense then and makes sense today since many shooters already know the controls of the M16/AR-15 series.

While many AR manufacturers over the years have offered kits to convert 5.56mm ARs, usually with a 9mm upper and a drop-in magazine block, Stag Arms' pistol-caliber rifles employ dedicated 9mm upper and lower receivers. The uppers feature heavy-profile, 16-inch, 4140 steel barrels with 1-in-10-inch twist rates. The bores and chambers are chromed, and the muzzles are capped with A2-style flash suppressors. As with all Stag Arms ARs, right- and left-hand versions are available.

What also sets 9mm ARs apart from the 5.56mm or 6.8 SPC is the operating system. Most AR carbines chambered in 9mm use a simple blowback system — not a direct impingement or gas piston configuration like typical ARs. There is no gas block, gas tube, or piston.

Test and Evaluation: Stag Arms Model 9T

The Stag Arms Model 9T uses a simple blowback system. The upper receiver is a one-piece bolt and carrier with a modified ejection port cover and an enlarged shell deflector. The lower receiver is also different as it uses an integrated magazine well plus a specially designed hammer, magazine catch, and recoil buffer. What remains the same are the AR controls. The safety, charging handle, mag release, and six-position collapsible buttstock all function the same. Also different with Stag's 9mm ARs are the magazines. They accept standard Colt-style 9mm AR magazines, which are similar to the modified UZI mags that Colt used back in the day — straight sticks with double-stacked columns of cartridges. With these, the bolt locks back after the last round is fired. Stag's Model 9T has a long, free-floating, 13.5-inch Diamondhead VRS-T modular handguard as well as Diamondhead's deluxe aluminum flip-up sights. With its full-length Picatinny top rail, the Model 9T offers plenty of room and options for mounting an optic. The handguard is drilled and tapped at the 3, 6, and 9 o'clock positions so rails can be added where needed for other mission-critical accessories. The handguard has several lightening cuts that help dissipate barrel heat, and the bottom and sides of the forend are grooved for enhanced control.

I had the opportunity to test the Model 9T variant and found it was an easy carbine to adapt to. Reloading the skinny stick magazine was the only new characteristic. Otherwise, it is pure AR but with less recoil, blast, and noise.

The Stag Arms 9T offers minimal recoil in the AR platform and feeds off the same ammo as your semi-automatic pistol.

As mentioned, the Model 9T employs a blowback operating system, and the bolt carrier group is noticeably different than that of a direct-impingement AR. The bolt carrier key is not needed, and the Model 9T's bolt carrier is heavier. This is necessary because the blowback system works off the resistance of the bolt and recoil/buffer spring.

A red-dot sight is a natural choice for an AR-style 9mm carbine, so I mounted a Meprolight Tru-Dot RDS with a 1.8-MOA dot reticle, an upgrade that offers rapid target acquisition with both eyes open. The RDS is a low-cost commercial version of the Metro M5 sights used by the Israeli Defense Forces. It's constructed with an aluminum body and tough polymer frame around the large viewing window. A single AA battery provides thousands of operating hours, and the sight has an auto shutoff capability for additional energy savings. The red-dot reticle has four switchable brightness settings — three for day/night use and one for night vision and magnifiers. The unit comes with an integral Picatinny rail mount with QD levers. It weighs 10.5 ounces and takes up 4.5 inches of rail space. Once mounted, the RDS is at the exact height needed for an AR platform.

The Model 9T's magazine features a steel body with a polymer follower that is molded bright orange so you can visibly see the mag is empty when the bolt is locked back. There are witness holes, and the steel floorplate is easy to remove for maintenance. I acquired three additional sticks from Brownells as I wanted to try some fast reload drills with the 9T. The Brownells mags are made of steel with steel followers and have a slick Xylan coating for smoother operation. They hold a whopping 32 rounds each. Manipulating the stick mag into the Model 9T's magazine well requires a bit of re-training because the stick is so long. I performed reloads by grabbing the magazines in the center with my index

There is no forward assist on the 9T. Note the large brass deflector at the rear of the ejection port.

finger extended — just as you would with a pistol magazine — to orientate the front of the mag into the beveled magazine well. I then pushed the fresh magazine home and tugged on it to ensure it was properly seated before running the bolt as I maneuvered my support hand back to the handguard while getting back on target.

Lessened risk of overpenetration is a benefit of the 9mm, but most operators know that swapping out ammo in a compact 5.56mm AR achieves similar results. Using 9mm ammo, however, means I can run my carbine with the same ammo I use in my full-sized and compact handguns. I can swap ammunition between my carry pistol and the Model 9T. I loaded all four mags using Winchester White Box 115-grain FMJs, Hornady 115-grain HAP, and Atlanta Arms 147-grain FMJs.

Some older 9mm ARs were known for being unreliable due to the way they

The 9T uses flip-up Diamondhead BUIS and the muzzle is capped with an A2-style flash hider.

were made, and inferior magazines. I have a few pals who could not say enough bad things about some of the older 9mm AR magazines. I was not jaded by their com-

SPECIFICATIONS

MODEL: Stag Arms Model 9T
CALIBER: 9mm
ACTION: Blowback
TRIGGER: Single Stage
BARREL LENGTH: 16 in.
OVERALL LENGTH: 32.25-35.75 in.
WEIGHT: 7.9 lbs. (unloaded)
GRIPS/STOCK: A2-Style, 6-Position
SIGHTS: Diamondhead Premium Flip-Up
FINISH: Matte Black Frame
CAPACITY: 32+1, Single-Stack Magazine

ments, however, and after running the Stag Arms and Brownells magazines through the Model 9T, I had to disagree with them. I had absolutely no issues with the Model 9T, and I ran it hard right out of the box, with numerous tactical and bolt-lock reloads. The extra

packing lube in the action cooked off with continuous shooting. I allowed magazines from bolt-lock reloads to hit the deck. Like I said, there wasn't a single issue.

The Model 9T uses a single-stage trigger with an average 5.9-pound pull. There is a slightly perceptible amount of creep before it breaks. The trigger works, and my accuracy downrange served as proof. Shooting the Model 9T from a rest I was able to get some nice groups. The best five-shot group, measuring 0.75 inch at 25 yards, was produced with the Winchester FMJs. Firing rapidly off-hand, the groups opened up to about 4 inches on average with all of the ammo tested. Loading one, two or three rounds into the magazines allowed me to practice bolt-lock reloads with the sticks.

The Meprolight sight is fast on target with both eyes open. Even in the bright noon sun, I could easily acquire the red-dot. The Tru-Dot RDS suits the Stag Arms Model 9T well. The sight co-witnesses with the all-metal Diamondhead sights, which use Diamondhead's proprietary diamond-shaped aperture. Turning off the red-dot, I flipped up the iron sights and

PERFORMANCE: STAG ARMS MODEL 9T				
9mm Ammo (bullet weight in grains)	Velocity (fps)	Energy (ft.-lbs.)	Best Accuracy (inches)	Average Accuracy (inches)
Hornady Steel Match 115 HAP	1,338	457	0.81	0.92
Atlanta Arms 147 FMJ	1,024	342	0.72	1.17
Winchester White Box 115 FMJ	1,339	458	0.48	0.74

Bullet weight measured in grains, velocity in feet per second, energy in foot-pounds, taken 15 feet from the muzzle by a ProChrono digital chronograph; accuracy in inches averaged from three, five-shot groups at 15 yards.

ran a few drills with them. The other Diamondhead enhancement, the VRS-T handguard, is slim in hand and offers a secure grip without any sharp edges.

Pistol-caliber carbines are an American tradition. In the Old West, cowboys favored long guns that were chambered in the same caliber as their revolvers. That way they didn't have to carry two types of ammo. This logic still makes sense today, and the Stag Arms Model 9T is an ideal partner for your 9mm pistol.

Test and Evaluation: Pair of Wilson Combat AR9s

Engineers at Wilson Combat took a fresh look at their cutting-edge ARs and decided to create a dedicated 9mm platform — the AR9 series. Available in carbine, SBR and pistol configurations, Wilson's new AR9s are compatible with Glock, Smith & Wesson M&P, and Beretta 92 magazines. These are three of the most popular handguns, so Wilson Combat has made it easy to pair your favorite 9mm handgun with a duty-ready, AR-platform pistol or rifle. Not only do the weapons use the same ammunition, but they'll also share the same mags.

The ability of these ARs to use common 9mm service pistol magazines makes them ideal candidates for cost-effective training, offering less recoil and muzzle blast compared to 5.56mm AR platforms. For home defense, the 9mm comes in a wide variety of bullet options to prevent overpenetration, yet the cartridge is finally being loaded to its full potential to stop threats. The FBI switching back to the 9mm round is *prima facie* proof that the round provides the required performance. Several manufacturers have converted the AR platform to 9mm over the years, but it takes some well-thought-out engineering to make an AR run consistently on a pistol caliber diet. According to Bill Wilson, "Those old Colt-style magazines were unreliable, and if you drop a fully loaded one, it will most likely bust open and leave you stuck." That is why Wilson Combat designed the AR9 series around proven, reliable mags like those from Glock, S&W, and Beretta. These magazines are du-

The Wilson Combat AR9 rifle (top) is a dedicated 9mm that feeds off Glock Gen4 magazines. The AR9 pistol (bottom) packs all the features of the rifle but in a compact package.

rable, reliable and quite common. Drop one on a cement floor and they won't split open. And while older designs use a magazine well block to convert an existing 5.56mm lower to be compatible with a skinny 9mm mag, Wilson's AR9s are built from the ground up for the nine.

I recently got my hands on the Wilson AR9G Carbine and AR9G Pistol for testing. These models use Glock Gen4 and Gen5 magazines, hence the "G" in their names. They work with any 9mm Glock Gen4 or later magazine, from tiny G26 mags all the way up to 31-round G18 ones. The guns start with Wilson Combat's proprietary BILLet-AR upper and lower receivers, which are made from 7075-T6 aluminum and designed to accept standard AR parts like triggers, charging handles, buttstocks, optics, and more. The lowers sport integral trigger guards and heavily flared magazine wells for fast reloading. Working a skinny magazine into a lower designed for a larger mag has its challenges, but the magazine wells on the AR9s I tested literally funneled the handgun magazines home with confidence. This lower/ magazine combination is designed so that the bolt will lock back after the last round is fired. Like most other 9mm ARs, Wilson's AR9s use a closed-bolt blowback operating system, and my test guns were very smooth shooters. Wilson Combat invests a lot of time and effort into making its ARs run smoothly, and the AR9 series is no exception. The internal parts are slick in operation; the charging handle and bolt carrier group work with you, not against you. In operation, the blowback system harnesses the force of the fired bullet to send the bolt carrier group rearward, and the recoil spring in the receiver extension sends the bolt forward. With such a wide

The magazine release on the Wilson Combat AR9 is oversized for faster manipulation.

SWAMP YANKEE MEDIA / SMALL ORCHARD PRODU

Wilson Combat guarantees that its AR9 will shoot 1.5-inch, five-shot groups at 50 yards with premium factory ammunition.

variety of ammunition on the market, it says a lot about Wilson Combat quality that the AR9s I tested ran so smoothly and flawlessly. No matter what bullet shape I tested — round nose or flat hollowpoint — all of it exhibited excellent feeding.

The uppers are rated for +P ammo, and since their barrels are longer than a G17's, I recorded higher velocities and energy with each test load. The AR9 bolt carrier group is a proprietary design with a heavy-duty claw extractor and plunger ejector tuned for enhanced reliability. The bolt carrier group looks similar to that of a direct-impingement AR, but it's heftier and without the bolt carrier key, cam pin, and a few other pieces. The extra weight of the bolt carrier group is needed for the blowback system to operate, and this is what makes some 9mm ARs recoil more harshly as the bolt slaps back and forth. You won't notice that on AR9 weapons, however.

The AR9 lacks the extended shell deflectors you'll see on other 9mm ARs; they use shell deflectors like those of other Wilson Combat 5.56mm NATO ARs, and the same-sized ejection port. Wilson optimizes its AR9 barrels for suppressors with minimal gas blowback. Made from carbon steel, the match-grade barrels feature 1-in-10-inch twist button rifling. The muzzles are threaded 5/8x24 TPI and come equipped with QCOMP flash suppressors, which have multiple ports to reduce muzzle climb. My test AR9G Carbine came with an unfluted 16-inch barrel (fluted 16- and 14.7-inch barrels are available) and the AR9G Pistol had an 11.3-inch barrel (8-inch tubes are an option). My test AR9Gs shared many similar Wilson Combat features, including the company's TRIM handguard, Starburst-textured Bravo Company pis-

tol grip, two-stage Tactical Trigger Unit (TTU) set at 4 pounds, and matte black Armor-Tuff external finish. Aside from their barrels, the Carbine and Pistol vary when it comes to their stocks. The Carbine has an adjustable, wiggle-free Wilson/Rogers Super-Stoc. On the other hand, the AR9G Pistol came equipped with a Shockwave Blade forearm support for greater stability while firing. I ran both on the range with some extra G17 Gen4 and G19 Gen4 magazines loaded with ammo from Black Hills, SIG Sauer, and Wilson Combat. For targeting, I added an Aimpoint CompM4 and Burris FastFire reflex sight to the Carbine and Pistol, respectively.

Wilson guarantees that its AR9s will shoot 1.5-inch, five-shot groups at 50 yards with premium factory ammunition, and it

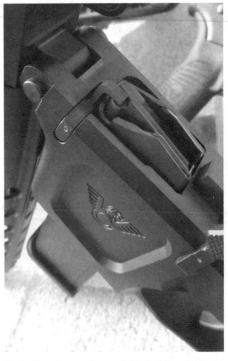

The AR9 series employs a dedicated 9mm lower for superior function and reliability.

SPECIFICATIONS

MODEL: Wilson Combat AR9G Rifle
CALIBER: 9mm
ACTION: Blowback, Semi-Automatic
BARREL LENGTH: 16 in.
OVERALL LENGTH: 31.25-32.75 in.
WEIGHT: 6.4 lbs.
HANDGUARD: Wilson Combat
         T.R.I.M. Rail
STOCK: Rogers Super Stock
GRIP: Wilson Combat/BCM Starburst
        Gunfighter
SIGHTS: Optics Ready
FINISH: Matte Black
CAPACITY: Glock Gen4 Magazine
Compatible, 17+1

SPECIFICATIONS

MODEL: Wilson Combat AR9G Pistol
CALIBER: 9mm
ACTION: Blowback, Semi-Automatic
BARREL LENGTH: 11.3 in.
OVERALL LENGTH: 24.25-27.55 in.
WEIGHT: 6 lbs.
HANDGUARD: Wilson Combat
         T.R.I.M. rail
BRACE: Shockwave Blade
GRIP: Wilson Combat/BCM Starburst
        Gunfighter
SIGHTS: Wilson Combat QDS Flip Up
        Sight System
FINISH: Matte Black
CAPACITY: Glock Gen4 Magazine
Compatible, 17+1

was finally time to put this claim to the test. My testing of the AR9G Carbine began at 25 yards, where I could easily keep five-shot groups under 2 inches offhand. This setup was near perfect, with the bolt operating smoothly and efficiently. The bolt and magazine release buttons are oversized with aggressive checkering. Combined with the flared magazine well, my reloads were very fast. The muzzle brake stifled muzzle rise when shooting rapid-fire strings, and I could still achieve tight groups.

Using a rest at 50 yards, my groups measured about an inch. With SIG Sauer's V-Crown ammo, I was able to squeeze out a five-shot group that measured 0.89 inch. That kind of accuracy is exceptional, especially when you consider that the 9mm was never designed for use in a rifle. In short, there are really no compromises in terms of the AR9G Carbine's performance or accuracy. The first thing I noticed about the AR9G Pistol was how great it looked and shot. The Burris FastFire's 3-MOA reticle allowed me to get on target quickly. The Burris red-dot allows shooting with both eyes open, so grasping the pistol with both hands and centered to my chest yielded excellent control in rapid fire. The AR9G Pistol performed exceptionally — it was smooth, accurate and consistent. With a tactical light mounted to the handguard, it'd make an excellent home defense weapon, especially paired with a handgun that shares the same magazines.

I keep saying it and it bears repeating: Pairing your sidearm with a rifle makes a lot of sense, and Wilson Combat has done a great thing by offering so many AR9 variants to satisfy shooters with Glock, Smith & Wesson, and Beretta magazines. And they're Wilson Combat ARs — so you're getting top-quality weapons that are truly accurate and reliable.

Test and Evaluation: Tresna JAG9G

Who doesn't have plenty of spare Glock 9mm magazines laying around?

PERFORMANCE: WILSON COMBAT AR9G RIFLE

9mm Ammo (bullet weight in grains)	Velocity (fps)	Energy (ft.-lbs.)	Best Accuracy (inches)	Average Accuracy (inches)
SIG V-Crown 115 JHP	1,587	643	0.89	0.97
Wilson Combat Signature Match 115 FMJ	1,393	539	1.12	1.22
Black Hills (new) 115 FMJ	1,552	615	1.17	1.29

PERFORMANCE: WILSON COMBAT AR9G PISTOL

9mm Ammo (bullet weight in grains)	Velocity (fps)	Energy (ft.-lbs.)	Best Accuracy (inches)	Average Accuracy (inches)
SIG V-Crown 115 JHP	1,376	483	1.00	1.47
Wilson Combat Signature Match 115 FMJ	1,185	390	0.95	1.5
Black Hills (new) 115 FMJ	1,341	459	1.12	1.22

Bullet weight measured in grains, velocity in feet per second, energy in foot-pounds, taken 15 feet from the muzzle by a ProChrono digital chronograph; accuracy in inches averaged from three, five-shot groups at 50 yards.

The magazine release on the Wilson Combat AR9 is oversized for faster manipulation.

The Tresna JAG9G 9mm runs on spare Glock G17, G18, G19 and G26 mags.

And who doesn't like the idea of a rifle that runs on the same ammunition as your pistol? The Tresna Defense JAG9G BU rifle enables you to do just that, but it takes that compatibility to another level because it can use any Glock Gen4 double-stack 9mm magazine. Do you carry a G19 or G26 concealed? The Tresna rifle accepts the 15-round G19 and 10-round G26 magazines. Plus, it will run 17-round G17 mags without a hitch. The bottom line is that the JAG9G is not picky — you can load it light or even with a 33-round G18 mag. If you have more Smith & Wesson M&P magazines laying around, Tresna Defense offers the JAG9MP BU, a model that accommodates any 9mm M&P magazine.

Tresna Defense is a division of Tac-Grip, whose CEO, Jose Jaurequizar, explains that "Tresna" is Basque for "tool." And as a tool, the Tresna JAG9G performed exactly as I expected, though I was skeptical about those shorter Glock mags I thought would have me fumbling during a reload. But that's getting ahead of the story.

Headquartered in Dallas, Georgia, Tresna Defense develops firearms for civilian shooters, including competitors, as well as law enforcement officers and military personnel. You may have heard about the company's LE/military-only JAG9F LE Tactical PTW, a short-barreled, select-fire, AR-15-style weapon that is compatible with 9mm Glock Gen4 and later magazines. This 9.5-inch-barreled carbine offers excellent control in full-auto and three-round burst modes. And Tresna has applied its PTW research and development to its civilian JAG9G and JAG9MP variants.

The Tresna uses a billet lower that is specifically machined to accept either Glock or Smith & Wesson M&P magazines. The relief cuts in the lower make operating the Tresna comfortable.

Both the JAG9G and JAG9MP have operating controls like a standard AR-15. The magazine release, bolt release, charging handle, forward assist, and safety selector are all standard AR fare. Both guns are 99 percent compatible with aftermarket AR parts. The Tresna JAG9G comes well-equipped from the factory with an adjustable Rogers Super-Stoc, an A2-style pistol grip, and an aluminum, quad-rail handguard. In fact, a cursory look at JAG9G may have you think it is a typical AR-15. But the JAG9G was designed from the ground up to use 9mm ammunition and feed from Glock mags. As such, it uses a blowback operating system, not the traditional direct-impingement arrangement like a standard AR-15.

The upper receiver is equipped with a 16-inch barrel that has a 1-in-10-inch, right-hand twist rate and a government-style profile. The barrel floats freely within an aluminum quad-rail that offers plenty of real estate for mounting accessories. Oblong cutouts along the handguard ensure the barrel cools quickly, especially after rapid-fire strings. The handguard's top rail mates with the flattop upper's for a full-length, uninterrupted plane on which to mount sights and optics.

The charging handle operates a massive bolt block due to the direct blowback operating system. Basically, the bolt and recoil spring move rearward after a shot is fired to eject the empty case and cock the hammer. As they transition from rearward to forward movement via the recoil spring in the buffer tube, the bolt lifts a cartridge out of the magazine and slams it into the chamber.

And, while some 9mm AR designs use a shortened dust cover and an oversized shell deflector, the JAG9G features a full-sized dust cover and a standard-sized shell deflector. The lower receiver is precisely machined from a billet of aluminum. The quality of the milling is evident, as is the thought that went into the design. Remember how I said I expected to fumble with shorter magazines? The magazine well is flared to quickly accept them, and it is designed so even the tiny 10-round G26 magazines can be manipulated with ease. The front of the magazine well flares outward and is textured in case you want to grip that surface to pull the carbine into your shoulder. The magazine well is angled to conform to the design of the Glock mags. Inserting a fresh magazine is quick thanks to the angle of the magazine well and position of your loading hand. (Older 9mm ARs tend to load magazine sticks perpendicular to the receiver, so a little more reloading finesse is required.)

The lower receiver has an enlarged, integral trigger guard, and relief cuts are present on both sides, just forward of the trigger, so right- and left-handed shooters can keep their trigger fingers comfortable yet ready. The adjustable Rogers Super-Stoc features a locking lever that removes any wiggle or play.

The single-stage trigger has a little creep but consistently breaks at 7.5 pounds. Finally, the Tresna JAG9G is designed so the bolt will hold open after the last round is fired.

I mounted a Meprolight Tru-Dot red-dot sight on the JAG9G prior to the range evaluation. It seemed like a perfect match for the carbine and, paired together, the rifle/optic combo still weighed less than 7 pounds. At the range, the Tresna JAG9G preferred 147-grain bullets. Atlanta Arms' 147-grain FMJs performed the best from a bench rest, creating a best five-shot group that measured 1.09 inches. Keeping five-round

The magazine well on the Tresna is flared for easy and fast reloads. The front of the lower is flared, offering a sure grip, especially when shooting rapid fire.

SPECIFICATIONS

MODEL: Tresna Defense JAG9G BU

CALIBER: 9mm

ACTION: Blowback, Semi-Auto

BARREL LENGTH: 16 in.

OVERALL LENGTH: 32 in.

WEIGHT UNLOADED: 5.6 lbs.

HANDGUARD: Aluminum Quad Rail

STOCK: Rogers Super-Stoc

GRIP: A2 Style

SIGHTS: Optics-Ready Picatinny Rail

FINISH: Matte Black Type II Hardcoat Anodized

CAPACITY: 33+1 (Glock Magazine)

groups under 1.5 inches at 50 yards was pretty simple and took little effort due to the carbine's nice trigger. I also shot the JAG9G off-hand at 25 yards for speed and fell into a two-shot rhythm that quickly decimated the center- mass portion of the target. Using several types of 9mm Glock Gen4 mags, the JAG9G performed without any issues.

It was very easy to run the JAG9G thanks to its AR-style controls and ergonomics. A pistol-caliber system like the JAG9G makes a good choice, especially when you want a long arm that takes the same ammo and magazines as your sidearm.

PERFORMANCE: TRESNA DEFENSE JAG9G BU				
9mm Ammo (bullet weight in grains)	Velocity (fps)	Energy (ft.-lbs.)	Best Accuracy (inches)	Average Accuracy (inches)
Atlanta Arms 147 JHP	1,014	336	0.87	1.09
Winchester 147 JHP	1,019	339	0.95	1.26
Seller & Bellot 115 FMJ	1,300	432	1.02	1.13

Bullet weight measured in grains, velocity in feet per second, energy in foot-pounds, taken 15 feet from the muzzle by a ProChrono digital chronograph; accuracy in inches averaged from three, five-shot groups at 50 yards.

CHAPTER 23

REFLEX SIGHTS, LIGHTS & LASERS

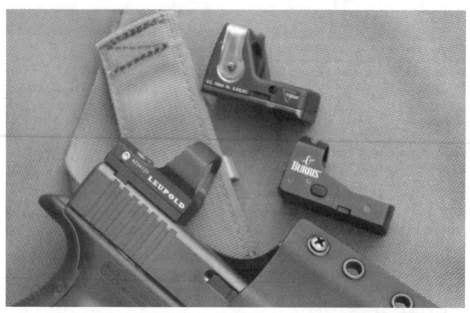

Reflex sights are made to be used with both eyes open and offer fast target acquisition. They can also be used for concealed carry.

Iron sights are standard equipment on pistols. They work plain and simple, but if you're in a parking lot at night and a bad actor comes at you with little warning you want an advantage. In real life, you don't have the luxury of time like you do at the public gun range. Life is fluid and so should be your shooting. An optic on a pistol is an advantage.

One notable example is the Meprolight FT Bullseye, which enables you to shoot fast and accurately while keeping both eyes open. The FT Bullseye is a micro-optic with a footprint that is a fraction of the size of the typical reflex sight. It replaces the rear sight and there is no need for the front blade. The design is streamlined and sits flush with the top of the

The Meprolight FT Bullseye viewed from the operator's point of view.

slide. There's no need for batteries, and you don't need to the change your holster to accommodate it. It runs on a combination of fiber optics and tritium. Simply put, there's no need to align front and rear sights. All that is required is to align the bright bullseye dot on the target and press the trigger. The unit is available with either a red or green dot.

Competitive shooters have been using red-dot sights on their pistols for over 40 years. Red-dots and other low-power optics are the norm on current military carbines. The next logical progression is optics on carry pistols. Red-dot reflex sights like the Trijicon RMR, Leupold DeltaPoint, and Burris FastFire III — to name but three — are touted as compact and rugged, and can make a concealed carry handgun better.

Pros and Cons of Reflex Pistol Sights

Adding a red-dot reflex sight to a carry pistol has pros and cons. First the

cons. The total cost of the weapon system nearly doubles, as the sights are almost as expensive as the guns. Not only that, reflex-style sights have a larger footprint than the typical rear sight, battery life must be monitored, and foul weather can diminish the capability of the sight. Then again, the pros are nothing to sneeze at: reflex sights offer faster target acquisition and ease of aiming. The ability to shoot faster and more accurately in situations under 25 yards are strong reasons to make the switch from irons to a reflex. Plus, as I found out, mounting a reflex sight on a concealed carry pistol does not change normal everyday carry.

I chose a full-size Glock as the test platform, a handgun popular among law enforcement and civilians. Despite it being a full-size pistol, with a proper holster from Bravo Concealment and a covering garment it can be invisible to the untrained eye.

As mentioned, reflex sights allow you to keep both eyes open and view your target through a small curved glass lens onto which a reticle is projected. A light-emitting diode projects a red dot, amber chevron or other aiming point, giving you an unlimited field of view since there is no magnification and the aiming point appears to be projected out to infinity. This means that parallax will not affect sighting. Simply place the aiming point on the target and, if zeroed properly, the target will be hit.

Many pistols are coming from the factory drilled and tapped, so you can mount a variety of reflex sights. Glock, Smith & Wesson, Canik, Kimber, and others are some of the more forward-thinking. For non-factory mounting options, there are two ways to attach the sight to a pistol. One is to mill an area near the rear sight on the slide and drill and tap it for the mount. This way you can keep iron sights as a backup and place the reflex optic closer to the bore's center axis. In this configuration, the iron sights are taller — like those used with a suppressor — so they clear the reflex sight. Some mount the rear BUIS in front of the reflex sight; others behind. The second method of attachment is to use the rear sight dovetail with a mounting plate. Since my full-size Glock is not a MOS model I opted for the second option. It was less expensive, and I wanted to be able to mount the reflex myself. Other than those included with the sight, the tools needed to mount it were a hammer and brass punch.

Test and Evaluation: Trijicon RMR, Burris FastFireIII, Leupold DeltaPoint

All three reflex sights tested — Trijicon RMR, Burris FastFire III, and Leupold DeltaPoint — consist of the sight and a mounting plate. Each has its peculiarities: The underside of the Leupold allows access to the battery, the Burris has a small cap on the topside, and the Trijicon does not use a battery for its power source. With all three, the sight and mounting plate sandwich together, forming a seal to keep out debris and moisture.

At the range, I pounded the sights using a variety of ammo: PMC 115-grain FMJ, Hornady 115-grain FTX, and Federal American Eagle 115-grain FMJ. Hands down the red-dot sights were faster to acquire than open irons. There was, however, a learning curve to find the aiming point in the sight window. The pistol needed to be held slightly lower than when using the irons. Ramp-up time was short, but a switch to the reflex sight requires

training. To evaluate durability and test a one-armed or injured-arm reload scenario, I used each sight to rack the slide by hand or catch it on the edge of the shooting table or holster. The sights stayed dead on, no change in zero.

Being parallax free means that the aiming point does not need to be centered within the sight window. I fired with the dot off-center to see if parallax had any effect. Out to 25 yards, there were no issues. The accuracy is more than adequate for action shooting competition and defensive purposes.

What separated the Trijicon RMR (Rugged Miniature Reflex) Dual Illumination sight from the others was that it operates without batteries. It uses Tritium to illuminate the reticle in low-light conditions, along with fiber optics that automatically adjust the brightness of the reticle level and contrast to available light conditions. The brightness of the reticle adjusts automatically when going from

From the operator's view, the Trijicon RMR's windage and elevation controls are clearly marked for direction and click value.

SPECIFICATIONS	Trijicon RMR Dual Illuminated	Burris FastFireIII	Leupold DeltaPoint
Magnification:	1x	1.07x	1x
Sight Window:	0.9 x 0.6 in.	0.8 x 0.6 in.	1.0 x 0.8 in.
Length:	1.8 in.	1.9 in.	1.6 in.
Width:	1.2 in.	1.0 in.	1.2 in.
Height:	1.0 in.	1.0 in.	1.1 in.
Weight:	1.2 in.	0.9 oz.	0.6 oz.
Reticle:	7.0 MOA Amber Dot	3 MOA Red Dot	3.5 MOA Red Dot
Parallax Free:	Yes	Yes	Yes
Eye Relief:	Unlimited	Unlimited	Unlimited
Activation:	Always on	Button	Knob
Automatic shut off:	N/A	No	Yes
Dot Intensity Settings:	Automatic	4	Automatic
Power source:	Fiber Optics & Tritium	1 CR 1632	1 CR 2032
Battery Life (@ medium intensity):	N/A	1,200+ hrs.	9,000 hrs.
Material:	Forged aluminum	Aluminum	Magnesium
Finish:	Cerakote matte black	Matte black	Matte black
Weather Resistance:	Waterproof to 66 ft.	Water resistant	Waterproof

bright to dim light and vice versa. All the tested sights have this feature. The sight window on the Trijicon is thicker than the other two sights and that tended to slightly block the view when aiming with both eyes open compared to the other units. The top edge of the sight window houses a translucent band that allows light to get in and power the aiming point.

The FastFire III has the smallest footprint of all the sights tested. A Torx wrench and screwdriver are included, along with a battery, lens cleaning cloth, protective cover, and a clamp mount that can be used with a Weaver or Picatinny-style rail. An additional base is required to mount the FastFire III on the Glock 20. The Burris was the easiest sight to install. A dovetail block easily slid into the dovetail in the slide. Center it, then attach the mounting plate with two screws, locking the mounting plate to the slide. A flexible, soft gasket goes between the mounting plate and the sight. The sight is mounted to the mounting plate via two screws. The battery compartment is on the top side of the sight and a flat blade screwdriver is required to change the battery. A tiny flat blade screwdriver is also required to adjust windage and elevation. The clicks were not as precise as the Trijicon, but I walked the aiming point around and back to zero and it was still on.

Like all the sights, numerous reticle options are available. The big difference between the FastFire III and the other two subjects was you could override the auto illumination of the aiming point and adjust it manually. A rubber button on the left side of the sight controls the illumination. Press it once for automatic illumination, twice for highest manual illumination, three times for medium illumination and fourth for the lowest setting. Pressing the button a fifth time turns it off. The

The activation button is located on the left side of the Burris sight. The battery compartment was easily accessible.

battery life is about two months with the sight constantly on. You can turn off this sight but just remember to turn it back on when it's needed.

The rear of the sight has a white vertical line that helps you acclimate to the sight and get on target. The sight window was like the Trijicon — square at the bottom and arched on the top. At the range, I could get on target fast with the Burris and stay there throughout the shot string.

The Leupold DeltaPoint features were in between those of the Trijicon and Burris. Like the Trijicon, the Leupold was always on and, like the Burris, it was powered by a battery. The DeltaPoint, however, is motion activated. It will shut down if left at complete rest for five minutes, which saves battery power. Once moved the sight automatically turns on. The battery should last 9,000 hours or over a year.

Included with the Leupold are 10 different mounting plates that fit everything

The top of the Leupold DeltaPoint houses the elevation screw. The two screws at the rear of the sight are adjustment lock screws.

from Smith & Wesson revolvers to numerous semi-auto pistols. Mounting the DeltaPoint is like the Trijicon — a dovetail mounting plate is slid into the slide's dovetail and secured with a screw, and finally, the optic is bolted to the plate. The sight needs to be removed from the mounting plate to change the battery and I found it was still zeroed after removing and reinstalling it.

The sight window of the DeltaPoint is oval with flat sides. It was the largest of all the sights and is slightly bulged over the sides of the slide. (The sides of the Burris and Trijicon were almost flush with the sides of the slide.) The DeltaPoint was the lightest of all the sights tested. Running through the same shooting procedures as the other units, I found the Delta-Point was very usable. The window frame, like the Burris, is thin, with slightly less obstruction of the field of view than with

the Trijicon. I could get on target faster with the Leupold. The DeltaPoint also has less reflection signature and the lens is crystal clear unlike the others, which are slightly tinted. Cocking the weapon using the reflex sight caused lens fingerprints on all sights. I wouldn't normally cock the weapon in this manner, but I wanted to know if the sights were durable and well-attached to the slide. They all were.

The battle-tested Trijicon RMR offers the convenience of battery-free operation. Since the FastFire III required a button to be pressed to activate the unit, there was an extra step. The upside: you could manually adjust the illumination of the aiming point. The DeltaPoint system is always ready, though it still requires a battery. The power-saving mode is an asset.

Target identification is necessary for any low-light situation. A tactical light that

Illumination is critical in a defensive or CQB scenario. Darkness hides both predators and prey, making identification of your target crucial.

punches a beam of white light on a target aids in identifying friend or foe. Backup by laser pointer makes shooting a weapon after target identification fast and sure. Lasers aid in firing an AR in unconventional shooting. Tactical lights expose dangers that lurk in the darkness, and can disorient an attacker, giving you the advantage. Remember: Distance is an advantage. A weapon-mounted light allows you to see and aim more accurately in the dark — the most likely time when creepy crawlies wait for victims. Today's tactical lights allow you to see farther into the night, and the farther you are from a threat, the better the chance you'll survive the encounter.

Crimson Trace is an innovator in the laser sight market. Since polymer-frame pistols do not allow for swapping grip panels, like on a 1911, the Crimson Trace Rail Master Pro attaches to any pistol with an ac-cessory rail. The Rail Master Pro combines a red or green laser with a 100 lumen LED tactical light. It has a tiny footprint and can be activated with your trigger finger from the ready position.

Another combination unit is the Viridian X5L — a powerful green laser and tactical light. The light throws 178 lumens on continuous mode and 224 lumens in strobe mode. The Viridian X5L has six modes: constant laser, constant laser/con-stant light, constant laser/strobe light, pulse laser, pulse laser/constant light, and con-stant light. Activating the unit is completely ambidextrous. Just press either the right- or left-side button to turn on or off or change the mode. Battery life is six hours in con-stant mode, 10 hours pulsing. It automati-cally shuts down in about 10 minutes after a brief warning period. Simply press either button to keep the power on. The X5L is

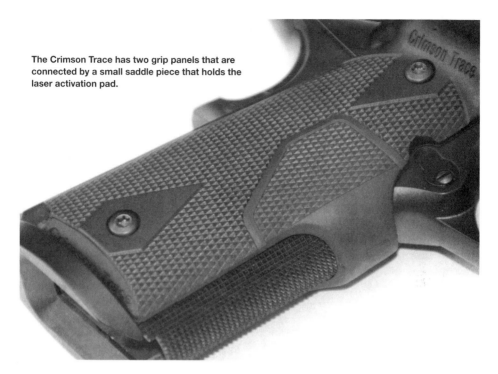

The Crimson Trace has two grip panels that are connected by a small saddle piece that holds the laser activation pad.

constructed with an aluminum housing so it is rugged. With the optional ECR Instant-On Kit, you can upgrade your existing light-compatible holster. The ECR instantly activates the laser/light when the pistol is drawn from the holster.

Pinpoint Placement: Watch the Bouncing Red-Dot

Early generations of laser sights were conspicuous bolt-ons — more gadget than gear. Current laser sights are integrated with the firearm. Many manufacturers offer model variants that come with factory installed lasers. Lasers, much like optics for pistols, have become the new normal.

Lasers are durable and concealable, not as fragile as one would think. I have drop-tested them from a height of 3 feet onto a piece of ½-inch plywood on a concrete floor. They've been dropped on the left and right sides, top, bottom, muzzle, and grip ends. I wanted to simulate a

drop from hip height due to a clumsy holster draw or a fumble from a nightstand drawer. I've also frozen the sights for 30 minutes to see if the buttons would work in a cold environment and then sprayed the sights with water to test water resistance. It's hard to kill these sights. The freezer had no impact on the operation of the activation buttons, though cold temperatures will shorten battery life. The water spray test does not cause lasers to fail, but water on the glass lens did distort the laser dot. Wiping it dry restored the dot to sharpness.

Light Amplification by Stimulated Emission of Radiation, or "laser" for short, is a way to emit electromagnetic radiation in the form of visible light. Physics aside, a laser sight is a laser pointer on steroids. The FDA regulates laser sights as Class IIIa devices that operate at 1 to 5 mW (milliwatts). Lasers can be hazardous. In fact, Crimson Trace instructs buyers to attach a tiny warning label on their firearm

The Crimson Trace master switch is set flush in the lower right-hand corner of the left-side grip panel. The author does not think this switch could accidentally be turned on.

The Crimson Trace LG-401 laser shown fitted into a one-piece grip. One battery snapped into the underside of each grip panel.

before the sight is installed. Do not shine a laser in anyone's eyes as it may damage the retina.

A laser can reflect off hard, smooth surfaces. When you hear a bump in the night and activate a laser, be aware of your surroundings. Mirrors, glass, TV screens, and other surfaces will reflect a laser's dot. The reflected light could temporarily disorient or deflect, looking like multiple lasers. Save the light shows for the concert arenas. Have a plan in mind.

Two perspectives dominate the laser signature debate. On one hand, the laser can be a deterrent. A bad guy can see the laser and back off knowing his position is compromised. On the other hand, if he is determined to do harm, the laser indicates your exact location.

Firearms with lasers require additional maintenance. Oil, dust, and other debris on the glass window of the laser's projection port can diffuse the beam. Clean the glass window and the laser's dot will be sharp and clear. Excessive oil can also affect circuitry. Replace the batteries, just as you would a flashlight. If you use the laser sights often, replace them more frequently.

Test and Evaluation: Laser Sight Face-off — Crimson Trace vs. LaserMax

A Springfield TRP 1911 served as my platform for this laser test. The Crimson Trace Model # LG-401 laser included one-piece grips, two dust panels, two batteries, hex wrenches, cleaning swabs, and instructions. The grips were attached to a small saddle piece that held the laser activation button, which Crimson Trace calls a pad. One battery snapped into the underside of each grip panel. A hex wrench was necessary to remove the TRP's gritty grip panels

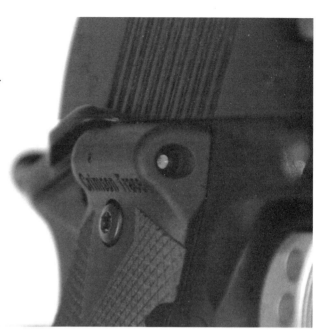

With the Crimson Trace master switch on, pressing the pad on the front of the grip turns the laser on; releasing the pad turns it off. It can be activated by the second joint of the middle finger or the fingertip of your firing hand. The right grip panel houses the laser projection port and adjustment screws. Tiny hex-head wrenches make point-of-aim adjustments.

prior to installing the dust panels, basically a thin piece of plastic that helps seal out debris and the elements. Then the Crimson Trace grip was secured using the original Springfield 1911 grip screws.

If you can disassemble a 1911 for basic cleaning, then the LaserMax Model # LMS-1911M will be easy to install. Remove the slide, pop out the guide rod, and replace it with the LaserMax rod. Instead of using the stock slide lock lever, LaserMax provides a replacement that acts like a traditional slide stop as well as the switch to activate the laser. Reinsert the LaserMax slide stop and attach on the right side a small tear-drop-shaped switch and lock it into place

To install the LaserMax LMS-1911M, disassemble your 1911 as you would for basic cleaning, remove the slide, pop out the guide rod, and replace it with the LaserMax guide rod/laser and its new slide stop/on-off switch.

with the provided Allen wrench. LaserMax provides a plastic bushing wrench in case it is needed, as well as clear instructions.

With the lasers installed on the Springfield, I headed to the range for live firing with Federal American Eagle ammo and Winchester white box on IDPA-style targets at 10 yards. Firing consisted of two-handed aimed fire and one-handed point fire from hip level. Iron sights were not used — only the laser's red dot. The goal was to fire five shots as fast as I could while hitting center of mass.

Laser sights make it easier and faster to hit a target. How much faster? On average .5 to 1 second faster depending on the shooter. Shooting with iron sights takes effort. Three focal planes need to be aligned: rear sight, front sight, and target. The laser sight combines the target plane and the dot. Place the dot on the target at the zeroed-in range and that's where the bullets will hit. Lasers allow you to hit targets with ease from unconventional or inconvenient shooting positions. Iron sight training should not be replaced by laser sight use, though, since I had a nagging thought throughout testing:

SPECIFICATIONS	Crimson Trace LG-401	LaserMax LMS-1911M
Compatible Firearms:	Any full-size frame 1911	Any 1911 with a 5.5-inch barrel
Installation:	Easy, tools required	Easy, no tools required
Activation:	Button under trigger guard	Switch on left and right side
Master on/off switch:	Yes	No
One-hand Activation:	Yes	No
Ambidextrous Activation:	Yes	Yes
Beam color:	Red	Red
Beam Modes:	Steady beam	Pulsating beam
Beam intensity:	5mW, 633nm, Class IIIa	5mW, 650nm, Class IIIa
Sight Adjustments:	Windage and elevation	Windage and elevation
Power source:	Two #2031 lithium batteries	Four #337 batteries
Battery Life:	4 hours constant	1.5 hours constant
Weather Resistance:	Water resistant	Water resistant
Material:	Polymer with rubber overmold	Aircraft-grade aluminum
Finish:	Matte black	Blue
Weather resistance:	Water resistant	Water resistant

What happens when the batteries die? That said, laser sights are a good training device. Dry fire exercises with the red-dot can reveal whether you are correctly pressing back on the trigger or exerting side pressure.

The Crimson Trace features a master switch in the lower right-hand corner of the left-side grip panel. This kill switch requires effort to operate, as it is flush with the grip surface, and it needs to be on for the laser sight activation pad to operate. You could not accidentally hit this switch to turn the laser on. Pressing the pad turns the laser on; releasing the pad turns it off. It is located directly under the trigger guard and can be activated by the second joint of the middle finger or the fingertip of the firing hand. It was easy to operate when I concentrated, which forced me to rethink my grip. There is no way that the laser could constantly be turned on. Pressure needs to be exerted on the pad. The right grip panel houses the laser projection port and adjustment screws.

The Crimson Trace works well with all holster types, but you will activate the laser upon drawing and undrawing from the holster. With the kill switch turned off this is a non-issue. At the range, the Crimson Trace dot showed up in bright light. It was slightly larger than the LaserMax dot. I did not have to sight in the Crimson Trace. It was good to go from the box, but I did adjust the windage and elevation anyway and then quickly brought the sight back to zero. The Springfield 1911 loved the Federal ammo and a five-shot group would have had all holes touching if not for a hot empty that landed in the crook of my arm, causing a flinch. I wouldn't necessarily mention this group, but I shot it from the hip by placing the laser's red dot on the target. I never looked at the 1911

The LaserMax replaces the 1911's factory guide rod.

The teardrop-shaped switch on the LaserMax can be operated from both sides of the pistol. Pointing the switch straight back turns the laser off; rotating it down turns it on.

The Viridian X5L green laser and tactical light throws 178 lumens in continuous mode and 224 lumens in strobe mode.

when firing. The Federal and Winchester loads did not affect point of aim on either laser after extended shooting sessions.

The switch on the LaserMax, Model # LMS-1911M can be operated from both sides of the pistol. Pointing the switch straight back turns the laser off; rotating it down turns it on. The switch can easily be rotated by the thumb of the supporting hand. The switch was difficult to use at first but soon loosened with use, making it easier to operate but not likely to turn on by accident. The sight could be adjusted by unloading the pistol and locking back the slide. Viewing the pistol from the front, there are two adjustment screws on the guide rod. The left screw adjusted for windage, the bottom moved elevation.

This laser sight was not activated by the holsters I wore. There is no way the LaserMax could be accidentally turned on while holstered. The LaserMax was not as bright as the Crimson Trace but had a natural pointing ability. The LaserMax needed two hands to be operated, though I could activate it with my trigger finger without compromising my grip.

The Crimson Trace is easy to install and use. You may need to rethink your grip since the middle finger activates the laser. I like the fact that the activation button just needed to be released to turn off the sight. The LaserMax, like the Crimson Trace, was well-integrated. Neither caused me to change my shooting hand grip. The support hand, however, had the new job of activating the laser.

CHAPTER 24

CARRYING HEAVY METAL – HOLSTERS FOR FULL-SIZE 9MMS

I t's no surprise that you can shoot a full-size pistol better a smaller one. There's more to hang onto, better sights, and the trigger is easier to manipulate — the list goes on. While some believe that full-size pistols should be your primary concealed carry choice, many armed citizens think full-size handguns are too heavy and difficult to conceal. The typical full-size 1911 weighs about 40 ounces or about two and a half pounds of naked steel. Add about five more ounces of ammunition and that brings the total weight of the thing to just under three pounds.

Think a polymer pistol of the same caliber is lighter? Not necessarily. Even full-size polymer-framed pistols like the Glock G17 Gen5 can pack on the weight due to higher magazine capacities. The 17+1 capacity G17 Gen5 weighs 32.1 ounces loaded. These 9mms are typically about 8 inches long and up to 1.25 inches thick.

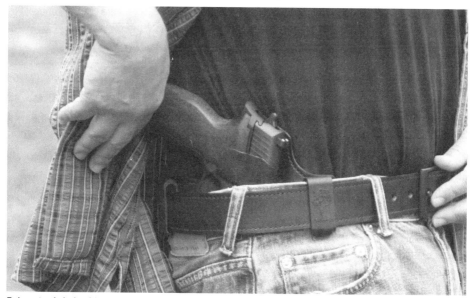

Pair a sturdy belt with a well-made holster to tote a full-size 9mm pistol for concealed carry.

The trick to carrying and concealing a large 9mm pistol is the belt and holster. Pairing up the correct components will make your concealed carry handgun easier to conceal and ready to perform the moment you need it. The first thing you need is a good belt. I'm not talking about a belt that you picked up at a flea market that has "Bad to the Bone" or "Good Ol' Boy" stamped on it, with a screaming skull belt buckle. Hiking up your drawers to reposition your concealed weapon every few minutes is unacceptable. A good gun belt is one that is wide and sturdy — specifically designed to bear the weight of a handgun and extra mags/rounds. The buckle needs to stay buckled, even if you scramble over a chain-link fence or belly crawl. A holster needs to be accessed in a hurry, so it must stay put in a consistent place on your hip. If you pair a holster with a lousy belt, you will have inconsistent draws and probably be fumbling when you should be shooting. A holster should hold the pistol close to your body, allowing the handgun to blend with the lines of your clothing and your body type. It should also offer a degree of comfort to avoid chafing skin, protect the weapon from perspiration, and be easy to put on and take off. Here are some holster/belt pairing choices I have used with my favorite 9mm handguns.

Bravo Concealment Adaptive (BCA)

Kydex is a thermoplastic that is vacuum-formed around a mold to form a rigid skin that will not stretch or shrink. Holsters made of Kydex have a slick quality that translates into a fast pistol draw. The Bravo Concealment Adaptive (BCA) holster is made of .08-inch-thick Kydex. It's tough stuff, as I purposely stood on the BCA with no ill effects. This is an outside-the-waistband (OWB) option that sits snugly against

your body and is very comfortable. Bravo Concealment will build the BCA to your specs, so I ordered 1.5-inch belt loops, a 10-degree cant, and a medium sweat guard. I carry a Glock 17 Gen4 in mine. That's 39.5 ounces of loaded, full-size 9mm pistol. The belt is a Galco 1.5-inch Reinforced Instructors Belt made of Type 13 nylon webbing. There is an internal polyurethane insert that reinforces the belt to make it rigid. The buckle is drop forged, parachute-type and uses a hook-and-loop closure. This setup secures the big Glock to my hip like it was epoxied on and it wears comfortably without any movement. For casual wear, this is a great combo.

Desantis Inner Piece

The DeSantis Inner Piece has long been a go-to IWB holster for 1911s. I like the leather snap loops and the old-school saddle leather. A stabilizer wing built into the back of the holster keeps a 1911 in position. I also am fond of the reinforced mouth so I can holster a 1911 with one

A DeSantis Inner Piece IWB holster with stabilizing wing is paired with a Galco SB3 dress belt.

hand. I use a Galco SB3 Dress Belt with the Inner Piece when I dress business casual in khakis or wool slacks. The 1.5-inch-wide Galco looks smart, and since the belt is rigid, it can carry the weight of a 1911 and look ready for the 10:00 a.m. standing meeting.

Blackpoint Tactical Mini Wing

The BlackPoint Tactical Mini Wing holster is a hybrid IWB design constructed of Kydex and small leather tabs that connect to the belt loops. The Kydex parts hold snug to a Springfield Armory 1911 while the leather tabs (or wings) easily adjust to the belt. These wings are small and thin and are perfectly comfortable. This IWB has a small footprint compared to others I've tested so it feels less bulky. To keep it all together I use the TUFF EZ-Feed 1.5-inch Ranger Belt with Cobra buckle. The TUFF belt is double layered for durability. It uses mil-spec scuba webbing and has a Keeper Retaining System, thus secures the heavy Springfield TRP 9mm to me no matter what I happen to be doing. The belt needs to be adjusted,

BlackPoint Tactical Mini Wing holster and TUFF EZ-Feed Ranger belt with Cobra buckle.

and that can be slightly complicated if you have never done it before, but once sized to the Mini Wing holster it's fast to put on for all-day carry. The TUFF Ranger belt is rugged-looking, and bear hugs the Springfield TRP and Mini Wing to my torso.

Desantis Intruder

A SIG P226 weighs 34 ounces unloaded but add 15+1 cartridges and that is some serious weight to pack. The DeSantis Intruder is an IWB hybrid that is

A DeSantis Intruder IWB hybrid holster made of Kydex and leather is teamed up with a DeSantis E25 Econ belt.

made of Kydex and leather. This holster is designed for comfort and uses a wide leather body to distribute weight. It's tuckable, meaning the plastic loops allow you to tuck your shirt over the pistol. The DeSantis E25 Econo Belt is 1.5-inches wide and has a rough-textured inner surface that sticks to fabric. When teamed up with the Intruder, they suck the P226 to my body. This is a very comfortable setup and, with the medium sweat guard, works well in warm weather.

Alternative Carry for Special Occasions

BlackHawk! offers several civilian-style casual shirts that are good looking and cover your weapon. The shirts can be tucked or worn out. I've used the button-style and polo shirts. Beltless options exist, and in a pinch, they work. A system that combines a holster and a concealment garment is the Rivers West Full Metal Jacket. This light-weight fleece has a built-in shoulder harness that connects to a holster. The holster has a concealment plate, so your handgun won't "print" through. There are two hand-warmer pockets, but a unique feature is that the holstered weapon is accessible via a hidden pocket. In fact, you can shoot through the garment with the weapon completely hidden. I've worn the Full Metal Jacket this past fall and winter carrying a Glock G17 and no one was the wiser. I've been told the slide won't hang up in the garment should you have to shoot through it, and the way it is constructed I'm inclined to believe that. I like the jacket so much I don't want to shoot through it. Another holster-type carry option is the Remora "No Clip" IWB holster, which does not need a belt. The outer skin of the holster is a rubberized, non-slip material that

The Remora "No Clip" IWB holster does not need a belt. The outer skin is a rubberized, non-slip material that clings to fabric.

clings to fabric. I've tucked a Glock G17 in the Remora and slipped the rig into my waistband and can attest that the weapon stays put.

Appendix Holsters for Full Frontal Carry

Appendix concealed carry means carrying your weapon up front. It is

The Rivers West Full Metal Jacket is a lightweight fleece with a built-in shoulder harness that connects to a holster. The holster uses a concealment plate so your 9mm won't print.

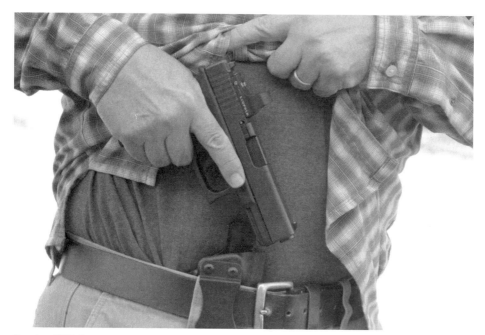

Carrying AIWB (Appendix Inside Waist Band) means your holster rides on either side of your belt buckle depending on whether you're right- or left-handed. Today's 9mm pistols are ideally suited to this type of carry in some situations.

controversial and, to some males of the species, a bit scary. (We tend to forget that in IWB 4 o'clock position the muzzle scans our femoral artery.) It took a while for American shooters to warm up to the 9mm, and acceptance of appendix carry seems to also be slow to catch on. Yet, this advanced carry method is ideally suited to today's 9mm handguns and should soon gain wide appeal when the benefits are considered.

Concealed carry safety needs to be taken seriously, no matter where on your body the weapon is located. If you have the right body type, appendix carry offers easier concealment and a faster draw than behind the hip or side carry. And, it's easier to protect your weapon from a gun grab.

Carrying AIWB (Appendix Inside Waist Band) means your holster rides just left or right of your belt buckle, depending on whether you're right or left handed. A loose-fitting t-shirt, pullover sweatshirt,

hoodie, shirttails, and other outer garments in your closet can conceal your weapon in appendix carry. Bending over with a behind-the-hip holster, it is easy for your weapon to be seen. On the other hand, large full-size pistols are less comfortable to carry AIWB, especially if you need to sit for long periods of time or bend over a lot. If you are on your feet all day it is not much of an issue.

Compact and subcompact pistols are by far the most comfortable to carry appendix-style, even while sitting. Try drawing a pistol from behind your hip while seated in a vehicle — good luck. Now try it with appendix carry — very doable. Appendix carry offers better access to your weapon if you're constantly getting in and out of your vehicle. Having a plan when you are in your vehicle is smart.

The reason I transitioned from behind the hip to appendix carry with compact pistols was the ability to more easily conceal

A Ruger LCR is less noticeable than other bulkier revolvers, and because it weighs less it was effortless to carry.

the weapon and because my pistol is close to where my hands naturally fall toward the front of my hips. My hands are almost always closer to my weapon at any given moment when I appendix carry. The draw is the thing, and with appendix carry I can grab the front of my shirt or hoodie with my non-shooting hand, yank it up to my chin, and grab the handgun with my shooting hand. The pistol is then in front of me and I can quickly gain a hold and shoot. You're more likely to be on the receiving end of a lethal confrontation, and never know when one will happen. You may only have a moment to react, so the ability to draw a weapon fast is important. Appendix carry is fast.

The author likes to carry revolvers in either a DeSantis Cozy Partner IWB or Galco SOB (Small of Back) holster.

Having the right holster makes all the difference when carrying any pistol concealed. Holsters designed specifically for appendix carry are made to be comfortable, provide support, and keep the pistol in a position for a fast draw.

Having the right holster but the wrong belt means your weapon will not stay in a consistent position. A good gun belt is part of the required equipment list. Here are a few examples of appendix IWB holsters and belts to keep your 9mm close at hand and ready for action.

The 5.11 Tactical Appendix IWB holster was designed in partnership with Viking Tactics and offers high-speed access and a secure fit. The holster is made of high-impact polymer, making it tough yet lightweight. This IWB can be worn front or back and features an integrated light clip for secure storage of your tactical flashlight.

The 5.11 Tactical Appendix IWB holster.

A good gun belt doesn't have to look tactical. Big Foot Gun Belts have a classic everyday look of premium leather. The Untamed Series features an 18-ounce double English bridle leather belt with a spring steel core for maximum support needed for all-day carry that will conform to your contour. A full-size 9mm won't leave your pants sagging

Bigfoot Gun Belt 18 oz. Leather with Steel Core

with this belt. It uses a premium roller buckle that is nickel plated and can be buckled without scratching the belt.

The Blackhawk! A.R.C. (Appendix Reversible Carry) IWB holster is designed for comfortable appendix carry. The A.R.C. is made of a soft, durable, injection-molded polymer that has a slight flex to it, making it comfortable for all-day wear. It uses a passive retention detent with an adjustment screw. This IWB is completely ambidextrous, so it will accommodate left- and right-handed users and comes with two cant angles and ride height-adjustable belt clips that work with 1.5- and 1.75-inch belts.

The Blade-Tech Klipt Appendix IWB holster was originally developed in conjunction with special operations forces, designed to be carried as a front strong-side appendix holster for extremely quick access in CQB (close quarter battle) environments. It is thin, making it comfortable to wear, and low profile even with minimal attire. It fits all belts up to 1 ¾ inches. The classic-looking EDC Belt is constructed of super-

The Blackhawk! A.R.C. IWB holster.

for concealed carry at the 2 o'clock position for a right-handed shooter. The Two O'clock gives you quick, easy access to your weapon and the ability to tuck your shirt into your pants. The Kydex body allows a smooth, low friction draw and easy one-handed holstering. A C-shaped clip grips the belt at the top and the bottom edges with little signature. The clip has

tough BioThane, which is a combination of polyester webbing and synthetic coating. This belt is abrasion resistant, waterproof and easy to clean, and will not crack or peel even in extreme temperatures.

Comp-Tech is constructed of Kydex and, as the name implies, is designed

The Comp-Tech Two O'clock holster.

five holes for adjustment and is made for use with 1.5-inch wide belts.

The compact Clinger Atom holster is is constructed of carbon fiber Kydex and features an adjustable ride height with four positions so you can have your 9mm ride lower or higher as needed for more grip. The clip is located close to the pistol's grip to push the grip of the pistol closer to your body for minimal printing. It is also completely ambidextrous and allows you to tuck in your shirt for deep concealment. Retention is adjustable via a screw. The Atom has a lifetime warranty.

The IWB DeSantis Slim-Tuk holster is a minimalist, ambidextrous design

The Blade-Tech Klipt IWB holster.

made of Kydex. This holster uses DeSantis' touchable 360 C-clip, so you can tuck in your shirt for maximum concealment. The clip is made of nylon, making it lightweight and flexible. And it securely fastens the Slim-Tuk to your belt.

The Compact Discreet Carry (CDC) Holster from DSG is constructed of smooth Kydex for comfortable all-

The DSG CDC holster.

DeSantis Slim-Tuk holster.

day carry and a fast, smooth draw. It has an adjustable retention device and is designed with sight channels that are compatible with night sights. The CDC provides easy on and off with a rubber-mounted belt clip for belts 1.5 inches wide, and is adjustable for either a vertical or forward cant.

The clip on the IWB Galco Scout holster features a rough outer leather exterior for better friction and stability with no cant. The interior of the holster is smooth leather, which facilitates a fast, buttery-smooth draw. It features a stitched leather sight rail and an injection molded nylon j-hook that secures under a 1.5-inch belt. The Scout is ideal for appendix carry, as well as cross draw and behind the hip carry.

The Tactical Series belts from Nexbelt feature one-size-fits-all in nylon that you trim to fit. They're constructed of two layers of heavy-duty nylon that provide the stiffness required for carrying a weapon. The backing is made of water-resistant nylon for enhanced wear and sweat protection. The belt tip is laser cut and heat treated to resist fraying. The cool thing about Nexbelt is its 1/4-inch increment adjustment for a perfect fit. (Traditional belts adjust in

1-inch increments.) It uses a buckle with a magnetic trigger for quick adjustments.

With four wear positions — Inside the Waistband, Belt, Small of Back, and Cross Draw — the new Four in One holster from Tagua can transition to whatever carry location you like. The Four in One has a minimal footprint so in appendix carry it is comfortable for all-day wear. It is constructed of premium leather with a soft layer inside and comes with both belt loops and belt clips.

The IWB Cordura holsters from Vega are thermal molded to the shape of

The Tactical Series belt from Nexbelt.

The Nexbelt Tactical Series.

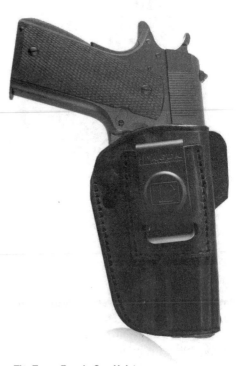

The Tagua Four in One Holster.

the pistol with a sight channel for secure carry, smooth draw, and easier holstering. The holster has a flexible yet sturdy polymer clip to attach over a belt.

The Versacarry is a unique minimalist approach to IWB concealed carry. The holster retains the pistol via a polymer rod that fits into the muzzle of the barrel. A metal core in the barrel is angled, securing the pistol. It is ambi-

dextrous and super lightweight since it is made of a flexible polymer. With minimal bulk, the Versacarry is very comfortable to carry all day long.

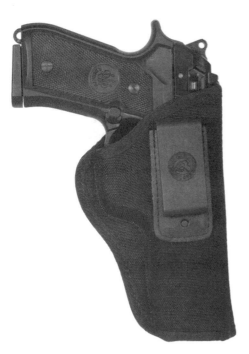

Vega IF2 cordura-molded holster.

covered with a button shirt or loose-fitting polo, it is easy to hide the your 9mm from sight in both profile and rear views.

No matter what you choose, pairing a sturdy belt with a well-made holster is the best method to ensure access to your full-size 9mm pistol when you need it.

Small-of-the-Back Carry

The opposite of appendix carry is the small-of-the-back position. Most belt-style holsters (IWB and OWB) can be worn — for right-handed shooters — behind your right hip and at the center of your spine. This type of carrying arrangement offers good concealment. Even if your jacket or shirt opens in front, your weapon remains hidden.

Revolvers are notoriously thick compared to semi-automatics — the Charter Arms Pitbull measures about 1-1/2 inches wide, a 1911 is about 1-1/4-inches thick. Using a sturdy 1-3/4-inch-wide belt, the Pitbull is completely hidden when viewed from the front and comfortable to wear in the small-of-the-back position. When

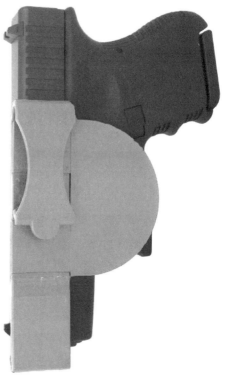

The Versacarry
Zerobulk holster.

CHAPTER 25

SUPPRESSING THE 9MM: SILENCERS GO MAINSTREAM

If you were to believe what you see on cable TV and in the movies, any silencer can be attached to any pistol. You would also believe that a suppressor completely silences the sound of a fired shot. Not so on both counts.

History of the Can

Blame Hiram Percy Maxim for suppressors being coined as silencers. Maxim, who was the son of Hiram Stevens Maxim, the inventor of the Maxim machine gun, invented the first commercially successful suppressor in about 1902. He trademarked the name "Maxim Silencer" and received a patent on his device in 1909. A suppressor never really silences the report of a fired cartridge — it just reduces the noise signature of the fired round.

Author firing the Beretta M9A3 suppressed using supersonic ammo. The noise was noticeable due to the supersonic ammunition.

The Arex Rex Zero Standard is well-paired with a Gemtech can. The setup balances nicely and there's no need for taller sights.

Shooters have always looked for ways to lessen the noise of their firearms, not because they were assassins as portrayed in the media, but because they want additional ways to mitigate hearing loss and not bother their neighbors. On Long Island at Saginaw Hill, Theodore Roosevelt used a Maxim Silencer to shoot rats with his kids in the local landfill. The former president did not want to disturb his fellow Long Islanders. In the early 20th century, Maxim Silencers were available via mail order and were advertised in newspapers. The cost was about $3.00 plus shipping.

A silencer is best described as a suppressor, or more commonly called a "can." The suppressor attaches to a firearm's muzzle and can be used on rifle, pistol, or shotgun. A firearm creates noise in several ways. The most obvious sources are muzzle blast and sonic boom. Muzzle blast is caused by high-pressure gas escaping from the firearm's barrel after the bullet leaves the bore. A sonic boom is created by shockwaves as the bullet exceeds the speed of sound. To a lesser extent, mechanical noise is also generated from the moving parts of the firearm. A suppressor helps eliminate the noise from the muzzle blast and sonic boom. Maxim's silencer features a series of baffles housed inside a cylindrical tube that stifle the gases and blast of a fired cartridge. Two additional advantages of suppressors are flash suppression and recoil reduction. Muzzle flash is contained inside the suppressor and less felt recoil is a result of slowing the burning gas.

Prior to 1934, the use of cans, short-barreled shotguns and rifles, and even machine guns were perfectly legal in the U.S. Criminals, however, like poachers and those involved in organized crime, were becoming an increasing problem. Think Baby Face Nelson, John Dillinger, Machine Gun Kelly, and the rest of those old-school gangsters. The U.S. Attorney General at the time knew firearms and suppressors could not be banned according to the Second Amendment, so a tax was levied on these types of firearms and devices. In 1934, Congress passed the National Firearms Act of 1934 and a tax of $200 was placed on the weapons and devices. At the time, $200 was a king's ransom, especially in the throes of the Great Depression. This virtually eliminated private ownership of suppressors.

During World War II, the OSS (forerunner of the CIA) regularly used suppressors during covert operations. An example is the rimfire pistol. High Standard manufactured .22 LR semi-automatic pistols fitted with a 7.75-inch suppressor for the OSS. These pistols were used later with SOG (Studies and Observation Group) in the Vietnam War. It was said that the amount of

With a threaded barrel, adding a suppressor is just a matter of screwing the can onto the end of the muzzle.

noise audible was merely the metallic sound of the mechanism cycling — about 90 percent noise reduction. The High Standard was a close-range, anti-personnel weapon. Other firearms were also silenced. Since then, our military special forces have used a variety of suppressed pistols.

Backyard gunsmiths have retrofitted everything from vehicle oil filters to plastic soda bottles to make homemade suppressors. These homemade devices have limited usage and in some cases one-time use. They are also illegal to make. Late in the 20th-century, interest in suppressors increased as military forces and law enforcement agencies began to use them more often and with less nefarious goals. Today, there are numerous manufacturers constructing cans for use on all types of guns from rimfires to centerfires, including shotguns.

Manufacturing processes, such as CNC machining and use of materials like aluminum and titanium, have propelled suppressor design forward. Brands like AAC, SureFire, YHM, Gemtech, SIG, Silent Legion, and SilencerCo to name a few build suppressors like the original Maxim design, a cylindrical metal tube housing a series of baffles. Depending on the use and type of firearm, the internal system of the suppressor may differ, but most modern cans typically have a large expansion chamber where the gas and bullet enter. The bullet and gas then flow or pass through a series of baffles. The number of baffles depends on the caliber and purpose of the suppressor. Designs like the Gemtech G-Core use a monolithic core in lieu of a series of baffles. The G-Core was designed using fluid dynamic models to study the way the gases flow when emitted from the muzzle. Some suppressors are designed to reduce noise level, some to lessen muzzle blast, while others are designed for accuracy.

Methods of attaching suppressors to firearms have seen great strides since the Maxim suppressor. Two basic methods include screw-on types for pistols and bolt-action rifles and quick-attach adapters secured to a muzzle brake or flash hider. Quick-attach types are used mostly for AR and other combat-style rifles with sustained full-auto fire, to ensure the silencer will remain attached.

There is still the $200 tax that needs to be paid to the government, and the price of the suppressor can be as much as the weapon itself. Depending on the manufacturer, suppressors can cost from about $300 to $700 for a rimfire. Cans for large-bore centerfire rifles can cost up to $2000.

In many states, suppressor ownership is legal and in some states, like Texas and Louisiana, they're allowed for hunting. Civilian ownership can be an arduous journey where the wait time from start to finish can take from six months to over a year. There are three ways to purchase a suppressor: through a trust, via a corporation, or outright purchase by an individ-

Suppressors are legal in most states, you will just need to fill out some paperwork, buy a tax stamp, and wait for your paperwork to clear. Photo: SilencerCo

Many suppressors are designed to be fired with different calibers. This Silent Legion .45 ACP suppressor can be used on a .45 ACP or 9mm pistol. Photo: Silent Legion

ual. All have pros and cons (see sidebar).

Suppressors have made a strong comeback. And as the process of ownership becomes easier you will most likely see more being used.

Mating a Can With a 9mm Handgun

Adding a suppressor to a 9mm pistol is easy, depending on the model of handgun and can. All that is needed is a threaded barrel. In fact, most manufacturers make pistol models with a threaded barrel as an option. If this is your case, you can jump ahead. If not, you'll need to add a threaded barrel. Adding a threaded barrel is easy, depending on the pistol. With handguns like the Glock, SIG, Springfield Armory XD, Smith & Wesson M&P, and others that use a tilting barrel with locked breech it's simple to swap barrels. Pistols like the Beretta 92FS/M9, 1911 platforms, and similar variants require that the barrel be fitted. Not a lot of fitting is required, but with some models a bit of file work is needed. A gunsmith is the right person to replace the barrel if you are not the DIY type.

There are many aftermarket threaded barrels from which to choose. SilencerCo, Lone Wolf Distributors, Faxon Arms, and Brownells are just a few companies that offer them. The OEM will most likely offer threaded barrels. The threads are typically standard ½-28 TPI for most U.S. manufacturers. Some European-made pistols may have a metric thread.

What you will find on nearly all suppressors made for pistols is a Nielson Device or recoil booster. Suppressors need a recoil booster, especially when the can is to be used on short-recoil operated semi-automatics chambered in 9mm or larger calibers. What's a recoil booster? When a centerfire pistol is fired, the barrel and slide assembly recoil a short distance, then the barrel unlocks from the slide. Typically, the barrel tilts to separate the interlocking lugs on the barrel breech block and the slide. The pistol uses the inertia of the fired shot to drive back the slide to cycle the mechanism and is designed to operate with a specific slide/barrel weight. When a suppressor is added to the barrel so is extra weight.

The 9mm Direct Thread suppressor from Silent Legion adds about 7.25 inches to your pistol and reduces sound up to 33dB. Photo: Silent Legion

This causes the pistol to improperly cycle. Without a recoil booster, the suppressed pistol will fire but the action will not fully cycle. You will need to rack the slide manually after each shot. By incorporating a recoil booster to the can, the weight of the suppressor is, in a sense, uncoupled from the barrel when the pistol is fired. This causes the action to function properly by boosting the recoil energy of the barrel and slide, and by temporarily decreasing the effective attached weight. The recoil booster is basically a spring inside the body of the can that attaches to the muzzle. When fired, the force of the expanding gas in the suppressor's baffles force the can body forward in relation to the barrel. The spring allows the barrel to recoil while the can stays in place. A recoil booster is not needed on a .22 LR pistol as the barrel on most rimfire handguns is fixed.

Most suppressors are made of lightweight material like aluminum or titanium, this to help keep the added weight to a minimum.

When choosing a can you can purchase a model that is made for a larger caliber, say .45 ACP, and use it with your 9mm. The decibel reduction level between a 9mm and .45 ACP can is negligible. To get the most reduction in sound, use subsonic ammo, which has a low muzzle velocity to reduce decibel rating. Some cans, like the SilencerCo Osprey, can achieve 125.2dB rating. This is so quiet you won't need earplugs. The Osprey is unique in that it is an eccentric suppressor design, meaning the baffles are not equally concentric around the bore, but below. This allows you to use the factory sights instead of needing to install taller ones. The 9mm Direct Thread from Silent Legion transforms your 9mm with a sound reduction of 33dB. This suppressor

has a 1.25-inch diameter, so depending on your pistol you might be able to use the factory sights.

MAXIM 9: INTEGRALLY SUPPRESSED 9MM HANDGUN

The SilencerCo Maxim 9 is an integrally suppressed 9mm handgun. That means the suppressor is built into the gun. The Maxim 9 is not only a low decibel shooter but is holster friendly. What's also cool about the Maxim 9 is it can be configured in short and long lengths. The front portion of the muzzle is removable, so the pistol can have an overall length of 9.54 inches in the short configuration and 10.75 inches in the long variation. In the short configuration, the pistol is hearing safe with 9mm subsonic ammunition assuming you shoot bullet weights of 147 grains or above. With 147-grain ammo the noise rates at 139.9dB. In the long configuration, all 9mm ammunition, including JHP, is hearing safe. Reduction levels shake out as 115-grain ammo with 137.1dB, 124-grain at 138.3dB, and 147-gain producing 136.3dB.

Photo: Silent Legion

Owning a suppressor is a simple process, but a process it is. If you want the instant gratification of walking into a gun retailer and walking out with a shiny new suppressor, you'll have to take a chill pill. The process takes time and the logjam currently is with the federal government, the ATF specifically, which approves Form 4 paperwork. Submitting paperwork either electronically or via old-fashion hardcopy varies the wait time. Fortunately, Silencer Shop (silencershop.com) can advise you on estimated waits and the best method to submit forms.

Using the services provided by Silencer Shop ensures a smooth, fast process. In the recent past, approvals have taken as long as 12 to 13 months. As of the date of the writing of this book (late 2017), approvals are four to five months depending on the submittal method. Prior to ATF approval, you must pay the SOT or Special Occupational Tax (also referred to as the $200 NFA tax), which is required to sell or transfer NFA items like suppressors. Here are the four steps that Silencer Shop uses to help you purchase a silencer.

STEP 1: Determine Suppressor Ownership in Your State

Silencer Shop and the ATF have a list of states that allow private ownership of silencers. These are the states where suppressor ownership is legal: AL, AR, AK, AZ, CO, CT, FL, GA, ID, IN, KS, KY, LA, ME, MD, MI, MO, MS, MT, ND, NE, NV, NH, NM, NC, OH, OK, OR, PA, SC, SD, TN, TX, UT, VA, WA, WI, WV, and WY.

STEP 2: Choose a Registration Method

There are three ways to register a suppressor — either to a trust, a corporation or in your own name. There are pros and cons to all three methods. Silencer Shop can walk you through the three methods to help you determine which method is right for you.

STEP 3: Buy a Suppressor

This step is the part where you choose a suppressor to fit your needs. Again, Silencer Shop can help you winnow through the various brands and types of silencers to match the best one for your needs. With the suppressor purchased, the paperwork is sent to the ATF for approval. Now the wait begins.

STEP 4: Take Ownership of Your Suppressor

Once you are approved, you can take actual possession of the suppressor from an NFA dealer, or if you live in Texas, Silencer Shop can ship your suppressor directly to your home.

Once you have gone through the process you will see just how simple it is. The waiting is the hardest part.

CHAPTER 26

RELOADING 9MM AMMO – CRANKING OUT NINES

If you reload today, it is not because you want stellar accuracy and consistency from your ammo. Sure, there are competition shooters who weigh each bullet and measure each case exactly, but for most of us reloading is an excuse to spend alone time in the man cave. You won't be saving a wad of money by reloading if that's your motivation. I've only seen a cost decrease per round cost when I purchased in bulk and then I never did figure in my time pulling the press handle. But I completely understand the desire to

These 9mm rounds are loaded with Montana Bullet 115-grain JHP projectiles. The author used this load for numerous Glock Sport Shooting Foundation (GSSF) competitions.

Nosler 115-grain JHP bullets are used in these cartridges. This load gave excellent accuracy.

reload. The 9mm is a relatively easy cartridge to handload, when you consider the variety of powders and how many bullet choices exist today. There are other pistol cartridges that are inherently more accurate, but for the most part, you can achieve excellent accuracy with the 9mm.

There are a few things to keep in mind when reloading the nine. The cartridge does

With Hornady 115-grain XTP bullets the author found consistent feeding in a wide variety of 9mm pistols.

not need a heavy crimp since it headspaces on the mouth of the case, though a light taper crimp is a good idea. Also, abide by the recommended minimum and maximum overall cartridge length dimension, which ranges from 1.000-inch minimum to 1.169 inches maximum. Keeping to the lengths recommended in your reloading manual will ensure the rounds function in your gun.

For a good, affordable competition and plinking load, I like the Rainier 115-grain LeadSafe plated hollowpoint bullet. This bullet has a good taper so it feeds well in modern 9mm pistols. The swaged lead core is completely encased in a copper plating. I load this bullet over 5.5 grains of Alliant Powder Unique. Out of my Glock G17, I get a muzzle velocity of about 1,200 fps. I set the bullet for a cartridge overall length (COL) of 1.120 inches in the case. This load cycles just fine in my G17 and other modern 9mms. I found some older 9mm pistols, like a Walther P1, that did not like this load. For a more vintage 9mm, stick to military loads. I load a 124-grain FMJ over 7.6 grains of Accurate No. 7 or 5.3 grains of Power Pistol. Rely on trusted reloading manuals like those from Lyman, Hornady, and Nosler.

Considering that today's ammo makers crank out enough 9mm to fill warehouses on a daily basis, coupled with the quality control and consistency inherent in modern machinery, it's hard to make the case for reloading the nine to save money or achieve better accuracy. However, there are lots of other reasons to tackle the cartridge at your reloading bench, and you'll become a better shooter if you do. Thankfully, components and reloading data for the 9mm are in abundance, so add this one to your reloading bucket list — and be ready for some serious fun at the range.

CHAPTER 27

9MM COMPONENTS – POWDER, BULLETS, CASES

Unique is an all-around powder commonly used in shotshells but is also popular for handgun cartridges like the 9mm.

Before you start handloading your very own 9mm rounds it would be best to review reloading manuals like those from Hornady and Nosler. I like reading reloading manuals as much as I like reading baseball stats and trajectory information. I guess that's just me. Since the 9mm is chambered in a variety of firearms with barrel lengths ranging from 2 inches up to 16 inches, you will need to choose the correct powder. You will also want to be sure not to load rounds with high pressure in older firearms that were not designed for it. In general, though, fast-burning powders work well in the 9mm. Here's a short list of powders that are well suited for the 9mm.

Accurate Powders

Accurate No. 2 is a very fast burning, double-base, spherical handgun powder suitable for use in a wide range of handgun calibers, including 9mm. It provides light recoil and low flash making it a good choice for use in short-barreled pistols. Plus, it's an economical choice for high-volume shooters. Accurate No. 5 is a fast burning, double-base, spherical handgun propellant that is versatile and can be used in many handgun calibers, and of course, the 9mm likes it. It offers a good balance between ballistics and cost efficiency. Another option from Accurate, No. 7, is a double-base ball propellant originally developed for high-intensity cartridges. It's a popular powder for 9mm loads used by competition action pistol shooters.

Alliant

Alliant's Bullseye powder has been around since 1913 and works with most pistol calibers. It is known for being fast burning, accurate, and consistent, as well as economical. Power Pistol, on the other hand, is designed for high performance in semi-automatics and is an excellent choice for 9mm. Another Alliant offering is BE-86 — an excellent option for the nine. It uses a special extruded flake formulation that yields tremendous ballistics in center-fire pistol loads, with high energy, a good burn speed, and less flash. Sport Pistol is good, too. It's a relatively new powder designed for precision and action shooters. It provides consistency, clean-burning with extremely reliable cycling, excellent charging and case fill, and ballistics. Sport Pistol also uses a low muzzle flash formulation that is optimized for polymer-coated bullets. Some comparable powders can burn off the polymer coating at the bullet base during ignition, Sport Pistol won't. Alliant Blue Dot is yet another one to check out. It's consistent, accurate and can be used for shotshell loads as well as handgun ammo. Needing no introduction and popular for a long time, Unique is an all-around shotshell and handgun cartridge powder that is clean burning.

Hodgdon

Hodgdon's 700-X is an extruded flake powder that is ideal for not only light field loads in 12- and 16-gauge shotshells

Alliant Bullseye has been around since 1913 and is a fast-burning powder well-suited for the 9mm.

Hodgdon Hi-Skor 700-X is an extruded flake powder that works well for 12- and 16-gauge shotshells as well as 9mm, .38 Special and .45 ACP cartridges.

but is just as good as a pistol target powder for cartridges like the 9mm. Another Hodgdon propellant worth knowing is CFE Pistol. It's a spherical powder that was originally developed for U.S. military applications. CFE Pistol uses the Hodgdon CFE formula, or Copper Fouling Eraser, virtually eliminating copper fouling while providing top velocities with clean burning and minimal muzzle flash. The stuff gives optimum performance in cartridges like the 9mm. If those don't do it for you, HS-6 is a fine spherical propellant with wide applications in pistol and shotshell reloading. In 9mm pistols particularly, HS-6 provides top performance. An additional good option from Hodgdon is Universal. It's one of those powders that handles a broad spectrum of cartridges for both pistols and shotguns.

IMR

IMR Unequal is a flake shotgun and pistol powder that is very versatile and works well for shotshells and handgun cartridges. IMR's SR 4756 is a fine-grained propellant popular with shotshell and handgun cartridge handloaders, offering top velocities.

Ramshot

True Blue from Ramshot is worth a look. It's a double-base, spherical powder with great metering properties, making it a good choice for progressive reloading equipment. An excellent choice for 9mm rounds.

Winchester

Winchester 231 is one of the most popular pistol powders around for duplicating standard 9mm loads. It is consistent, clean burning and has low flash. Winchester also makes AutoComp — an extremely fine powder used by competition shooters. It has a high burn rate with minimal muzzle flash. Yet another option is 572 from Winchester, a relatively new powder that not only works with shot-shells but pistol calibers. It is versatile, to say the least.

Bullet Options

When I reload for the 9mm I think of the sweet spot in bullet weights as being 115, 124 and 147 grains. With bullets in these three weights, you can cover training, plinking, competition, and self-defense. There are 90- and 100-grain 9mm bullets and these are a good choice for small game hunting. Hornady makes an excellent expanding bullet that covers these weight ranges called the XTP. There are other oddballs like the 105-grain solid copper lead-free bullet from Lehigh Defense that are purpose-built for defense. This bullet is designed with Controlled Fracturing Technology, meaning four separate petals separate — plowing four wound channels. Sierra's Tournament Master is a 95-grain FMJ bullet used for competition shooting. Here are some other options divided by usage: Blasting/Training/Plinking, Self-Defense, and Target/Match.

Blasting/Training/ Plinking Bullets

Hornady's 110- and 115-grain FMJ bullets are all-purpose projectiles that are excellent for autoloading handguns, ensuring reliable feeding and cycling. The 124- and 147-grain FMJ round-nose bullets are similar in design and terminal performance to the lighter weight ones. These two bullets are a good choice for small game hunting.

Rainer has a dandy 115-grain copper-plated, lead core round-nose bullet that is low in cost yet accurate. I have used these bullets in Glock Sport Shooting Foundation (GSSF) matches over the years and can attest to their quality. I have also used the 115-grain plated hollowpoint bullets, which are also winners. The 124-grain plated hollowpoint and plated round-nose give you economical blasting in a heavier bullet. The 147-grain plated flat-nose and plated hollowpoints feature a lead core that is completely covered by copper plating.

Remington has good choices, including the 115-grain FMJ and jacketed hollowpoint bullets, which are very consistent. They cost slightly more but are worth it. The 124- and 147-grain jacketed hollowpoints print with great consistency in a heavy projectile.

Federal Premium is no stranger to the game. The Federal Syntech 115-grain bullet is unique. The polymer-encapsulated Syntech prevents metal-on-metal contact in the bore, thus eliminating copper and lead fouling, which means you have to clean your gun less frequently. Plus, since it does not use a copper jacket, it minimizes splash-back on steel targets.

Montana Bullet makes excellent 115- and 124-grain FMJ bullets designed for high-volume shooting. Don't overlook some of the lesser-known makers, they are pushing the limits!

Montana Bullet 115-grain FMJs. The author reloads these 1,000 rounds at a time.

Winchester's 115- and 124-grain FMJ hollowbase bullets are near perfect for low-cost target practice. Get some.

One last option in the plinking bullet category I can't forget is Speer. Speer's 115- and 124-grain total metal jacket bullets feature Uni-Cor construction that bond the jacket to the core for near-perfect uniformity, eliminating the opening found at the base of other bullets. It's another high-volume bullet to consider.

Self-Defense Bullets

When it comes to personal protection, Hornady's 90-, 115-, 124-, and 147-grain XTP hollowpoint bullets are hard to beat. They have a swaged core and drawn copper jacket to ensure uniform expansion and in-flight stability. Hornady adds a cannelure to this bullet to keep the core and jacket locked together while allowing the cartridge case to tightly crimp, adding security at high velocities.

The aforementioned Speer company is favored by armed citizens and law enforcement alike. The 90-, 115-, 124-, and 147-grain Speer Gold Dot hollowpoints could be considered the benchmark in self-defense bullets. They feature Uni-Cor construction that bonds the jacket to the core for uniformity.

The Lehigh Defense Extreme Penetrator bullet comes in 90- and 115-grain weights. These things are solid copper, and use a progressive nose geometry that allows for deep, straight penetration while creating a permanent wound cavity diameter. The Lehigh 105-grain Controlled Fracturing bullets are solid copper and pre-stressed at specific points so that after a predetermined penetration depth the razor-edge petals deploy, releasing an energy spike and then separate and radiate outward from the primary path of the bullet. Meanwhile, the bullet shank continues penetrating. Unlike traditional expanding bullets, controlled fracturing projectiles create an initial energy transfer, multiple wound paths, and a deep penetrating base. The 124-grain Extreme Defense bullet is designed to create a permanent wound cavity that is two times greater than an expanding bullet.

Remington makes the 115-grain jacketed hollowpoint. It's a traditional design that offers dependable cycling in pistols and controlled expansion. Big Green's 124- and 147-grain Golden Saber hollowpoint bullets feature a jacketed nose with spiral cuts completely through to promote controlled expansion to well over 1.5 times the bullet's original diameter.

The 95- and 115-grain TAC-XP bullets from Barnes are designed primarily for personal defense. These full copper bullets maintain their original weight when shot through barriers like wood, glass, and metal.

Commonly known for producing supremely consistent target bullets, Sierra has some defensive choices worth considering. They make a 90-grain SIG Sauer V-Crown bullet that features optimal accuracy, weight retention, and expansion at all effective distances. The bullet uses a stacked hollowpoint design with an additional cavity.

Winchester's well-known 115-grain Silvertip is an iconic hollowpoint with a reputation for reliable functioning due to the uniquely engineered jacketed bullet. This bullet delivers penetration and rapid energy release with virtually no weight loss or bullet fragmentation.

Target/Match Bullets

Hornady has long been a player in the match shooting scene. The company's 115-grain HAP (Hornady Action Pistol) hollowpoint bullets have a swaged core and drawn copper jacket that protects the nose, ensuring smooth feeding.

Not all 9mm brass is the same. Case volume can differ between manufacturers. Make sure you consult reloading manuals before using one-size-fits-all cases.

Rainer brings a selection of 115-grain copper-plated, lead core round-nose and hollowpoint bullets to the contest that are low in cost yet accurate. Use them for plinking and competing.

The traditional 115- and 124-grain jacketed hollowpoint bullets from Nosler are designed with a tapered copper alloy jacket and form-fitted lead core. These things were built for accuracy as well as defense.

Sierra's top-performing 90-, 115-, and 125-grain Sport Master bullets are engineered to provide consistent, reliable expansion over a wide range of velocities. The jacket ensures uniform expansion along serrated lines and doubles as a defensive round. But don't ignore Sierra's 95-, 115-, and 125-grain Tournament Master bullets. They're built for competition and designed for accuracy, too.

HSM is making a big splash with its 115-grain FMJed bullets. The projectiles are constructed with a lead core and copper jacket that completely encapsulate the core. Think cheap in price yet very competitive.

Remington is no slouch on the firing line. The 124- and 147-grain jacketed hollowpoint bullets give good accuracy. They have a proven history of producing results in match shooting.

9mm Case Options

I have reloaded nearly all major U.S.-made cases and many from foreign ammunition manufacturers. For the most part, specs between them are very close. Only if you measure each would you know the difference between, say, a Remington and Winchester case. Sometimes you find some can hold slightly more powder, or the rim is somewhat different, or other minor differences. One thing to note is the headstamp on the case. Companies like Starline stamp cases with the +P designation. These cases tell you the loads are +P or higher pressure.

I typically use once-fired brass. I put it through a tumbler, and as I feed the empty case into the reloading die, I examine it looking for cracks, deformations, worn rims, etc. My rule of thumb is: If it looks bad throw it in the recycling bin. Do not reload it. I've seen some reloads where the cases were used numerous times and the case wall was corroding. These are guaranteed to jam up your weapon or cause a harmful situation. Discard ammo in this condition if you come across it. Or, if you choose, you can use a bullet puller and yank the bullet to use in a fresh case. If you choose to shoot this ammo, at the very least you could get a case head separation in your pistol's chamber —

and in a worst-case scenario you could blow up your pistol and cause grave bodily harm to yourself or a spectator. I had a spectacular head case separation using a 9mm AR. The AR spit out a head blown open like the petals on a daisy and the rest of the case was lodged in the chamber. Game over. The AR would not run. Not an issue at the practice range, but if I had not known about it and stored the rifle for defense I would have been in a pickle with a rifle that could not provide any protection.

Steel and aluminum cases cannot be reloaded, but Shell Shock Technologies manufactures the NAS3 two-piece 9mm nickel alloy shell. The two-piece case consists of a solid nickel-plated aircraft aluminum head and a proprietary enhanced nickel alloy stainless cylinder. The 9mm case is 50 percent lighter and costs significantly less than conventional brass cases. The combination of materials offers greater corrosion resistance and tensile strength — two times stronger — and better elasticity than brass. So all of this is interesting, but can you reload them?

The answer is yes — using Shell Shock's custom reloading dies. I have been told that the cases can be reloaded up to 40 times. The proprietary nickel alloy stainless cylinder offers uniform wall thickness and a case capacity that is fractionally larger than a standard 9mm brass case. Outside dimensions comply with SAAMI specifications. The NAS3 cases eject cool to the touch and can be picked up with a magnet, which makes them great for outdoor and indoor ranges.

The nickel-plated aircraft-grade aluminum head provides greater lubricity than brass and will not abrade, clog, foul, wear out, or damage the breech or ejectors. The cases can also be loaded to +P and +P+ levels. In fact, NAS3 cases have been tested successfully with pressures up to 65k psi.

The case design also prevents 'ballooning,' a condition caused by autoloaders with an unsupported breech. The head of the case can be anodized in different colors for easy load identification.

I have started to reload with these cases in my Dillon RL 550C and don't see any difference from brass. The Shell Shock dies fit the Dillon tool head. Use a mechanic's magnet, one with a telescoping handle, to pick up the empties. If you reload and train often, Shell Shock cases offer a long reloading life and you don't have to bend down to pick them up.

Shell Shock Technologies manufactures the NAS3 two-piece 9mm nickel alloy shell. The two-piece case consists of a solid nickel-plated aircraft aluminum head and a proprietary enhanced nickel alloy stainless cylinder. Special dies (right) are required to reload Shell Shock cases.

CHAPTER 28

BECOME A 9MM PROGRESSIVE

I think of progressive reloading presses as one-armed bandits, but instead of feeding coins into a slot machine and hoping for a payout I feed components into the press and count my wealth with each crank of the handle and the number of rounds loaded. Progressive reloading presses allow you to produce upwards of 500 rounds per hour, and for anyone who is an action shooter like a 3-Gunner or who does high-volume training, reloading with a progressive press makes sense.

With the pull of the handle on a progressive, several different operations happen simultaneously. Typically, at Station 1 a case is resized and deprimed. At Station 2, the case is primed, powder dropped into the case, and the case flared to accept the bullet. At Station 3, the bullet is seated into the case and, at Station 4 the case is crimped to the bullet. Some progressives have more stations for additional operations. Since one pull of the handle performs multiple operations in the reloading process, a progressive press is more efficient if your end goal is the maximum amount of cartridges loaded in the minimum amount of time.

Progressive presses fall within two types: manual indexing and automatic indexing. With an automatic index, the shell plate rotates the cases to the next station automatically with each pull of the handle. The

The Dillon RL 550B progressive press can crank out a whole lot of 9mm ammo in a hurry. Photo: Dillon Precision

tomatic indexing presses. On a manual, you need to manually rotate the shell plate. Two examples of manually indexed presses are the Dillon RBL 550 and RCBS Pro 2000. In progressive presses you can install a powder measure, primer feed, case feed, and bullet feed system, so essentially all you do is fill the powder measure, primer tube, case feed hopper and bullet feed tube, then sit back and start cranking the handle. Once started, every stroke of the handle completes a reloaded cartridge and drops it into the bin. Set up is more complicated with a progressive machine, but once ready it is like a tiny ammunition factory.

Another feature I like about progressive presses is the ability to swap out die plates when I change calibers. No need to adjust dies each time I swap caliber. Here are a ew progressive presses my pals and I use.

Dillon Precision RL 550B

SPECIFICATIONS

MODEL: Dillon Precision RL 550B
INDEXING: Manual
STATIONS: 4
RATE: 400-600 per hour

The RL 550B uses any standard 7/8x14 TPI dies (the dies must deprime in the resize die). You can reload rifle and pistol cartridges in the RL 550B — from the small handgun calibers like .32 ACP all the way up to large rifle cartridges like the mammoth .338 Lapua Magnum. This four-station press comes with a powder measure, priming system, dies, tool head, hex wrenches and catch bin. Just add components and adjust the dies to start. The press is manually indexed so you must rotate the shell plate by hand to advance a case to the next station.

Hornady Lock-N-Load AP

Hornady Lock-N-Load AP. Photo: Hornady

The Lock-N-Load AP is a five-station press that uses Hornady's patented Lock-N-Load bushing system, which makes it one of the quickest change-over progressive presses available. With its quick-change metering inserts, you can switch from one powder to another with the push of a button. The universal case retainer spring affords quick, easy removal and replacement of cases at any point in the loading process.

SPECIFICATIONS

MODEL: Hornady Lock-N-Load AP
INDEXING: Automatic
STATIONS: 5
RATE: 500 per hour

Lee Precision Pro 1000

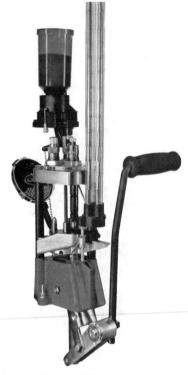

you can load only one case at a time. Caliber changes take about three minutes.

RCBS Pro Chucker 5

The Pro Chucker 5 from RCBS is a five-station auto-indexing press that features quick-change die plates for fast caliber changes and greater efficiency. The large 4.6-inch operating window means you can load all pistol and even large magnum-length rifle cartridges. Plus, the Pro Chucker 5 can be converted from five- to seven-station operation.

SPECIFICATIONS

MODEL: RCBS Pro Chucker 5
INDEXING: Automatic
STATIONS: 5
RATE: 500-600 per hour

**The Lee Precision Pro 1000 progressive press.
Photo: Lee Precision**

The Pro 1000 from Lee Precision is designed for pistols calibers — .32 S&W Long through .45 Long Colt — and small rifle calibers like .223 Rem. It works by feeding a bullet and pulling the lever, with a finished cartridge dropping into the bin. Each stage of operation is automatic except for manually placing a bullet into the case mouth. Alternate loading sequences are available, so

**The RCBS Pro Chucker 5.
Photo: RCBS**

SPECIFICATIONS

MODEL: Lee Precision Pro 1000
INDEXING: Automatic
STATIONS: 4
RATE: 250-300 per hour

DEFENSIVE AMMO

What Matters? What Doesn't?
Get the Answers Here!

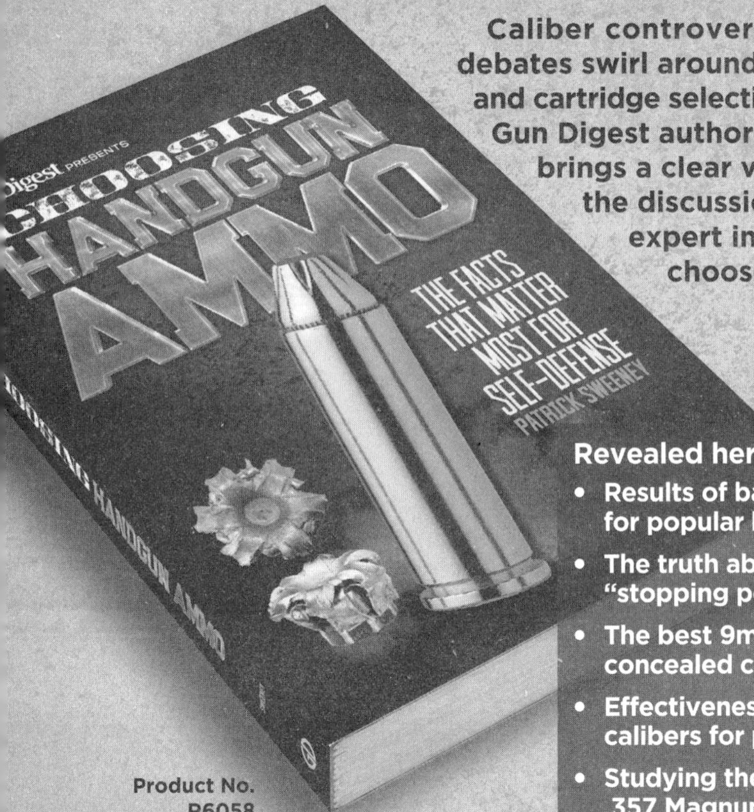

Caliber controversies and endless debates swirl around handgun caliber and cartridge selection. Now, leading Gun Digest author Patrick Sweeney brings a clear voice of reason to the discussion, with data and expert insight to help you choose the right ammo for your needs.

Revealed here:

- **Results of ballistics testing for popular handgun rounds**
- **The truth about so-called "stopping power"**
- **The best 9mm rounds for concealed carry**
- **Effectiveness of small calibers for personal defense**
- **Studying the heavy hitters: .357 Magnum, .45 ACP and 10mm**

Product No. R6058

Choosing Handgun Ammo is a must to help you make smart decisions about concealed carry, home defense, and personal protection ammunition.

Order online at
GunDigestStore.com
or call 920.471.4522

GunDigest
WE KNOW GUNS SO YOU KNOW GUNS

GET YOUR FREE BONUS DOWNLOAD TO **9MM: AMERICA'S MOST POPULAR CALIBER!**

WANT MORE 9MM GUNS AND GEAR?

Your **FREE Bonus Download** from *9mm: Guide to America's Most Popular Caliber* contains extra material — from chapters on the latest and greatest striker-fire handguns and large-capacity carbines, to 9mm Derringers and the best full-size nines for your bug-out and survival plans ... it's all here!

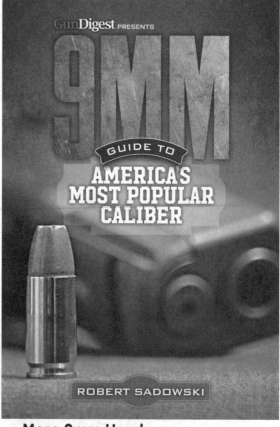

- **More 9mm Handguns**
- **Top Pistol-Caliber Carbines**
- **Top Secret Spectre 9mm Build Kit**
- **And More!**

Visit gundigest.com/9mmBook for your **FREE Instant Download!**

WE KNOW GUNS SO YOU KNOW GUNS